ALSO BY DEREK LEEBAERT

To Dare and to Conquer: Special Operations and the
Destiny of Nations, from Achilles to Al Qaeda

The Fifty-Year Wound: How America's Cold War
Victory Shapes Our World

The Future of the Electronic Marketplace
(co-author/editor)

The Future of Software
(co-author/editor)

Technology 2001: The Future of Computing and Communications
(co-author/editor)

Soviet Strategy and New Military Thinking
(co-author/editor)

THE DELUSIONS OF
AMERICAN FOREIGN POLICY
FROM KOREA TO AFGHANISTAN

MAGIC AND MAYHEM

DEREK LEEBAERT

SIMON & SCHUSTER
New York   London   Toronto   Sydney

Simon & Schuster
1230 Avenue of the Americas
New York, NY 10020

First Simon & Schuster hardcover edition September 2010

SIMON & SCHUSTER and colophon are registered trademarks of Simon & Schuster, Inc.

For information about special discounts for bulk purchases,
please contact Simon & Schuster Special Sales at
1-866-506-1949 or business@simonandschuster.com.

The Simon & Schuster Speakers Bureau can bring authors to your live event. For more information or to book an event, contact the Simon & Schuster Speakers Bureau at 1-866-248-3049 or visit our website at www.simonspeakers.com.

Designed by Renata Di Biase

Manufactured in the United States of America

10 9 8 7 6 5 4 3 2

Library of Congress Cataloging-in-Publication Data

Leebaert, Derek.
  Magic and mayhem / Derek Leebaert.—1st Simon & Schuster hardcover ed.
    p.   cm.
  "Simon & Schuster nonfiction original"—T.p. verso.
  Includes bibliographical references and index.
  1. United States—Foreign relations—1945–1989. 2. United States—Foreign relations—1989– 3. Magical thinking—Political aspects—United States. 4. United States—Foreign relations—Philosophy. 5. United States—Foreign relations administration. 6. Political culture—United States. I. Title.
    E840.L417 2010
    327.73009'04—dc22   2010011182

ISBN 978-1-4391-2569-4
ISBN 978-1-4391-4167-0 (ebook)

To Genevieve

I don't believe in magic.

J. K. ROWLING

CONTENTS

MAGIC AND MAYHEM

INTRODUCTION

FOR A LIFETIME, AMERICA HAS STUMBLED AND STUMBLED AGAIN in its political and military dealings with the rest of the world. We have found ourselves entangled in Afghanistan, Iraq, Vietnam, and, from 1950 to 1953, with China on the frozen Korean Peninsula—these being just the worst moments of miscalculation. To pick at random, other letdowns include illusory arms control deals with Soviet Russia rather than demonstrable limitations on weaponry; "nation-building" in places where nations have never existed; attempts off and on to fine-tune, just for starters, the futures of Iran and Pakistan; and faddish intellectual obsessions with counterinsurgency or nuclear terrorism that burst forth in one decade, as they did respectively in the 1960s and '70s, only to lie in oblivion for thirty years, then undergo frantic resurrection at one more surge of "crisis."

Two great accomplishments happily offset this unnerving record: the ultimate defeat of the Soviet empire and the triumphant creation of a global web of trade that boosts the lives of billions of people.

These profound successes are nonetheless surrounded by a host of dangerous self-deceptions that I sum up as magical thinking. I call it "magical" because shrewd, levelheaded people are so frequently bewitched into substituting passion, sloganeering, and haste for reflection, homework, and reasonable objectives. Goodness knows that American energy and excitement have combined to cause financial boom-bubble-busts at home for some 250 years. But magical notions are much less apparent in the pragmatic ways that America goes about its domestic affairs. America would not generate unsurpassed enterprise, still be the richest nation, or now lead software and biotech innovation if the geopolitical frame of mind permeated Silicon Valley, Walmart, or the heartland's equally cutting-edge agribusinesses.

When we think magically, we expect to produce astounding outcomes of our own design. This element of taken-for-granted power is what distinguishes magical thought from mere wishful thinking. In wishful thinking, we believe that what we wish for is actually true. We interpret events as we would like them to be, as opposed to what they really are. But the magical perspective convinces those who hold it that gigantic desires can be brought to fruition in the snap of an American election cycle—to "transform the Middle East and the broader world of Islam politically," or to crush the Viet Cong.[1] There's nothing misty-eyed about this determined, solipsistic temperament. That degree of willfulness is also what distinguishes magic from religion, in which we implore the divine to intervene. At worship, we seek to deserve the favor of supernatural might. In the grip of magical belief, we position ourselves at the center of profound events and believe that such vast, apparently worthwhile objectives must be fulfilled out of their sheer righteousness.

Magical thinking entails seductive, familiarizing rituals. In the excitements of global policy, we court some truly grim entities as imaginary friends, such as venal client states that eventually implode and splatter us in their collapse. We put our faith in silver bullets like the Superfortress bombers confidently relied on to deliver victory in North Korea, and onward to the assault helicopters of Vietnam and today's Predator drones in Afghanistan. We resort to bad analogies and inferior quantitative techniques while stilling our doubts with mantras of "stability" and "democracy" accompanied by the usual creepy euphemisms like "collateral damage," "enhanced interrogation," or percentage of "DOE," meaning "Death on Earth." When outcomes do not match expectations, as has been all too often the case, it is magically assumed that it was the particulars that were gotten wrong, not that the overall objective was misconceived. We misphrased the wish or bungled the follow-through: someone tripped in the war dance. How could the original proposition not have been sound? Therefore new shibboleths arise, as we repeat with a revived certainty that—next time—America will get things *right*.

Hubris draws on magical certainty, or indeed may derive from it. In either case, many men and women in power keep fueling hopes with unreason and calling it analysis. Magic entails illusion, whether on the stage or in National Security Council meetings where good minds prove that one's intelligence is no better than the assumptions it works from. When uncomfortable evidence is waved aside, illusion passes into delusion—and it's then that willfulness becomes deadly. Throughout, when we think magically, we believe that our desires override those of anyone else, peasant warriors in Asia and Kremlin apparatchiks alike.

Magical thinking simplifies. It fills in for ignorance and substitutes for critical, distanced consideration. Intricate alien phenomena are set up as more or less of one piece, like "communism" or "terrorism." It becomes the epitome of magic to believe that the most complex of aims can be realized on our terms among people whose languages we don't speak, whose histories we don't know, and whose interests we have not fathomed. Yet surely if we believe with enough resolve that we'll make something happen, it will. To believe that this country can accomplish whatever it sets its mind to is reasonable enough in business, science, and social change. That's much less so as we advance into faraway places about which we not only know little, but hardly bother to understand.

Magical thinking is rooted in a deep mulch of culture, misused legend, and misapplied experience. All countries draw on their own forms of it. Myths have conquered logic for millennia of hopes and alarms. But since America is the superpower, its illusions are more consequential. They are also particularly robust, stemming as they do from the country's dream-driven origins of being a City on a Hill, its unparalleled achievements of constitutional government as well as industry, and the ever-richer diversity of its people.

Of course, America doesn't inevitably succumb to the latest waft of magic when it faces challenges abroad. If it did, it wouldn't be the supreme power, securing the seas for global commerce and serving as the ultimate guarantor against threats to international order, as in the Persian Gulf War, when the country responded to Saddam Hussein's conquest of Kuwait. And there are other salutary examples of American strength wisely applied. The point remains, however, that a willingness to don magical lenses usually arises once excitement, peril, and ignorance combine. Magical thinking builds up in the time between disillusionments: initially, there's a fantastic sense of possibility, as when the obligation took hold to "liberate" North Korea on the doorstep of Mao's China. Then a bewildered reckoning follows. Before long, however, the country gathers itself for another death-defying leap, as in Vietnam a dozen years later, and so it goes.

Magical notions get injected into U.S. decision making with an ease rarely found in other advanced democracies. In part, that's because of the political appointments system on which America relies to staff its government. The White House has the responsibility to fill eight thousand or so senior jobs throughout the federal departments and agencies. The result is a kaleidoscope of new arrivals and random talents. The effectiveness of the country's professional civil service as well as of its Foreign Service is diminished. In addition, the boisterous spontaneity of the decision-making process of a continental republic—with its passionate advocacy groups, endlessly recombining coalitions, and opposing branches of government—creates lots of opportunity for focused, forceful people to weigh in with burning agendas.

This union of fresh high spirits and amateur overexcitement

leaves the door open to a certain type of enthusiast—whether from government, academia, the press, or think tanks—whom I call the "Emergency Man." Such are the clever, energetic, self-assured, well-schooled people who take advantage of the opportunities intrinsic to the American political system to trifle with enormous risk. They are drawn to the national security policy arena by its atmosphere of decisiveness, secrecy, and apocalyptic stakes. A particular civilian temperament finds wrestling with decisions about fleets, Delta Force, Stryker Brigades, Moscow summitry, and regional crises a lot more exciting than the dreary disputes surrounding Amtrak or tackling African poverty.

Of course, emergency men show up in the ministries of other nations. In France, professionals at the Quai d'Orsay mutter that their boss, Foreign Minister Bernard Kouchner, is so "in love with crisis" that he openly neglects the subjects that bore him, such as the European Union.[2] But, for better or worse, France—like Britain, Japan, Brazil, Germany, China—has a more constricted decision-making system, as well as intellectually impressive and usually dispassionate civil servants on the scene to lower the heat. There are strengths and weaknesses to both approaches. But the American one is well primed to inject the nation's love of the bold, optimistic, and grand into the mix.

Emergency men come in different flavors, from the "neocons" of recent years to the "the best and the brightest" national security cadre—as that remarkable observer of the American scene, David Halberstam, forever stamped them—of the Kennedy and Johnson presidencies, determined to bring Hanoi to its knees. (And it is chilling to now to hear the media call the latest arrivals in Washington, without irony, "the best and the brightest.") Emergency men can be found among the "daring amateurs" of the early 1950s, conspicuously in the CIA. Some were on the staff of General Douglas MacArthur, supreme commander of U.S. and UN forces during the fateful first ten months of the Korean War, and were to be found as well among his admirers on Capitol

Hill. They have been repeatedly on hand to fire up resolve against perils that, to them, have never been greater than at that very moment.

Emergency men furnish an endless stream of answers, usually before the penetrating questions have been asked. They radiate an aura of intensity, though their demeanor may be cool. They are united by an uncanny ability to amplify the drama of the moment. In the run-up to war and in debates over the nation's deepest interests, their demands for swift, vigorous action stand in for command of detail, whether of terrain, precedent, or the alleged support of allies. Oftentimes what seems the unassailably clear-cut moral quality of their convictions persuades many more of us, beyond that small part of the citizenry professionally concerned with foreign affairs, to unite behind their certainties.

How does this habit of ill judgment sustain itself, and where does its supply of bad ideas keep coming from? Why do they haunt us decade in and decade out? Why are patriotic, capable people in lofty office—as well as opinion leaders in universities, think tanks, and the press—entranced by the prospect of high-stakes action and by half-baked theories that are pretty well discredited even before the start? How does so much talent and spirit get co-opted from Main Street? How might the right discerning skepticisms be induced instead? How can we call on our better angels and apply the country's unmatched strengths to its own enlightened self-interest?

We can go a long way to answering those questions by exploring the six compelling illusions that typically are in play when the country lunges in dangerous directions that it never intended to go. The faces of our country's friends and foes may change over the years, as do the modes of war or parley, but the paths of folly are remarkably consistent and the language of crisis is rather unoriginal.

By dismantling the pattern of magical thought, and examining each strand of illusion, we get a sharper understanding than what has been offered to date as to how Americans imagine, confront, live with, and, sometimes, invite danger.

The individual strands are:

1. A sensation of urgency and of "crisis" that accompanies the belief that most any resolute action is superior to restraint; it's a demeanor that's joined by the emergency man's eagerness to be his country's revealer of dangers, real and imaginary.

2. The faith that American-style business management—as practiced in Silicon Valley startups soon to join NASDAQ or, not long ago, at the River Rouge plant in Dearborn or at steel mills along the Monongahela—can fix any global problem given enough time, resources, and appropriately "can-do," businesslike zeal.

3. A distinctively American desire to fall in behind celebrities, stars, and peddlers of some newly distilled expertise who, in foreign affairs especially, seem to glow with wizardry—and whom we turn to for guidance while believing, for a fatefully long moment, that they only have to wave their wands for success to fall from the sky.

4. An expectation of wondrous returns on investment, even when this is based on intellectual shortcuts—in fact on lack of seriousness and mental flexibility, as described, for instance, in trenchant analyses of the Iraq War—though the same shortcuts were apparent in Vietnam and North Korea, as well as in many politico-military efforts in between.

5. Conjuring powerful, but simplified, images from the depths of "history" to rationalize huge and amorphously

expanding objectives, a technique of foreign policy artistry resorted to by high officials, professors, and field
commanders alike.

6. The repeated belief that America can shape the destiny of
   other countries overnight and that the hearts and minds
   of distant people are throbbing to be transformed into
   something akin to the way we see ourselves.

What has not been done before this book is to pull together
these vexing compulsions in order to explain why we keep acting on them—and how to get out of them. To that end, the first
chapter lays the groundwork, such as how the peculiar types of
threat that America has confronted since 1945 have affected our
perceptions of the world. Thereafter each strand of the pattern
has its chapter. Each of those six chapters opens with a vignette
that illustrates the particular illusion being addressed, followed
by the key questions to be answered. Portraits of the emergency
men who embody the specific problem being discussed are also
included. Significant events of past decades then appear in a very
different light.

By story's end, we should have discovered how to make our
way around these strange temptations and will have come to
understand how the country can truly play to its strengths.
We'll recognize that America's promise is also to be found in its
faults—knowing that our country's greatest gift is that of endless
re-creation.

1.

SOURCES OF MAGIC

RALPH WALDO EMERSON CALLED OURS "THE COUNTRY OF tomorrow" because of our astounding ability to turn dreams into reality. Whether the issue at hand has been settling the continent within a nineteenth-century lifetime, the wearing down of Soviet tyranny, or assimilating the latest wave of immigrants, America has advanced confidently into the future, pressing its visions to completion.

Consider Franklin Roosevelt's vision at the outset of World War II. Within a month of America's entry into the greatest of wars, he pledged to double the 1942 production of tanks and planes, and then to double it again. This goal made no sense to the British, who had been fighting for more than two years and whose booming steelworks were fully mobilized. Visiting Washington in 1941, the great economist John Maynard Keynes had smiled politely at the young American planners. Like some tough-minded U.S. industrialists, he would not find Roosevelt's vision reasonable. Yet production roughly kept tripling.[1] FDR had no empirical basis to expect this achievement. But he had a rational sense of possibility and intimately understood his country and its people. He knew that U.S. manufacturing genius had been stalled by the 1930s Great Depression; this challenge offered a cause perfectly suited to American energy, speed, and enterprise.

Forty years later, Ronald Reagan understood that the Soviet Union was dying—so long as America helped with the euthanasia. No other national leader held this belief, nor did the CIA or most any foreign policy expert. He was an inheritor of both FDR's optimistic intuition and his self-efficacy, as well as of his insouciance—FDR having remarked that most of what he knew about the world came from his stamp collection. Reagan was the first postwar president to take the offensive against the Soviet Union across each mode of power: political, ideological, economic, and military. And when the decades-long contest was just about over, in the spring of 1988, he walked the streets of Moscow through crowds chanting, "U.S.A.! U.S.A!" At a time when extremely few politicians, professors, or CEOs understood the significance of twenty-first-century information technologies, he held up a microchip to students at Moscow State University as a symbol of freedom's power and material abundance; and when asked about the "evil" he had denounced only five years before, he cheerfully replied, "That was another time, another place."

A vision, after all, is not magical just because every bit of previous experience and prevailing wisdom says that it is impossible. A vision only passes into magic when it has to overcome difficulty by pure assertion, or by self-hypnosis, when we refuse to accept that more than a few of our high aspirations are unlikely to be pulled off. But those shortcomings have by and large been standard procedure if we consider the deadly reversals of Iraq, Vietnam, and North Korea—and the many ancillary attempts to fine-tune the world. U.S. practice has frequently been like the Gary Larson cartoon showing a couple of scientists contemplating a blackboard that bears two series of equations wistfully linked by "Then a Miracle Occurs." Miracles would have had to happen for the hypotheses that generate a lot of this activity to prove out.

First, some background before distinguishing the specific strands of illusion: How does magical thinking reveal itself in U.S. foreign and defense policy? What are the unique influences in American public life—particularly the approach to recruiting for high office—that open gateways to such intense willful dreaming? How does "Cold War" followed by what the Pentagon originally styled the "Long War" against terror shape our perceptions of the world? And how did magic begin to grip the public imagination so early in our post–World War II journey?

Foreign affairs by its nature is imbued with a mystique on the edge of magic: the secret dispatches, the untouchable sacredness of ambassadors, conclaves of wise men ruminating on Armageddon, the "3 A.M. phone call" to the White House that heralds the next hinge moment of history. President Kennedy called thrillingly on Americans to "dream of things that never were"—as his brother Robert would put it, quoting Shaw—whether men on the moon or, for that matter, U.S. health-care reform. But mingled with these visions of human advance were geopolitical fantasies of "America's frontiers . . . [being] on the . . . Mekong and the Tigris and the Euphrates."[2] The notion of America holding a crucial line on Vietnam's Mekong River marched us into a lost war. And there would be little good news some forty years further on by the time America actually deployed its army on the Tigris and Euphrates.

"Communism" was casually spoken of, as in the 1950s and early '60s as extending from East Berlin to the China Sea, little heed being given to the ancient abrasive powers of national difference. Likewise—by the simplifying spell of magic—Al Qaeda, Hamas, Hezbollah, the Taliban, the Muslim Brotherhood, Iranian fundamentalists, and Saudi Wahhabists have been lumped together as one single evil of "radical violent Islam." Under this spell, an amalgam of terror cells is tossed in with resistance fighters, national political organizations, a premodern religious movement, and even the secularist Baathist party, as if all wished the United States the same deadly harm.

Under the spell of one kind of magic, "friendly" dictators are believed to share our ideals. If they're not democrats, they have democracy in their souls. In the 1970s, at the U.S. Army's School of the Americas in Panama, the United States trained one of the most brutal of Latin America's officer corps, the instruments of Nicaraguan dictator Anastasio Somoza. Because the modern U.S. military is the armed force of a democracy, it was somehow taken for granted that modernizing Nicaragua's armed forces would democratize them. Yet murder and world-class embezzlement continued energetically in that country. During the 1960s, as the Kennedy administration expanded internal security funding and training to some of the world's grossest violators of human rights, several members of the Shah of Iran's notorious SAVAK gestapo were embedded in the Kansas City Police Department.[3] The Shah was fond of speaking about his affinity with the West; therefore the State Department's new Office of Public Safety believed midwestern values as well as constabulary teachings would rub off on his "policemen."

Practically by definition, magic is invoked to get us there fast. The lantern is rubbed, out swooshes the genie, and wish fulfillments rain down. So a defense secretary eager to flex additional U.S. muscle against "terror" can convince himself that so Herculean a task as taking over the Arab world's most populous oil-producing state will last "six days, six weeks"—at worst "six months"—before a satisfying departure. Or so Secretary of Defense Donald Rumsfeld promised U.S. troops a month before invading Iraq.

That hopeful half-year timeline keeps popping up. America intended to reconstruct North Korea and meld it with South Korea in the half-year over autumn 1950–spring 1951; and that was going to be the time needed, said General Paul Harkins, U.S. commander in Vietnam, to flatten the Viet Cong, "by Christmas" of 1963. "Six months" is the same critical duration that the *New York Times'* columnist Tom Friedman has offered, on a dozen occasions since 2003, to determine whether the United States has built democracy in Iraq.[4] And, judging from precedent, just "six months more," or so, will be heard from the White House in 2011, the year which President Obama has anticipated that U.S. soldiers can start to leave Afghanistan.

In Korea, in Vietnam, and on to the Tigris and Euphrates, the problem has not just been one of underestimating an enemy. Everyone has done that at least since Thermopylae. The problem is that the magical thinker has marched confidently forward, and complexity has been trampled out of sight. A great deal can be random in the "game of nations," a term coined by famed CIA operative Miles Copeland to catch the amorality of power politics. Luck and happenstance play their roles. The way forward can be obscure. But the magical thinker proceeds with the valor of ignorance, compounding the chances of disappointment.

To that end, former secretary of defense Robert McNamara had to confess with authentic contrition, long after the Vietnam War was lost, that neither he nor others in President Kennedy's national security cohort had "truly investigated what was essentially at stake" in Indochina.[5] The national security adviser, McGeorge Bundy, was even vague as to how the beleaguered Republic of Vietnam had come into being.[6] Bundy's successor forty years later, Condoleezza Rice, would explain with surprising lack of embarrassment that, with the White House knowing so little about Afghanistan, officials on September 11, 2001, raced to the map to find out where this threatening country might be.[7] Nonetheless, the magical thinker takes far-reaching action, barely inhibited by weighing the risks or well-argued alternatives.

Even basic arithmetic gets overridden. China, for example, has long been the most populous nation in the world, with limitless reserves of infantry; the U.S. Army, however, kept pressing deeper in 1950 through the eight-thousand-foot mountains and river gorges of North Korea onto that great country's very doorstep. It was matchless ground for history's biggest ambush. Or, midway in the Vietnam War, General Harkins's successor, William Westmoreland, adopted a strategy of "attrition": conscripts from Hartford, Tempe, and Macon were thrown against an opponent who had been fighting inexhaustibly on his own terrain for nearly twenty years. Commanders deluded themselves with "body counts"—statistical scorecards with minimal concern as to whether the Vietnamese bodies being counted were the enemy's—to show victory at hand.

Six months into Iraq and with no exit in sight, Mr. Rumsfeld asked his staff, "Are we capturing, killing or deterring more terrorists every day than the madrassah and the radical clerics are recruiting?" only to turn away from the worrying reply.[8] To be master of the answer before you have asked the question, ready to "stay the course" no matter what you hear, is the mark of the self-deceiver, not the public servant.

Magical thinking, in addition to trampling down complexity and mythologizing efforts "to stay the course," nourishes false connections that entangle themselves with our best-intentioned quests. America opposes "evil," and thus the "Axis" of World War II is drafted into the ritual analogy-making: Terror is the moment's paramount form of evil; Saddam, unambiguously evil, consequently has "a long-standing relationship" with Al Qaeda, as said Mr. Cheney.[9] No matter that on the issue of radical Islamic terror Saddam was closer to our side than to theirs—hated by Al Qaeda not as a tyrant but as a secularist enemy of Islam. The Vietnam War had its own basic false connection: Chairman Mao's China was communist; communism is expansionist; so all of Vietnam, its neighbor to the south, would soon be swallowed. It didn't matter that Vietnam had successfully fought the Middle Kingdom for centuries, as it would again four years after America left.

Reasonable objectives disappear under magical thinking. Resistance to one assault on a relatively well-defined U.S. interest, such as protecting South Vietnam from the communist North, or hunting down Al Qaeda, finds itself conflated into an overarching plan of action to put down all apparently connected problems—"containing China," say, in the 1960s or "ending tyranny in our world" after 9/11.[10]

The most dangerous of illusions is to believe that we are working under no illusions at all. The homework has been *done*. Options have been *weighed*. Precedents have been *considered*, intelligence *assessed*. And it's reassuring when the White House lets it be known, as in 1962, that Barbara Tuchman's *The Guns of August*, about how Europe's great powers stumbled into World War I, has been required reading in the family quarters. But such study didn't prevent President Kennedy from taking decisions that sped us into the swamps of Vietnam. Assurances of prudent reflection were similarly pressed on the citizenry when a spokesman insisted that Camus' *The Stranger*, which depicts a world more chillingly other than we can imagine, was being pondered on George W. Bush's Crawford, Texas, ranch. But fixed thinking tends to stay fixed under the thrall of magic—at least dangerously long enough to remake the world in ways entirely different from those intended.

Whether illusion or delusion, magical thinking colors both perceptions. Illusions at least are tamer. It was an illusion when the Defense Department's deputy secretary assumed in 2002 that any differences between Iraq's Sunni and Shia were surely "exaggerated"; it passed into delusion when the carnage stoked by religious, economic, and political hatred was brushed off as the last efforts of "dead-enders" and "thugs."[11]

Fortunately, America's most formidable rivals keep entertaining their own fantastical scenarios. When we pay attention, those can be used to our advantage.

"I thought I would issue a few proclamations," reminisced Leon Trotsky, commissar of foreign affairs after 1917's Bolshevik seizure of power, "and shut up shop." Workers of the world would unite. They didn't. Full of delusions about the truth of

Marxism-Leninism, the Soviet Union carried its brutal, irrational, collectivist economic doctrines right into the colossally dispersed information age of Microsoft, Oracle, and Dell.

Russia's belief in the fitness of arbitrary authority endures today. That is its own version of magical thought, and one that rationalizes corruption of anything that the powerful want to touch, whether stifling the press or using Gazprom as the Kremlin's cash cow. China, for its part, is a land with a terrifying record of magical notions. They span two millennia from the Burning of the Books to the Boxer rebels' faith that Western bullets would melt into water against their chests, and then on to the insanities of Maoism, in which "scientific socialism" legitimized endless hocus-pocuses—infant piglets expected to spawn litters, broken glass used to fertilize crops. It's a worrying record as that giant swells into the next candidate for superpower status. In any event, we can hardly count on an opponent's self-deceptions to keep offsetting our own.

All nations and peoples have their magical beliefs. Magical thinking has often blinded Britain to the fact that each phase of the ongoing Industrial Revolution has ratcheted down its power. France appears to dwell on past greatness, evoked by centuries of subtle diplomacy or memories of empire, to claim a unique understanding of the present world. Notoriously, the Germans long believed themselves to be justly vengeful victims of less civilized powers, as in the 1920s and, climactically, in 1939 when an unappeasable tyrant cried "retribution" to expand his Thousand Year Reich.

For America to have an abundance of magical beliefs might seem odd for so pragmatically commercial a culture. But consider how Americans nonetheless contemplate risk at home. The country's spasms of boom-bubble-bust offer telling implications. No other great nation has so consistently exposed itself to market turmoil, from canals in Andrew Jackson's day to subprime in those of Goldman Sachs. This desire for miraculous payoffs has gripped us at least since the American Revolution. And these private intensities work their way into America's gravest international undertakings. In the euphorias and letdowns can be seen an affinity for carrying the truly possible to the point of calamity. We believe that we can shirk elementary due diligence or, overseas, offhandedly squelch our very real opponents. The Iraq War itself, observes Richard Haass, who when it began headed the State Department's policy planning office, "was equivalent to investing $100,000 and thinking you'll make a million." [12] We build an outsized confidence in how our friends will assist us, only to plunge, when our hopes in Saigon or Kabul are dashed, into irrational despair. Plus there's a sourly applicable truth about bubbles: smart people who've learned about them the hard way nonetheless line up for the next one.

The many appointments that the White House disburses are not just cabinet secretaries and ambassadorial postings but all the deputy secretaries, undersecretaries, assistant secretaries, deputy assistant secretaries, associate deputy undersecretaries, office directorships, and other senior positions at State and Defense, on the NSC staff and at Treasury, as well as through most of the executive branch. The CIA and other parts of the intelligence community—as America's sixteen distinct organizations responsible for this function are called—have relatively few appointees. Yet for other reasons that we will see, they too have no shortage of self-deception.

There is nothing like this system in any other advanced democracy. For better or worse, the ministries are filled by permanent, though frequently rotating, career officials; those mandarins hold important roles sometime effectively up to cabinet level. In Britain and France, the civil service is an elite calling. In America, however, even the Foreign Service is weakly positioned, its carefully sieved career officers often cast as upper-servant types in

flight from the competitive economy that rages outside the poli-
tesses of diplomacy.

There's no harm in the fact that, since the Kennedy administration, around a third of U.S. ambassadorships have usually
gone to political appointees, a practice routinely denounced by
America's professional diplomats. Some political appointees,
such as President Obama's ambassador to Japan—a Silicon Valley
high-tech lawyer with a career of trans-Pacific deals—can be a
better fit than a Foreign Service officer or a policy generalist from
academia. However, what can become significant as a source of
magical thought is our method of filling decision-making slots in
Washington itself beneath the cabinet level.

Peter Rodman advanced one of the most ringing endorsements
of the status quo in his penetrating analysis, *Presidential Command*.
A Harvard-trained lawyer too restlessly imaginative ever to practice, he became an admired career noncareerist who, for nearly
forty years, alternated between think tanks and government,
working effectively in appointive office at the NSC, as director of
the State Department's Policy Planning Staff, and finally serving
from 2001 to 2007 as assistant secretary of defense for international
security affairs.

Rodman argued that a president most effectively exercises
power by personalizing the instruments of state right down to
the level of daily execution. In a system that depends heavily on
the qualities of the one person in charge, the chief executive can
only succeed, particularly in international policy, by assuring
authoritative political direction over the departments. How else
to make his hopefully clear-minded perceptions felt? Strong appointees loyal to his beliefs then work to fulfill his vision, perhaps
compensating for his own executive inexperience. The alternative, it is feared, is that White House policies might be stymied by,
say, a State Department that the Kennedy White House believed
lacked "energy" or that President Nixon and Henry Kissinger
found "disloyal," or that today, Rodman has written, "can rarely

ever bring itself to admit that diplomacy is not working." [13] As the line of reasoning goes, professional public servants—not just at State but also at Langley and even the Pentagon—are similarly beset by bureaucratic inertia, at best.

Yet to every victorious administration belong the legitimate spoils of government. An advantage of this practice is to pull into the system dynamic public-spirited people like Rodman who have the authority and the appetite to act on bold initiatives—in contrast, say, to the jaded career mandarins who inhabit European foreign ministries. When it succeeds, a valuable tension exists between the more original, articulate, and generally better-educated appointees, intensely alert to the short term, and an ongoing inherited staff that concentrates on longer challenges. Politically connected outsiders act as catalysts and innovators to turbocharge the process while not getting bogged down by repetition and past disillusions. In such a system, bright but relatively uninformed people interact intensely with informed but not cutting-edge ones. The results can be either creative tumult or administrative hell.

This diverse, multifaceted, adrenaline-charged method of policymaking, found only in America, can resemble a reverberatory furnace. Temperatures rise as Pentagon assistant secretaries, NSC directors, and unnamed senior officials at State alternately team up or joust with each other as well as with advocacy groups, think-tankers, policy consultants, entrepreneurial professors, and significant legislative assistants on the Hill. Lobbyists for foreign governments move back and forth to advise presidents and defense secretaries about their for now shrugged-off clients. Journalists abet this process and occasionally take high office themselves. It can even be difficult to tell who's "in" and who's "out."

America's freewheeling mode of policymaking, particularly in foreign affairs, also blurs lines of responsibility between branches of government and between government and the public. "Outsiders" can fast become "insiders," given enough passion and resources. Coalitions within the bureaucracy, as on Capitol Hill, can quickly be formed or pulled apart by shrewd players—Senate staffers, midlevel civil servants, citizen activists, legislators themselves as well as appointees—who know the policy process. Unusual benefits can flow.

For instance, George Crile's sardonic chronicle *Charlie Wilson's War* details the bureaucratic fights and citizen influences that secretly steered about $5 billion to the Afghan mujahideen's resistance to the Red Army in the 1980s. In this instance, a few political appointees worked closely with several farsighted career people to inflict a crippling wound on Soviet aggression. A fixated, Scotch-guzzling, hedonist Democratic congressman spontaneously gathered allies among committee staffers, political angels, and a maverick clandestine services officer at CIA to short-circuit entrenched resistance in State, at Langley, and among the Joint Chiefs.

And Wilson's exploit, with its mix of career officials and appointees, is not unique. It is matched by equally dramatic sagas still untold—as when midlevel political appointees in the Nixon, Ford, and Carter years took it upon themselves, entirely outside official channels, to collaborate with keen, truly expert insiders to obstruct the biggest-ever Soviet espionage setup in America. The CIA had refused point-blank to believe that such a masterpiece of thievery existed, and the FBI, never having counterintelligence as a priority, showed minimal interest. These twenty men and women instead went to informants in U.S. high-tech companies, buttonholed key congressmen, got pointers from the National Security Agency's wealth of electronic intercepts, and deployed back-channel leaks from Helene Boatner, then an officer in the CIA's operations center and later the founder of its Office of Leadership Analysis. Vital time was bought against further Soviet penetration for about five critical years until the evidence became undeniable to all concerned. Then, of course, every part of the national security apparatus lunged forward, desperate to be part of the sub-rosa blocking and tackling.[14]

One drawback of a system that depends so heavily on political appointees, however, is that these men and women know they must act *right now* before being swept out of office. Filled with the rightness of whatever their cause may be, they push their targeted, cogently argued priorities through bureaucracies less certain or obsessed. And they do so quickly, before rival approaches are brought to the table. Dreadful ideas can ricochet through the corridors of power more easily in the absence of intellectually demanding career officials who are permanently in place to argue and, if necessary, to push courteously back.

Institutional memory becomes spotty as appointees from an earlier administration vanish after elections and as their successors serve for two or three years, then to return to law firms, lobbying shops, corporations, or academia—leveraging public service as new clients, contracts, and center directorships arrive.

This form of (un)-planned obsolescence encourages "crises" to be hurried forward, only to fade under the tinctures of time, perhaps to reassert themselves in new guises. Since few appointees combine both the durability in government and the continuously fresh-eyed acuteness of the late Peter Rodman, the decision-making system is tilted steadily against weary career functionaries who try to explain that the "crisis du jour"—a cautionary term favored by Lieutenant General Brent Scowcroft, savvy national security adviser to both Presidents Gerald Ford and George H. W. Bush—might just be the eleventh iteration of a more or less similar commotion.

The White House Office of Presidential Personnel further randomizes the deployment of top talent. WHOPP is likely to be in the hands of the latest true believers. They may not always be the sons and daughters of political donors, but usually they're former campaign workers and people well connected through congressmen or other party nabobs. Thomas Schweich, a smart, politically active attorney who entered the George W. Bush administration as a deputy assistant secretary of state and who would serve as chief of staff at the U.S. mission to the United Nations, recalls how his own appointment was "preceded by an effort by a 20-something in personnel to place an unqualified friend in the job." "You know you have arrived when you get interviewed by the 29-year-old instead of the 22-year-old," a Foreign Service Officer and three-time ambassador chuckled to Schweich after having been grilled in 2005 for another top post at the State Department.[15]

And this type of randomness occurs in every administration.

Party affiliation may prove insignificant, provided one is of the right faction. Neocon Democrats in quantity proved useful to the last Republican presidency, and being a registered Republican—or an independent like Secretary of Defense Robert Gates—is itself no barrier to appointments under the Obama presidency. Once basic thresholds of qualifications are crossed, friends recruit friends or people they may have worked with in an earlier administration. The snag, besides the subjective assessment of appointees, is that the world is changing at an order of magnitude faster than are the thoughtful reflections of one's associates. Meanwhile, layered patronage networks accrete over the decades with catastrophic results.

Other influences in American life besides the political system make the country prone to passionate, simplifying foreign policy decisions. These include such deep-rooted characteristics as America's tempo of change, its eagerness to embrace the new, and a moralism that has taken many forms and motivations. These will be discussed later in the story. But magical thinking is also shaped by recent historical experience. Three key influences stand out over the last two generations.

One is the type of overarching global conflicts that America has faced almost continuously since 1945—the Cold War, which ended in 1991, and the response to transnational terror that began in earnest in fall 2001. By their nature, open-ended conflicts offer dangerous, diversionary enchantments. In an all-out war for survival, as much of the world experienced during 1940–45, governments are compelled to call in the most competent people to wage them. Everything is at stake and time is short. A nation submits itself to a stern, self-imposed audit of institutional focus and individual merit. In World War II, America went flat out— maximizing production, in which the country's genius is unrivaled. The graver the issue, moreover, the faster it passes into the hands of those who command the highest trust; Franklin Roosevelt's firmly Republican secretary of war, Henry Stimson, is a good example.

But in the ongoing, murkier struggles that have since gnawed at America, the country works itself into predicaments much less suited to its talents. Passionate agendas and mammoth objectives at best tangential to its vital concerns deflect attention. A lot more tough questions come to rest on opinions about what should and shouldn't be proper responses. These open-ended conflicts are easily seized on by moralists and ideologues, all the more so given the U.S. political system. In practice, this foments the illusion that problems are black or white. Specific national interests get obscured. Secondary urgencies are rationalized by third-rate arguments.

America then finds itself at war in places and with people that have little to do with the country's primary opponent. So in 1950–53 we're fighting China in North Korea while the Soviet Union throws in money, munitions, and, behind the scenes, pilots, gunners, and technicians. The following decade we're at war with North Vietnam, while this time both China and the Soviet Union sit back to serve as arsenals of tyranny.[16] Or, as in fighting Al Qaeda yet invading Iraq, we end up in combat against the real opponent's own enemies, who we've convinced ourselves are his accomplices—while leaving behind a "token" U.S. force in Afghanistan.[17]

A second influence from the past that helps to inject magic into decision making goes back to the total war that fell upon America in December 1941. It was a horror different from anything previously faced, not only in the number of dead but in being the first time that war rested on the mobilization of every element of the civilian complex of services and manufacturing. As the largest industrial power, America pulled it all together: leaps in aviation design; statisticians cost/benefiting Army air force bombing sorties; shipping boards run by industrialists; assembly lines retooled overnight; artillery trajectories calculated on "thinking machines"; physicists swept off to New Mexico; and a strange new kind of civilian organization for America, the Office of Strategic Services, precursor of the CIA.

In Washington, eminent lawyers, bankers, and academics began planning for postwar "national security" well before the fighting ceased. For the first time, military "defense" became just a subset of a nation's well-being, rather than the primary focus of part of its government. With the peace, the country would find itself far deeper in world events than even proponents of "the American Century" had dreamed when that term was coined in 1941. The United States trusted neither its friends nor its former enemies to rebuild themselves properly; and it had reasons.

It was apparent that "national security" was something that had to be worked at. It became broadly defined as America's ongoing capacity to pursue its internal life without serious outside interference. Moreover, as we will examine in depth in the following pages, the particulars of national security were increasingly to be worked out by civilians rather than by generals. And no longer would an assistant secretary at the State Department, then its third most powerful official, spend a thirty-eight-year career without once leaving the country.[18]

Open-ended wars like the Cold War and the one against terror, however, can make the term *national security* troublingly abstract. Year by year, decade by decade, "national security" has been stretched toward an endlessly receding horizon, eventually to include the country's defense-related priorities in science, transportation, education, energy, and, in due course, environment, climate, terror, and global unemployment and crime. The problem is not that everyone's business may be nobody's business. Rather, over time, it is that specific necessities—destroying Al Qaeda, for instance—can end up as sprawling quests, like expecting to "transform the Middle East." Everybody with establishment credentials can play. As U.S. politico-military involvements mounted after Korea, then to multiply on President Kennedy's "New Frontier," men and eventually women could increasingly commit their careers to national security, whether or not they wore uniforms. "National security policy" became a calling like any other, promising to cover a lifetime.

There is a third recent historical influence that enables magical thinking. It comes from the way the United States arose as a superpower.

Contrary to today's hoopla about America assuming "the leadership of the world" after World War II, the country did not yet fit the definition of a "super power." [19] The political sense of that term surfaced in the conflict's final year and meant a state that combined an armed global presence with a readiness to act in defense of worldwide interests. America, in contrast, was still a super island state, rather than the new island superstate. There was relatively little room for magic to intrude until about five years later.

Peace busts had habitually followed war booms. There was no guarantee that a renewed depression would not wither the tentative wartime prosperity. The bold commitments were, at this early point, enveloped in caution. The 1947 Truman Doctrine, largely directed again communist "terrorism" in Greece and shielding Turkey and Iran from Moscow, relied on the continuing capacities of the British Empire to an extent still unrecognized today. So did U.S. assumptions about the defense of Western Europe.[20] For the time being, America had had its fill of crusades.

In the sort of reorganization that usually follows convulsion, in autumn 1947 the National Security Council (chaired by the president and including the vice president, the secretaries of State, Defense, and Treasury, the assistant to the president for national security affairs) became the focal point of the peacetime objective of coordinating all U.S. military, diplomatic, and intelligence procedures. A small group of worried practical men—notably Truman's secretaries of state, George Marshall and his successor, Dean Acheson—were improvising a broad-scale strategic doctrine that got America's response to a nuclear world as remarkably right as could have been hoped. It underscored the prudent generalities of holding firm in Europe, of protecting Japan while not pushing into the Asian mainland, of working hand in glove with Europe's reviving democracies. Details could prove awkward. Mistakes were inevitable, such as offering useful refuge to scores of Nazi scientists, and ignoring petitions from Vietnamese nationalists for aid in winning independence from France. But overall strategy was sound.

Each man was of different temperament and background, yet each personified a levelheaded approach to extreme, world-risking matters: General Marshall had been the wartime chief of staff of the army and, according to Churchill, the "organizer of victory." Acheson was an eminent corporate lawyer, former undersecretary at Treasury and at State, and accustomed to the white-knuckle negotiations of high finance; he could make a deal stick. Of course, each man had his flaws; Acheson's anger could be epic. But along with a relatively small group of men such as Lewis Douglas ("the most important diplomat of the most powerful country in the world," said *Time* magazine), Marshall and Acheson helped to create an institutional frame of mind that could hold the worst sorts of emergency stampeding in check: America would not embroil itself in China's civil war before Mao Tse-tung won out in October 1949, nor would it attempt to corner the Soviet Union, as encouraged in wild declarations like *Fortune* magazine's insistence that "the American people [have] placed their frontier in the Caucasus."[21] Each man had a sense that actions have pitiless consequences, half of them unforeseen. Each knew how to separate what was important from what was not. All were qualities that left minimal room for illusion, or for tolerating the obsessions of others in Washington.

In 1948, Marshall refused to "play with fire" with a military response to the Soviet blockade of Berlin, and in fact voiced the hypercaution of the moment by opposing an airlift as well. There was reason to hesitate. In 1949, America signed the North Atlantic Treaty, which notably lacked steps for specific transatlantic defense collaboration. The U.S. Army still deployed just twelve tanks in Europe capable of fighting anyway.[22] Constricted defense budgets, the on-again-off-again draft, and a 180-degree turn in public opinion about any showdown with Moscow once Stalin indeed "got the bomb" in 1949—all fed into a nervous minimalism that was allergic to dreamy ambitions. Even the classified interdepartmental report NSC 68, completed in April 1950, and which has since received enormous attention as a founding document of the Cold War, was essentially a fantasy: there was no chance that Congress would agree to triple defense spending, let alone to directly support French and British colonial wars in Southeast Asia.

What, then, catapulted America into circumstances that have encouraged magical thinking in foreign policy for sixty years? The Korean War, which was quickly dubbed the "Come as You Are War" for America's complete lack of preparedness. It's a condition that has been seen again since—as in Iraq, where U.S. soldiers were ill-equipped for bloody occupation—and has been similarly described: "You go to war with the army you have," said Defense

Secretary Rumsfeld in 2004, "not the army you might want or wish to have." The difference, of course, is that Korea was anything but a war of America's own choice and timing.[23]

"The Korean conflict marked the end . . . of the Fortress America era," wrote Matthew Ridgway, one of the few hero-generals of World War II whose fame would be polished in that hard country.[24] The events of 1950–53 would institutionalize the means of open-ended conflict and marked the moment when magical thinking began regularly to insinuate itself with decisions of "national security."

In June 1950, eight North Korean divisions lunged across the 38th Parallel to try to overrun the entire south, the new Republic of Korea having been nurtured by the United States. The assault was backed, organized, triggered, and altogether "started" by Moscow, as Truman and Acheson rightly concluded.[25] With Korea only 120 miles across the China Sea from U.S.-occupied Japan, the challenge was stark. In Washington, every congressmen but one leaped cheering to his feet when word arrived on Capitol Hill that President Truman had ordered U.S. forces to intervene. Gallup reported that 81 percent of Americans agreed.

North Korea's disciplined mechanized units easily mauled the GIs sealifted in from Japan. Raw, shoddily equipped units were rushed over from America and fed into the same meat grinder, to be cornered by superior numbers on a dwindling beachhead at the southeastern angle of the peninsula. In one of America's ultimate military achievements, undertaken against the sober judgment of the entire Joint Chiefs of Staff, General Douglas MacArthur, supreme commander of Allied Powers in the Pacific, reversed disaster on September 15 by landing rapidly assembled Marine regiments, followed by the U.S. Army's 7th Infantry Division, 150 miles behind the enemy lines at Inchon. The "Sorcerer of Inchon," as Acheson described him for the spell he thereafter cast over Washington, retook Seoul within a week and swung north. Before him lay the prize of overthrowing the brutal North Korean state, as well as of putting an end to its "Great Leader," Kim Il Sung, father of the current demigod.

And then befell what Acheson would call "one of the most terrific disasters that has occurred to American foreign policy," entailing the longest retreat in U.S. military history. As he would lament to the former president five years after the armistice, this horrific retreat and the remaining eighteen months of war "destroyed the Truman administration."[26] For the first time since Western Europe itself had been liberated, friends abroad would ask in rising chorus *"What are they thinking?"* as Americans blustered about using atomic weapons against China, an ally of atomic-armed Russia since Valentine's Day, 1950.

The conventional explanation is that disaster in Korea was plain military miscalculation, whereas Vietnam and Iraq were politically induced failures, their chief architects being civilians.[27] But that is incorrect. The U.S. decision to "liberate" North Korea was no simple military misstep. War is fought for political objectives, and this was as much a political operation as had been the conquest of Japan. It was the pursuit of a "complete victory," out of which could be forged a new united Korea—a "liberalized" north, its dams and power plants deemed essential to the postwar reconstruction of the south.[28] The architects were civilians, as in Vietnam and Iraq. MacArthur was not just following his star but executing a policy behind which—briefly—stood the nation; we were all in it together.

The next chapter discusses the decisions, the men who made them, and the particular follies of that catastrophe. What concerns us here is how the initial blood-soaked war of that first decades-long, open-ended conflict set bitter precedents.

By the time the war stalled to a close in June 1953, roughly along the lines where it had begun, Beijing had thrown in its massive People's Liberation Army of tough peasant soldiers; 36,516 Americans were dead, plus at least a half million South Koreans, most of them civilians. The compromise "die-for-a-tie" armistice left some fifty thousand U.S. troops in South Korea and a state of war with the North that technically exists to this day. The armistice terms that President Eisenhower obtained that year—and which a bellicose North Korea renounced in 2009—were ones for which Truman rightly said he would have been impeached. And when America fails at a war, further poor choices ensue.

The Korean War introduced illusions that compromised then and future U.S. policies in three truly American ways.

One has been an unreasoned emphasis on high technology. If the silver bullet of airpower didn't deliver quick victory in Korea, there was at least no shortage of opportunities for envisioning high-tech magic thereafter. Following Korea, U.S. defense would rest heavily on the country's nuclear forces, since no other exhausting ground war would possibly be tolerated again. The Vietnam War and the war in Iraq have had their own silver bullets, including helicopters and so-called computer-laden "net-centric warfare" respectively.

Second has been the lawyer's magic of signing treaties, an activity that reflects the U.S. belief that getting one potentate or another to scrawl on the dotted line, or to serve as a cat's paw for U.S. purposes, means the leader can bind his subjects to long-term American advantage. After Korea, "pactomania," as it was called at the time, induced us to sign many such defense treaties, including the Baghdad Pact in 1955, which bound America to Iran, Iraq, and Pakistan, among other signatories, for the sake of Middle Eastern stability. More recent, Americans keep envisioning outsized roles for their NATO allies, as in Vietnam, Iraq, and Afghanistan—roles that somehow go unfulfilled.

Third is the practice of notionally isolating an opponent— no need to negotiate, talk, or even note the existence thereof. After the Korean armistice, there arrived the true irrationality of imagining that some 500 million Chinese had departed the planet except as vaguely grasped menaces: Taiwan, to which the American-backed Nationalists had fled, would henceforth be

China as far as Washington was concerned. There would be no contact of any sort with the mainland for twenty years, displaying a mind-set that has reappeared since: no talking at all to the Viet Cong or to Hanoi until 1966; shunning the Palestine Liberation Organization, which today has a mission based in Washington, for twenty-seven years; and, after 9/11, no direct diplomatic contact with Iran, Syria, and still-totalitarian Pyongyang.

With Korea also came U.S. determination not to repeat past sins in doctrine and preparedness: never again, Americans insisted, would they allow themselves to be so ill-equipped or vulnerable to surprise. Disaster south of the Yalu drove the nation to accept the inevitability of "neither war nor peace," which after sixty years still frames our view of the world.

Cries of emergency in the years since Korea have not been continuous: they rise and fall in response to passing fears and excitements. America moved into its two successive long, open-ended struggles in a very American fashion. The country displayed its usual enthusiasm, fleeting attention span, and short-term welcome of the various high-energy problem solvers drawn to national security policymaking. There would be fits and starts, lots of high-toned pork-barreling, indirection, and bureaucratic tussling, as well as moments of true courage. Korea at its start had been declared a "crusade," as would be the Vietnam War and the initial determined response to 9/11. Yet in each case every crusading quality soon evaporated. Unlike a crusade, there was rarely any sense of specific high purpose, of commitments to national unity, unlimited sacrifice, or consistent objective once reality failed to adhere to fanciful notions about what could be accomplished and how.

Korea was far from a complete loss—nor for that matter was even the Vietnam War, which arguably bought time for teetering states such as Thailand and Indonesia, confronted by subversive parties loyal to Moscow or Beijing, to fall more or less into the American orbit. The initial decision to rescue South Korea enabled Japan to recover unthreatened from its World War II devastation. And it's not likely that Japan, now the world's second or third largest economy, would have forgone returning to military power had *all* of nearby Korea become a glowering unified enemy. U.S. intervention also had the benefit of deterring Stalin from another imperial predation he had planned on the far side of Eurasia, that of bringing mutinous Yugoslavia to heel.[29] Three and a half decades later, as the 1953 armistice still held, an authentically democratic South Korea would emerge as a respectable ally of the United States.

Public consciousness about the Korean War would change year by year, and in that change we find evidence of magical thinking. What had been regarded as a bloody stalemate transformed itself in Washington's eyes; ten years later it had become an example of a successful limited war. Already by the mid-1950s, elite opinion began to surmise that it had been a victory, perhaps not a glorious one, but that the decision to fight in Korea had nonetheless been "a hard choice . . . incontestably right," which is true if one wishes to look only at the original objective of rescuing the South. But that recollection passes over the nightmare defeat and appalling withdrawal from the frozen North. A magician's wand has swept away the extent that the war turned out to be a hideously taxing minimization of disaster, and the fact that it took almost two years to establish our lines securely where they had been a month after Inchon. Yet "America has never lost a war" remained part of the national myth, and the notion of having "prevailed" in Korea became a justification for going big into Vietnam.[30]

To look now at the Iraq War, we can see similar illusions taking hold of eager imaginations. Iraq, it is to be hoped, will struggle its way into democracy or at least a not-too-oppressive oligarchic state friendly to America, and not violently opposed to Israel. Then one might conclude with the still-outspoken formulators of this adventure that "victory" can indeed be declared.[31] To be sure, it would be a hard-won victory by their own standards, but "victory" nonetheless, including the ouster of one of the world's more barbarous tyrants.

Yet the notion of "victory" in Iraq, even more so than in Korea, requires a substantial retreat into fantasy. To call the war a victory, no matter what now results from the withdrawal of U.S. combat troops, leaves the door wide open to future magical self-deceptions. Talk of "victory," a term no U.S. commander uses to discuss Iraq, turns upside down the seven-year agony of an exploit assumed to be crowned with democratic fulfillment before autumn 2003. Dangerously, it encourages us to believe that *next time* we can get it right, providing we correct the mistakes of Operation Iraqi Freedom, whether ones of military tactics, diplomacy, or of all-around "management."

Meanwhile, due largely to the Iraq War, WANTED posters for Osama bin Laden fray on the walls; nuclear-equipped Pakistan rots in place, as does ever-bloodier Afghanistan; Iran is a grimly rejoicing third party; the Israeli-Palestinian antagonism is more intractable yet; and a trillion dollars have been spent. The cornered, toothless Saddam is gone, but virtually every objective of 2003 has turned into its disastrous reverse by 2010. To portray the Iraq War as in any fashion a success is symptomatic of the magical thinking being addressed here.

Americans know what military success looks like: engagements that, for one, don't end up unrecognizably, disastrously far from the mission declared at the start.

The Persian Gulf War in 1991 was an exemplary large-scale intervention—a classic tactical triumph of technological supremacy over a ruinously self-exposed enemy. This was a focused, deliberately restrained mission to expel Saddam Hussein's army from Kuwait, his wretched conscripts being strung out across two hundred miles of desert. It "stands alone in over two generations of constant military engagement," Defense Secretary

Robert Gates would reflect in 2008, "as a more or less traditional conventional conflict." [32] And if the Pentagon could not accomplish that task, with more than a half-million American warriors plus sturdy NATO backing, in about one hundred hours, well, the building might as well be shuttered. Given prominent, hands-on coalition participants from nearby—such as Syria, Saudi Arabia, and Pakistan—it was clear, as Fred Kaplan, *Slate*'s "War Stories" columnist, reminds us in his well-titled account of the later Iraq fiasco, *Daydream Believers*, that this first Middle East war looked like a considered intervention for limited geopolitical objectives. And so it was, rather than an improvised crusade.

Similarly, the 1999 eleven weeks' war over Kosovo was undertaken by a coalition of Western governments, preceded by two months of negotiation that legitimized and clarified its objectives, then followed by a UN peacekeeping mission. The presence of overwhelming backup forces nearby as well as American military leadership resting on political good sense and seasoned diplomacy further increased the chances of success. "No bomb strike was more important than maintaining NATO's cohesion," recalls the U.S. general in command. "The cutting off of any other alternative through diplomacy and the ultimate consequences that NATO could bring to bear against a small country [Serbia]—*that* brought the success." [33] Ten years later, a democratically stable Serbia applied to join the European Union. Excluded from both the Gulf and the Kosovo shoot-outs were illusions that have taken hold since Korea, including beliefs that tangible contributions from strategically significant allies are to be optional and that the theater at issue can quickly be transformed in America's image.

The Gulf and Balkan conflicts were, on one hand, each relatively simple, because they were brief, due in no small part to overwhelming force and constrained objectives. But on the other they were complicated because America was the lead nation of an alliance. In each case, however, it's significant that the conflict broke out in the ten years between the end of one long, open-ended engagement and the start of another. There were no morally tempting magics—as against "communism" or "terror"—to possess men and women in power.

Otherwise the cadre that the media describe as the "national security establishment" does much, with the best will in the world, to suffuse U.S. foreign policy with illusion.[34] These men and women spend much of their lives wrestling in and out of government with politico-military problems, and, regardless of party or style of presidential command, they have been the most vulnerable of all to the appeals of magic. The miracles expected in the Middle East and in Southeast Asia, the fantasies that attend U.S. dealings with Moscow and Beijing, and the planetary self-deceptions after 9/11 serve as only a few of the recurring indicators.

We will now meet some of the more excitable members of this calling, as well as elected officials of much the same disposition whose urgencies raise the heat worldwide when they seize on issues supposedly of their country's utmost danger.

2.

EMERGENCY MEN

Few Americans in August 2008 had ever heard of South Ossetia and Abkhazia. Yet within twenty-four hours of Russian tanks rolling through the Roki Tunnel, which connects South Ossetia with Russia, the answers flew out of Washington. Surely America could easily "get it right" on behalf of the plucky little democracy of Georgia, from which those two regions had broken away. From the White House came the usual declaration: "It must not stand," a phrase last heard when Saddam invaded Kuwait. Briefed on the tensions, Republican presidential candidate Senator John McCain discerned "a matter of urgent moral and strategic importance." He insisted "we are all Georgians," as if just rallying to his party might be insufficiently patriotic.[1]

From policy institutes, op-ed pages, radio shows, and the weekly magazines that five years earlier had urged war against Iraq, impassioned Democrats and Republicans alike thundered about appeasement by "Old Europe," as did conservative columnist Charles Krauthammer. Georgia, it was said, was like Czechoslovakia in 1938—an analogy offered by Richard Holbrooke, who'd soon return to government as a high State Department official in the Obama administration. Some enthusiasts wanted to double the stakes by hurrying this semi-authoritarian borderland into full NATO membership. Others thought it a splendid idea to equip Georgians with shoulder-fired antiaircraft missiles, as America had very quietly done for the Afghani mujahideen in the 1980s.[2]

Similarly excited responses will likely flavor, too, whatever "crisis" breaks out in the summer of 2011 or in presidential election year 2012. Many people, not just heated adventurers in Moscow and Tbilisi, are ready to play with dynamite. Maybe one in a hundred of these events will explode—but it only needs one to detonate a cataclysm. Meanwhile, today, Moscow has established new basing rights and diplomatic ties with the separatist territories. Yet the immediate assumption that Russia's other neighbors would be cowed into obedience proved wrong; former Soviet republics like Ukraine and Kyrgyzstan instead have grown even more protective of their sovereignty. And, a year after the five-day war, an independent European Union inquiry concluded that Georgia had set it off.

What kind of people are the emergency men?[3] How do they make their urgencies felt? Where and why has their influence been decisive in America's journey from the creation of the postwar world after 1945 through to Iraq, Afghanistan, and perhaps other battlegrounds soon to be entered? What can offset their influence and prevent us from embracing the same misleading passions?

John le Carré, a savvy observer with firsthand experience in secret intelligence, identifies one segment of the genre in a way that covers everyone. He describes them as "global architects, the world-order men, the political charm-sellers" who convince themselves—and too often the rest of us—that the country is safer, and the world a better place, for their manipulations.

Cries of emergency can still frame other public policy issues. Former vice president Al Gore compares fighting global warming to fighting fascism. Serious people like the superinvestor Warren Buffett compared Wall Street's burst bubble of 2008 to a "nuclear winter" and an "economic Pearl Harbor." [4] But it is to the excitements of war and peace that emergency men rally most often, and "crises" can always be found.

Being an emergency man is not a chronic condition. It can grip reasonable people suddenly faced with outright horror: lists of teachers, doctors, and village elders beheaded by the Viet Cong in the Mekong Delta, or cables about Shiite rebels abandoned to Saddam's executioners, or reports of a thirteen-year-old rape victim in Somalia being stoned to death for adultery before a crowded soccer stadium. Their energies are abruptly mobilized. They must *do something*.

Of course, emergencies arise. Emergency men wouldn't flourish if periodically their proclamations of disaster didn't mesh with the ghastliness of the larger world. Think of Rwanda, in which the fastest, most efficient killing spree of the twentieth century murdered eight hundred thousand Tutsi. But Rwanda is an example of what comes from overdosing on emergency as Washington shamefully led the effort to evacuate most of the small international deterrent force already there. That was because by 1994, the United States had endured decades of alarms false and otherwise about unknown places. For years, messy engagements on the ground had rarely turned out right. Nineteen brave soldiers had just died in 1993 to no purpose in the "Black Hawk down" debacle. And who really knew where Rwanda might be anyway? The secretary of state, for one, pulled an atlas off his shelf midway through the slaughter to help locate this heart of darkness. [5]

Emergency men and idealists are closely related. But emergency men, often occupying a pulpit of sorts, can tend toward being moral bullies as well. They know they're right and are quick to show how you are most assuredly wrong. A specific question—such as "*How* many maimed?"—gets turned around on the questioner, clearly a weakling "invested in defeat." Those doubtful toward staying the course in Afghanistan or the Middle East or Southeast Asia are surely indifferent to our (truly) gallant dead, and no doubt eager to abandon courageous Iraqis or Vietnamese or Koreans to the bloodbaths of "Islamo-fascism," "godless communism," or from wherever comes the latest "implacable enemy whose avowed objective is world domination by whatever means."[6] Emergency man rhetoric doesn't change much, whether one is confronting Moscow in 1954 (when that last call to arms was sounded in Washington) or denouncing extremism today. Choose any predicament that Washington labels a "crisis" and watch habits unfurl. See too the ease with which even the minor pests of international affairs, such as Venezuela's strongman Hugo Chávez, are labeled as "threatening U.S. national security."[7]

America has not always been so excitable in the world. The caution, measured tone, and quiet authority of the years of Marshall and Acheson bespeak a different epoch. Yet even at that time, excitable voices began urging rash exploits abroad. The Soviet occupation of Eastern Europe, Bolshevik designs farther west, Moscow's nuclear detonation in 1949, and then the Korean aggression chilled a steadily more terrifying climate. Rasher men than Secretaries Marshall and Acheson, such as *Fortune* magazine publisher C. D. Jackson, who would become a White House adviser on psychological warfare, were before long able to shoehorn themselves into significant government positions. Year by year, the perilous Cold War decades gave them increased running room. The 9/11 atrocity and the subsequent frantic American response have afforded the latest generation of emergency men and women solid footing in public life.

Today the emergency enthusiasts are less often found among diplomats or military officers. It is political appointees who now enjoy visibility and wield clout in the ever-expanding labyrinth of national security. But at the start of America's rise to global politico-military power after World War II, two significant figures helped to define the genre—a newly prominent Foreign Service officer and the most famed of fighting men.

Impulsive and occasionally reckless, George Kennan became the first intellectual as emergency man within the policymaking system. Unlike many of the aspirants to authority in the national security arena who would follow him, he possessed the credentials of a fine career diplomat. He had the languages, years lived abroad, a profound knowledge of his specialty (Russia), good negotiating skills, and an articulacy all his own. He is now regarded as a wise man of the postwar world, largely due to his sparkling writings during a long life and to an absence of interest among Americans at looking deeply into their own history.

A year after the fall of Germany, as the forty-two-year-old chargé d'affaires in Moscow, Kennan sent Washington his famous "Long Telegram," which correctly discerned in Soviet conduct a mortal threat to America's way of life. It set the foundation for a principle of "containment"—the doctrine that American strength should firmly countervail all points of Soviet expansion. But when in the following year he moved from theorist to problem solver on becoming the State Department's first director of policy planning, he increasingly came to work outside the regions, topics, and procedures he knew best.

In his office at State, Kennan was ever less the grave diviner of Russia's ancient and now frightening ambitions. Instead he was doing a lot more work in the national security arena— choreographing futile parachute missions behind the Iron Curtain and shaping a paramilitary role for the new CIA. Yet nearly in tandem he opposed the North Atlantic Treaty as an entangling alliance against Moscow, eventually urging that the European allies try to defend themselves against the Red Army through some form of passive resistance. To the Foreign Office mandarins in London, he remarked that America, like the nineteenth-century Victorian British Empire, would also have to become accustomed to "frontier wars" on the Soviet Union's far-flung periphery. In

Washington, he urged that at least two fully mechanized U.S. Army divisions be dedicated to the purpose. The Joint Chiefs of Staff brushed off the notion.[8]

For better or worse, Kennan didn't include Latin America in his "frontier." After his first and only trip there in 1949, he recommended to Acheson that the United States simply ignore that continent, which could only become ever more decrepit because its peoples were heavy with the "human blood" of "Negro slave elements," due to "extensive intermarriage." As for Japan, he believed that its future lay in reconstituting an "empire" in Southeast Asia—bringing down the last one having just cost America 97,121 dead in the Pacific and East Asia.[9]

Finally too frenetic for Acheson, Kennan was sent back to Moscow in 1952, this time as ambassador. He insisted that the CIA provide him with a poison capsule should he be singled out for abduction. It didn't and he wasn't. In conditions already rife with fears of communist subversion, he ludicrously warned the State Department that Moscow was inciting tensions between "blacks and whites" in the American South. There was hardly the need to do so. And after an unprofessional bêtise while returning from leave in Berlin, Stalin declared him non grata except for long enough to pack his bags.

Kennan had nonetheless been practical enough to back, initially, Truman's defense of South Korea in June 1950 and, by early fall, to recognize that disaster lay right around the corner as MacArthur drove north. Few in government cared to listen.

Meanwhile, Douglas MacArthur's ambitions transcended what is considered appropriate even for the republic's most successful generals while in uniform. In the autumn of 1950, he was seventy—mentally sharp, but afflicted by poor eyesight and Parkinson's syndrome. Behind him stretched the army's most glittering career: First Captain and first in his class at West Point, a Medal of Honor in World War I, youngest chief of staff at age fifty. Far beyond the rows of ribbons, more important, MacArthur remains the greatest synthesizing field commander of modern times. He superbly combined the arms of land, of sea, and by then, of air. No one in all history has led any comparable seaborne assault, let alone against such a brave and daunting foe as Imperial Japan. He alone envisioned at the start of the Pacific war how American fighting power could master the ocean as a highway and advance from Australia to Okinawa and straight on to Tokyo Bay. Once there, his rule of Japan was a political masterpiece. His egotism was notorious, but none of this could have been achieved without cool, sustained judgment and an intellect easily the most powerful among U.S. commanders of the era.[10]

In September 1950, Washington debated whether to storm across the 38th Parallel after the "sorcery" of the Inchon landing— only the debate wasn't really a debate. The initial mission of rescuing the South had essentially been accomplished. Washington, as well as MacArthur, believed that a larger purpose was just about to be fulfilled as North Korea's army crumbled once the GIs and marines struck it from behind. The terms of the UN resolution under which America fought were elaborated to ensure "a unified, independent, and democratic Government of Korea." Some midlevel officials at State wanted the UN forces to stop at the defensible Pyongyang-Wonson line. But now the purpose was to "liberate" the North in a sweeping "complete victory," not just to regain what had been lost.[11] A victory parade was planned in Tokyo for several months hence—just as one would decades later be planned for New York in May 2003, after President Bush declared the end of significant combat operations in Iraq and Afghanistan.

Who in Washington was going to oppose such an alluring objective, or refute a magician like MacArthur? Not anyone in the chain of responsibility. Truman dismissed China's oblique threats to intervene as "blackmail." To yield to communist intimidation now would invite Moscow to "take over the whole Middle East," which U.S. and British planners suspected Russia coveted at least as much as it did Western Europe. Acheson uncharacteristically spouted clichés: any show of "hesitation and timidity" would increase, rather than decrease, danger to the United States, so the country must be "firm and courageous." [12] Having returned to service as secretary of defense after brief retirement, Marshall would not undercut a commander in the field. Given China's new alliance with Stalin, the decision makers in Washington understood that what they called a "police action" held the potential of becoming the first—and the last—world war of the new atomic age. Yet crossing the parallel was endorsed by all concerned, except the enemy.

The temptation to build on success, to believe that once events start to move in one direction they will just continue going in that direction, was overwhelming. Before Inchon, the Russians, Chinese, and North Koreans were deemed nearly unstoppable. Yet after one extraordinary triumph, these two huge backers of a suddenly deflated client state were assumed to be cowed. This was a magical reversal between extremes. Likewise, an illusion formed that Mao Tse-tung's regime, flush with the mandate of heaven after twenty-two years of civil war, would tremble as Americans advanced to its borders—perhaps, as Beijing imagined, eager to go even farther to crush its revolution.

In Washington as at Tokyo headquarters, no one wanted to know more, a classic danger signal. The basic aversion to pulling back from mounting winnings, to knowing when to stop, had shut down ordinary prudence. The push north was like a stock market paying off fabulously in the early part of a boom; all the players were signing on.

By the time UN forces crossed the 38th Parallel, 5,394 Americans had been killed. There would be 28,345 more battle deaths by the armistice.

Victory was already "won in Korea," MacArthur reported to Truman that fall. China would not intervene, he added almost as an afterthought. Should it nevertheless do so, his B-29 Superfortresses, each carrying seven tons of bombs, would turn the

Yalu River that divided the two countries into "history's bloodiest stream." Here two illusions played out, as they have now through several decades. In Korea, as in Vietnam and in Iraq, a high-tech American silver bullet was believed to be at hand to dispatch the opponent easily. And in each case, as well as in so many instances between the Korean War and today's fight in Afghanistan, the U.S. leadership convinced themselves that they knew how an opponent was thinking. MacArthur believed that no one better understood what he repeatedly called "the mind of the Oriental," or the mysteries of the East. But evidently he was not thinking like a Chinese revolutionary.[13]

Bitter winds swept in from Siberia as the GIs and Marines slogged through the closing autumn, oblivious to the fact that under darkness and fog China was slipping 300,000 battle-hardened veterans across the Yalu into the North Korean mountains, leaving few traces by mid-November except strange footprints in the snow and some captured scouts whom Mac-Arthur's headquarters insisted must be Korean.

Officers at the front grew uneasy. But headquarters was unconcerned, and Washington, whatever its growing anxieties, was going along. A colonel reporting in to Tokyo HQ slammed the door when storming out of his briefing: "They're living in a goddamn dream world."

"You could almost see it coming," another officer recalled, "those young men moving into that awful goddamn trap."[14]

On the night of November 25, the jaws snapped shut. Many American outposts were never heard from again. A long, agonizing retreat passed down the freezing peninsula, leaving liberated Seoul to the victors' mercy behind it.

Hubris is but part of the story. "Magical thinking?" asks an old soldier who was MacArthur's official spokesman and thereafter an engineering brigadier in the drive north. "It was all part of the confusion."[15]

MacArthur had remained steely during the war's first disastrous months. The triumph of Inchon, after all, had been conceived, planned, and ultimately launched all within those eighty-one days following the initial invasion. Taking the offensive, MacArthur was again remaking Asia. But as his forces reeled back down the peninsula that winter, he did not concede that he had made a horrible misjudgment. Instead he insisted that he—and the interests of the United States—were being stabbed in the back at home.

From a cerebral, indomitable, and ultimately overconfident persona, MacArthur tipped into an unsoldierly emergency-man mode. This most political of generals let it be known to congressional war hawks and to the Truman administration alike that what he concluded was Washington's sudden timidity about China, and its attraction to "the concept of appeasement," compelled him to fight under "extraordinary inhibitions." He didn't have enough troops to make "a 100-percent difference" and "to clear out all Korea." [16] He urged that the remnants of the Chinese Nationalist military huddled on Taiwan be unleashed against the mainland. Since the White House forbade him to take the war directly into China by striking bases behind the Yalu River, he also let it be known that North Korea, and perhaps the South as well, was being surrendered. Dismissed on April 11, 1951, for defiantly contradicting Truman once too often, he returned immediately to an America he had not seen for fifteen years.

The biggest ticker-tape parade ever greeted MacArthur in New York City on April 22. In speeches and in Senate testimony, he argued that China's intervention had handed America a God-sent opportunity to create "a free Asia" that might just be the beginning of rearranging the world. Calm in manner but employing language redolent of ultimate danger, he insisted that "all-out forceful effort" would be required, an implicit reference to the Strategic Air Command's atomic weaponry.

"Alone if necessary," he averred—if other nations "haven't got enough sense to see where appeasement leads." Sure of his truths, he depicted the alternative as the slow death of the West. America faced "Communist Jehad."[17]

MacArthur, and the hawks to whom he gave eloquent voice, observed JCS chairman General Omar Bradley, were "perfectly willing to propel us into an all-out war with Red China and possibly with the Soviet Union, igniting World War III."[18] Theirs was a formulation we have seen since: if "atheistic communism" or "terror" or radical Islam is the enemy, and if there is no substitute for victory, then the logical conclusion must be that victory cannot be achieved until communism or terror or radical Islam has been eradicated everywhere.[19] Americans cheered MacArthur from the heart, but the cautious policies of Truman, the failed haberdasher, appealed more to the sensible, pragmatic nation than did the world-transforming thunders of the American Caesar.

The more literary of MacArthur's critics dusted off their hands. They had used a new epithet, *unilateralism*, to condemn his reasoning, though they had the grace to acknowledge the term as academic gobbledygook.[20] The seesaw war continued. What little remained of Seoul was lost again and then once more retaken by the Americans. The Chinese People's Liberation Army reinstalled the Great Leader Kim Il Sung in Pyongyang. And the "coalition" led by America turned out to be far less than it sounded, and not for the last time—"token forces at best," MacArthur testified.[21] Americans opposed the war in greater numbers than they would Vietnam at its worst.

MacArthur did not entirely fade away. He entered a long twilight as chairman of that grand but obsolescing corporation Remington Rand. As for the war that ended his stellar service, it took strange shapes in national memory. Even the vaguely determined number of its American dead shows the odd angles: the Pentagon did not get the number right for fifty years, and the *New York Times* still got it wrong on Memorial Day 2010.[22]

• • •

Although Dwight Eisenhower's record in international meddling is less than admirable, the five-star general entering the White House in January 1953 set a tone of calm routine. America's best fighting men are rarely prone to frantic belief. An officer seldom rises in the U.S. military by harping on emergency, and Eisenhower possessed "the long patience of the soldier."

Unlike MacArthur, he appreciated the candid feedback of sound staff work. He had spent too much time delegating the problems of one trouble-fraught day after the next to believe that he could burst from a phone booth to remake the world on the fly. He also enjoyed the minutiae of economics, essential to understanding national and global difficulties. He read reports, studied the financial pages, and had a crackling command of statistics. Altogether anything but an emergency man, he employed the time given by a chilly peace to deliberate on events, to examine contingencies, and to do so by as rigorously composed a process as the pains of those years permitted. Scholars today cite his shrewd, forward-looking direction of the National Security Council as an example for the Obama administration.[23]

This was one of the few presidencies since Korea without relentless, systematized feuding at the top between "vicars of foreign policy" at State and "steel-trap minds" at Defense, with sharp-elbowed national security advisers jockeying in between.[24] Eisenhower's secretary of state, John Foster Dulles, conducted the nation's diplomatic business firmly, and clearly under his chief's authority. The dour, reliable senior partner of Sullivan & Cromwell was not someone likely to be rolled over if faced in court. In office, Dulles was like a lawyer employed to argue positions that he hesitated to believe. He talked the language of emergency— "massive retaliation," "agonizing reappraisal," going to "the brink." Yet he was the only top official on record to ever express doubts that America should be the world's greatest military power in the first place.[25] He kept circling the globe in the hope of spreading the burden of opposing Moscow and Beijing among as many accommodating regimes as possible. Repelled by French and British colonialism, he resented American entanglement in the most fateful alliance he would help to create—the Southeast Asia Treaty Organization, SEATO, intended explicitly to be an East Asian NATO. Here the United States joined with those colonial powers, as well as with Australia, New Zealand, Thailand, the Philippines, and Pakistan, to guarantee the defense of Cambodia, Laos, and the newly created South Vietnam against unspecified "aggression."

Of course not all was prudent during the Eisenhower years. The stalemated Korean War was closed out by quietly letting China know that, this time, nuclear weapons might in fact be used. And Eisenhower signed off reluctantly on a 1952 Republican Party platform that had called for America to "roll back" communism from Eastern Europe. Four years later, the emergency men percolating in the middle ranks of his administration succeeded in fostering a doomed rebellion in Hungary. Washington also staged feckless coups in Iran and Guatemala, tried to do so in Syria and Indonesia, and sent five thousand marines in 1958 to hit Beirut's quiet summertime beaches to counter what was perceived as a communist-inspired power play by Egypt. The reigning belief was a mechanical conviction that if one "domino" fell to Moscow, then row upon row would collapse around the globe. The fear was palpable.

But caution from the top by and large prevailed—and for reasons worth heeding. Eisenhower had no appetite for America "to police the entire world," and to try to do so without allies, he said, was behaving "no better than Genghis Khan." [26] He pulled back from intervening in Vietnam in 1954 when he recognized he had little support in Congress and no overseas backing other than France. He stepped away from Hungary, saying America would not be a knight-errant in a place "as inaccessible to us as Tibet" (where, inanely, the CIA would soon play at fomenting rebellion against China). [27] And each move he took in thwarting the British-

French-Israeli invasion of Egypt in 1956 was based on principles of the UN Charter. Yet among the dominos stood Laos, where, as a new analysis concludes, "action was substituted for any real examination of national interests."[28] America got secretly involved in a civil war in this backwater of some 2.3 million people that set the stage for its self-entanglement in the much larger one in adjacent Vietnam.

Meanwhile, Eisenhower slashed spending on his beloved army. Another Soviet-sponsored assault like that in Korea, let alone an outright invasion in Europe, would be met by nuclear weapons, courtesy of General Curtis LeMay, the cigar-chomping head of Strategic Air Command. And here Eisenhower was rather less wise. How might the administration then deal with "little wars," critics asked, if its preferred response was nuclear? Contemptuous of that horrible term, the president offered an all-too-glib answer: if the country could win a big one, it could certainly win a little one.[29] It was as if the police department was supposed to drop blockbuster bombs to break up sidewalk quarrels. It was also an answer that previewed illusions to come of easy victory in Vietnam and in Iraq, each of which was expected to be a "little war" that could be handled in conventional, high-tech-intensive ways.

Before retiring to Gettysburg in January 1961, the general delivered the farewell address that introduced the phrase "military-industrial complex" and warned against the "scientific and technological elite" who were making their hunt for money and influence "virtually a substitute for intellectual curiosity."[30]

Not particularly an elite of science or technology—rather more one of law, business, and political science faculties—the vigorously youthful men who arrived in power three days later saw few limits and acted accordingly. The term *New Frontier* had first been embraced by Kennedy at the Democratic National Convention in July 1960. Now it became their catchphrase for bold, high-energy initiatives. Kennedy's inaugural, the only one ever to be devoted exclusively to foreign affairs, set a milestone in consolidating the emergency-man presence within the American system. The era would be a time of talking up "heroic leadership," a classic alchemy of practical issues into magical menaces and remedies.[31] Heroic leadership invokes means and makes them ends: a drowsy citizenry will be exalted by all the challenge and excitement, at least until the flag-draped coffins return home.

In early autumn of 1960, the emergency-man-in-full strode onto the national stage as the magic of television entered nearly every American household. John Kennedy was the first such figure to attain the presidency, and—like Richard Nixon, whom he would defeat—was a believer that the world was an endless chain of extremities converging on himself. Kennedy denounced the aging complacency of the Eisenhower years, which had become a "decade of inaction" when "the tide began to roll out for the United States" and a red one began to pour in. No one carried more conviction than the dashing young small-boat commander, now our president, in depicting his country's "hour of maximum danger."

Americans were hailed as the "watchmen on the walls of freedom" in a world half slave and half free. Kennedy offered nothing remotely regretful about this predicament. President Eisenhower had spoken of the painful necessities. "Every gun that is made, every warship launched, every rocket fired," he declared, consumed money that could better be spent on schools, hospitals, highways: a world in arms left "humanity hanging from a cross of iron." Kennedy's speech, however, trumpeted the pledge to "pay any price, bear any burden, meet any hardship, support any friend, oppose any foe," which amounted to a blank check tossed before the world.[32] Misjudgment was inescapable as appeals to emergency became part of an institutionally underwritten way of life.

Kennedy's language canonized the alarmist vision, but he pressed well beyond rhetoric. His was a simplifying view of the world, manifested in a profligate resort to covert operations, a secret endorsement of assassination as ongoing policy, the self-avowed personal "excitement" over pointless exile raids on Cuba, and a fascination with elite, glamorous outfits like the Green Berets, whose weapons and headgear he helped to select.[33] His zeal included "nation-building" in places where nations had yet to come into being, police aid was no longer scattershot but would be systematized under a newly created bureau, the Office of Public Safety, whose name could have come out of Orwell. That office promptly bestowed its gifts on some of the worst violators of human rights outside the communist world.

"Vigor" is a basic preoccupation of the sick, and Kennedy—having twice received the last rites for Addison's disease—knew that death stood near. He faced down its specter with a frantic sexuality and clamorous saber-rattling. Through the excitement, he inspired a hundred thousand law partners and executive vice presidents to recover their youth and a sense of simple urgent objectives. All were part of a generation that had fought its way to victory in the greatest of wars only fifteen years earlier. Now they recalled the days when they had discovered unimagined strengths in themselves, when they were the spearhead of an unequivocally united nation.

"Great crises produce great men," Kennedy concluded in *Profiles in Courage*—the title a classic emergency-man formula to finding solutions in existential transcendence, not in technical achievement; in demigods, not in inventors. And, consciously or not, this most impatient of men did not intend to be left out of the pantheon. Three and a half hours before he died, his last speech cataloged his thousand-day military whirlwind: Minuteman missiles boosted 75 percent; Polaris submarines increased from twenty-four to forty-one; nuclear warheads doubled; counterinsurgency forces in Vietnam multiplied sixfold. It didn't matter that he knew soon after entering office that the "missile gap" with Moscow—a keynote alarm of his campaign being that

Eisenhower had allowed the Soviets to develop a superior ICBM force—had never existed. After endless denunciations of Eisenhower's lassitude there was not much room for second thoughts.

Our nation remembers Kennedy as a champion of peace, and like any civilized man he had elements of peace in him. The Test Ban Treaty stands witness, as does his "seething" attempt to prevent Israeli development of an atomic bomb, which he believed undercut the U.S. stance against nuclear proliferation.[34] So does his genuine shock over the Cuban Missile Crisis, which he handled calmly despite urgings from General LeMay, the retired Dean Acheson (ever more of a hard-liner once out of government), and other advisers to strike first and ferociously. But this overall trick of memory is best explained by a desire to keep him with us as an ideal leader, distanced from how his proud commitment to Vietnam would end. The people around him, writing the insider accounts, were also eager to forget how their militant idealism had led to the war. During these troubled but exhilarating years, Americans were promised they would henceforth "live on the edge of danger" not only as watchmen but as nation makers, not just defending the world but reshaping it to press freedom forever forward.[35] Such ambitions were unlikely to pay off. Adrenaline may be a servant of greatness, but it is not its incubator.

For the brisk and eager men who joined him, ahead lay more thrilling tasks than splitting stocks or teaching GOV101, let alone reviewing corporate contracts—as one of the best of them recalled when leaving a tedious legal practice to join Defense Secretary McNamara's civilian general staff at the Pentagon. Professors, previously for the most part advisers to the departments dealing with national defense, now became true line practitioners. Journalist Theodore White proclaimed the emergence of "a new priesthood of action intellectuals."[36]

A variation of this term was *defense intellectual*, designating men and eventually women in academia who moved in and out of government as appointees or consultants. They gained inordinate influence by default as the national security apparatus expanded and the politicians whom they advised walked ever deeper into the dark. Policy agendas were becoming truly strange, and multiplying to such an extent that a politician couldn't keep up: nuclear escalation ladders constructed by RAND (then a U.S. Air Force–backed think tank in Santa Monica); social development programs for Sumatra; counterinsurgency tactics taught in Tay Ninh, and so on. Of course the defense intellectuals were as much in the dark as anyone.

An admirable sense of possibility, even of compelling obligation, often accompanies the actions of emergency men. But their passions habitually segue into a confidence that pushes into commitments wise and foolish. The same "Special Message on Urgent National Needs" that Kennedy delivered to Congress in May 1961, challenging the nation to send a man to the moon, presented a second urgency. He upped the ante on what Eisenhower had much more tentatively started, laying the groundwork to deploy some 17,492 military "advisers" to South Vietnam. He vividly conveyed a just revulsion at Hanoi's means of delivering liberty. Its killers, he added correctly, had murdered "four thousand civil officers" over the preceding twelve months, a number that includes entire families. Who could turn away? It was all "a thrust of action and purpose," glowed Arthur Schlesinger, Jr., the distinguished historian whom Kennedy brought down from Cambridge to chronicle his eight years in office.[37]

Informed voices of caution offered quieter alternatives. Laos was the deadly "crisis" of spring 1962; Moscow and Hanoi's support of one of the two Laotian political factions led Secretary McNamara to suggest ordering forty thousand American troops into its misty hills. Meanwhile the Joint Chiefs recommended using nuclear weapons should China intervene.

Kennedy finally resisted open involvement, saying privately that a stand over the South Vietnamese border would be better than a stand in landlocked Laos. The army chief of staff, General George Decker, bitterly resisted the temptation to intervene in either place. "We cannot win a conventional ground war," he argued, elaborating that, in Laos alone, hundreds of thousands of soldiers would be required to attain such an objective.[38] Though he would argue that guerrillas could be handled by any good soldier, he didn't believe that additional Green Beret teams would make much difference in South Vietnam, a state of some 17 million people. There was no such panacea, he warned. Deeper military involvement in the region needed to be looked at as a major war. This wise officer had fought valiantly in New Guinea, the Solomon Islands, and the Philippines; he knew something about jungle combat. Kennedy and McNamara forced him to retire after serving just two years. "We have a problem making our power credible," the president concluded, "and Vietnam looks like the place."[39]

The administration firmly believed in developing a capacity to respond across the whole spectrum of violence with precision. National security aides spoke matter-of-factly about their power to inflict one-eighth "DOE" ("death on earth"), about trading a dozen American cities for a half-dozen Soviet ones—an attitude popularized as "thinking about the unthinkable." The alternative to all-out destruction or "massive retaliation" against the Soviet Union would involve intricate scenarios of ever-less-limited war—weirdly proportionate, its targets growing in magnitude in a gradual "escalation" right up to apocalypse, depending on what the Kremlin did to deserve it.[40] Nearly every working assumption tended to forget the real-world human reactions that would be awakened. For decision makers to climb coolly, rung by rung, up the escalation ladder would require that U.S. cities be evacuated methodically at the start of the ascent. To imagine that the roads of, say, Washington, D.C., might be any less gridlocked during a red alert on the brink of total "DOE" than during the evening rush hour was, perhaps, illusory.

It took Eisenhower to say from retirement that all this talk of general war was "preposterous." He was right and most Americans came rapidly to agree; the family-fallout-shelter mania of 1961–62 collapsed into one more popped bubble on Wall Street.

Similar creative nips and tucks were being applied to the other end of the spectrum of supposedly surgical force. Within three weeks of departing Harvard's Massachusetts Hall for the West Wing, national security adviser McGeorge Bundy met with the CIA's deputy director for operations and unblinkingly reviewed the means of expanding Langley's capacities to do murder.[41] This blind faith in what happy outcomes assassination would bring to the game of nations descends straight from the sixteenth-century fantasy worlds of *Utopia*. Fidel Castro, to be sure, would be high on the list. But tweaking of the direction of history might apply to China as well—to "strangle the [nuclear] baby in the cradle." A genocidal communist regime thought for good reason to be insane might not be able to restrain itself from "stepping on the capitalist cockroach," as Chairman Mao promised. So means of cleanly doing away with China's weapons scientists got on the agenda, the president adding the twist of "anonymous planes" to preempt China's entire nuclear program.[42] Military adviser General Maxwell Taylor proposed some sort of paramilitary feat. Prudent opinion at the State Department stood in the way, the matter ultimately becoming moot eleven months after President Kennedy's death as China set off "Device 596" at Lop Nur.

The magical belief that intense risk inescapably confers exalted rewards worked its way through the political bloodstream. It is a strange attraction that draws us in to circumstances from which we should run screaming. A willingness to walk along the edge of extremity is apparent in Kennedy's heroic, truly kamikaze claim that "any dangerous spot is tenable if men—brave men—will make it so." [43] He was heedless that peasants-turned-warriors in the Mekong Delta might agree.

Succeeding as president after the gunfire in Dallas, Lyndon Johnson retained his predecessor's entire national security cohort. Johnson had minimal interest in global excitements, traveling to Europe only once, for the funeral of the former West German chancellor. Tragically, he did not push back against the sparkling, hardworking advisers he had inherited. "It looks to me like we're getting into another Korea," he confided anxiously to McGeorge Bundy in spring 1964. [44] And there's no record that LBJ shared the encroaching illusion that the Korean War had been an American victory. Yet, like pushing forward to liberate North Korea, the decision to go big into Vietnam was a debate that wasn't much of a debate. In 1964, Congress overwhelmingly authorized the president to "take all necessary steps, including the use of armed force" to protect a regional ally. But it was based on faulty intel-ligence that indicated U.S. warships had twice been attacked without provocation in the Gulf of Tonkin. The White House had as much latitude as it wanted, with no declaration of war—as would be true for Iraq, and as it had been for Korea.

In his final years, Eisenhower advised Johnson that "if you are going to do this," at least "swamp the enemy with overwhelming force." [45] Yet the carefully crafted worst course of all was chosen—deep, direct involvement without enough force for the fully demanding task, which the Joint Chiefs had estimated might require something like a million American combat troops. Instead a step-by-escalating-step of "graduated" air war against North Vietnam got under way in February 1965. And that July, one hundred thousand soldiers were dispatched to South Vietnam.

A decade after Kennedy's first rousing confrontations with Moscow, now often styled "the Crisis Years," such drama was already becoming the stuff of parody. Woody Allen captured the tone in

his short film *Men of Crisis* (1971), which celebrates a nation's por-
tentous "men of power" as they go forth to battle self-inflicted
emergency.

By that time, 53,849 Americans had already been lost in Vietnam, and many more would follow. Richard Nixon had arrived as
president—riding the "lift of a driving dream," a revealing phrase
truly his own.[46] It unites the American-approved word *dream* with
the more troubled *driving,* an utterance from deep in the heart of
that driven man. Like Kennedy, he was fascinated by those international theatrics that, he asserted, were the only real grounds
for the United States to need a president.

But while the socially insecure, deeply uncollegial Nixon resented the polished, assured "Ivy Leaguers" who had surrounded
the fallen president, he still chose to bring close the most complicated one of all, the Harvard professor who had been among
the louder voices invoking the nonexistent "missile gap" when
Nixon had run for president in 1960. Nixon knew an intellectual
adventurer when he saw one, but found Henry Kissinger useful as his national security adviser. He observed that Kissinger
was one of those people who foment crises "to earn attention
for themselves," adding that the professor would have set one
off over someplace like Ecuador had not Vietnam been in play.[47]
Nixon was mocking his adviser's tendency to build on fears that
Nixon himself had less artfully exploited on his own way up. Each
referred to the other as "paranoid," the abiding insult from men
and women who believe they have their own obsessive suspicions
under control.

Meanwhile, the State Department would be marginalized
as it had been under Kennedy, who dismissed it as a "bowl of
Jell-o," and as it would be again during the run-up to Iraq in 2003.
A self-described "big-league operator," Nixon imposed the tight-
est, most centralized of presidential command structures over
foreign affairs.[48] In this case, however, such single-minded authority failed. The much-overrated summits and pirouettes with Mos-

cow and Beijing rested heavily on fantasy and will be examined anew in the next chapter. They were not even effective enough to stop each of the communist behemoths from sending Hanoi an endless flow of munitions that killed Americans daily.

The title of the book Nixon wrote before his presidency, *Six Crises* (1962), captures the hyperexcitable culture of political power. Extraordinarily, it often shows the author on the point of losing his head as he obsesses with maintaining self-control—from the first "crisis" of investigating communists as a junior congressman in 1948 to the last "crisis" of campaigning against JFK in 1960. Nixon's unique contribution to diplomatic strategy was to have his intermediaries confide to his opponents that they had a borderline psycho on their hands. Kissinger, for example, had to let it be known in Moscow that the president was "out of control" on Indochina. Another White House emissary was directed to imply that Nixon was somewhat "crazy"— experienced and brilliant, to be sure, but capable of the utmost ruthlessness.[49] It is an intriguing diplomatic method rather hard to picture being conceived, let alone applied, by Eisenhower, Marshall, Acheson, Dulles, or, in fact, Kennedy.

Typical of emergency men, both Nixon and Kissinger were bored by the slow, dismal science of economics, however much that probing discipline can illuminate the nature of cost and choice, let alone reveal how business and much else in the world functions. Economics was not his "central field of study," the national security adviser admitted modestly.[50] Power to Nixon and Kissinger meant military might. To the extent they even thought of it, a member of the NSC staff recalled, international economics "enjoyed equal rank with U.S. policy in Haiti" but less than that in Peru.[51] Using America's financial clout to pressure the Soviet Union wasn't in the cards. Moscow would instead gather in a windfall of trade, loan, and technology benefits offered in the unfocused hope of military and diplomatic cooperation.

"I refuse to believe that a little fourth-rate power like North

Vietnam doesn't have a breaking point," insisted Kissinger in the fall of 1969.[52] He was blind to a basic fact of strategy outside the struggles between first-world countries; bombing an undeveloped, agricultural, essentially invertebrate society—like North Vietnam with its primitive infrastructure—would have minimal useful impact. And given the relatively restrained level of damage that the American nation could stomach inflicting in any event, he was proved wrong about a "breaking point." But Kissinger had a sardonic view of disengaging that he shared with the president: "Withdrawal of U.S. troops will become like salted peanuts to the American public; the more U.S. troops come home, the more will be demanded." [53]

Whether in his dealing with the Soviet Union, China, or the Vietnam War, each has been acclaimed as a "realist," a decision maker who grasped global forces and their outcomes as they truly, harshly are. They have been credited with having grimly reckoned balances of power while writing off unneeded, unsustainable involvements. Nixon's effusive toasts to Mao at the Forbidden City in February 1972, as the bloody Cultural Revolution ground over the Chinese people and as those munitions rolled south, is commonly offered as Exhibit A of that realism. Exhibit B is the deals with the Soviet Union. And few in Vietnam War–seared America were paying much attention to the fates of Kurds, Bangladeshis, Timorese, and Hmong caught up in the "grand strategies" of the time. Yet given the minimal curiosity that Nixon and Kissinger shared toward technology, economics, and demography, their being characterized as "realists" tells us more about the pundits of that day, and of our own era, than about this president and his diplomatic chancellor. Both men were dreamers of power, each imagining that the purely political, dramatic objectives pursued over the tactical short term would prove creative and enduring in the long.

Emergency men often call on the idiom of "realism," proud in meeting the nastier aspects of the world head-on while supposedly demonstrating prudence and self-restraint. But emergency men can be surprisingly unworldly, particularly those who are incurious about the larger world of achievement in economics and business. Being preoccupied with the higher statecraft, they can also be vague about places and peoples. Impatient with the planet's minor irritants, for example, Kissinger brushed off the killing by Jakarta's generals of fifty to eighty thousand Catholics in remote East Timor, only four hundred miles from Darwin, Australia. After all, he asserted, it was "self defense" occurring "in the middle of [Muslim] Indonesia."[54]

This bad-moon presidency collapsed in 1974, at the midpoint between World War II victory and the start of the Iraq War. Its dishonest assertions of "national security" to cover up the Watergate break-in and other criminalities were exposed. But blood in the streets, goes an old saying, brings opportunity to a certain kind of talent.

During the two-and-a-half-year presidency of Gerald Ford, the men who would devise the Iraq War were beginning to make their names. These included two successive White House chiefs of staff moving into a vacuum of power. The first was Donald Rumsfeld, former congressman and a man "who always reminded me of the Wizard of Oz," scoffed William Seidman, chief of the White House's Economic Policy Board, since "he thought he was invisible behind the curtain as he worked the levers, but in reality everyone could see what he was doing."[55] The second was Rumsfeld's protégé Dick Cheney, future defense secretary and vice president. Opportunity also came for even younger men, such as Democratic senate aide Richard Perle and defense analyst Paul Wolfowitz, who would become prominent, deeply informed critics of the Nixon/Kissinger effort to manage Moscow via compromises reverently known as "détente." Among their contemporaries in the national security arena were up-and-comers like diplomat L. Paul Bremer, one of the scores of assistants who had first tasted executive power while on Kissinger's bloated National

Security Council staff. Passing in and out of government, most of these participants would contribute usefully to peeling away the nation's security delusions during the years leading to the Soviet collapse in December 1991. They, at any rate, had yet to catch fire as emergency men and ignite what lay around them.

In 1977, the newly arrived President Carter announced that America had overcome its "inordinate fear of communism." One more secretary of state, this time the distinguished lawyer Cyrus Vance, warmly endorsed that sentiment, arguing that Moscow's party boss, Leonid Brezhnev, "is a man who shares our dreams."[56] Unfortunately, these dreams were discovered at an awkward time, during an arms race in which only one side was racing. "When we build weapons, they build," said Carter's defense secretary, the physicist Harold Brown. "When we stop, they nevertheless continue to build."[57] And what they were building included a new class of missiles targeting Western Europe. In December 1979, Carter—an unusual emergency man whom we'll get to know later—changed his opinion overnight about these apparently not-too-threatening people when they invaded Afghanistan. But such dramatic oscillations are part of the emergency sensibility.

Meanwhile, the Vietnam War, which had ended with Saigon's collapse in April 1975, quickly slid down the memory hole, much like its Korean predecessor. New national security studies programs at elite universities ignored it. It was not examined seriously at West Point or the Army War College, and the U.S. military jettisoned just about anything to do with counterinsurgency—all those counterguerrilla, "little-war" tactics and doctrines so romantically invoked during the Kennedy years. Overall, Vietnam was considered only in passing. It was a "syndrome" that pundits concluded would keep hindering America from involving itself on such third-world killing fields as those of El Salvador, Angola, and Afghanistan.

The fall of Vietnam and the still-clinging hopes for détente show another facet of emergency men. Emergency men overreact to failure, as when their supplications to Moscow proved worthless. Binges of optimism are followed by deep pessimism, as in a bank run or stock market crash. The same men who had been overstimulated in the early 1960s about competing with Moscow, and who had urged an exemplary stand in Vietnam—Bundy, McNamara, Arthur Schlesinger, all honorable men—now raised a histrionic chorus of despair. The 1970s were the worst years of American economic performance since the Great Depression, and as the country suffered its severest recession since World War II, there were all the more reasons to compromise, they argued. They referred respectfully to the "legitimacy" of the Soviet regime as they gave their own country at least half the bleak responsibility for the arms race.[38] The only way to deal with that co-superpower was through deep understanding of what made it so fearful of the West. Anyone extremist enough to suspect Moscow of violating arms control treaties, suborning peace groups in Western Europe, or backing urban terror was simply spurning the peaceful intentions of those who truly understood.

Time was by no means on the side of the West, I wrote in 2002, a decade after the Soviet collapse; the fiercely armed yet sclerotic giant might not have been long for this world, but no one knew what convulsions, fatal to far more than itself, might disfigure its last moments.[59] Like Eisenhower, Ronald Reagan let it be known that America's strength did not rest on military might but on industry and ideals. Foreign policy was not Reagan's preoccupation, nor had it been Eisenhower's. From his 1981 inaugural on, Reagan made it clear, as had Eisenhower, that the country's future depended on strengthening an economy that ultimately rested on the energies of individual Americans. He revived Eisenhower's calm assumption that the United States was in fine shape, not lethargic, faltering, in need of desperate overtures to the east, or burdened by malaise. In contrast with Kennedy's self-described years of "burden and glory," Reagan could focus relatively sustained efforts toward sufficiently enduring ends, like Eisenhower, because less adrenaline (a substance of short-term effect) was being pumped into the game of nations. There was none of the heat and little of the excitement that characterized the White House of twenty years earlier: men always "in a constant hurry, taking last-minute decisions to last-minute meetings, making last-minute corrections to last-minute statements, as if they were always trying to catch up with events." [60]

A man who had seen the theatrical from the inside, Reagan disdained the frantic rhetoric of "crisis" and "emergency." Nor did he speak of "balances of power" and "spheres of influence." He crossed out contentious phrases in drafts of his staff's NSC directives, which he read thoroughly. He kept insisting to his closest advisers that his purpose was "quiet diplomacy." To call the Soviet empire an "empire" and to add that it was evil and its days numbered, which he did, was merely to say the obvious. He also used the word *crusade* before Britain's parliament to describe the struggle. But the procedures taken to this end were measured. They were reinforced by felicitous timing, America's resurgent economy, frequent cooperation with Congress, and steady collaboration with two firmly supportive governments—the conservative one of Britain and the socialist one of France. For the first time, a cabinet-level apparatus was created to integrate international economic and financial matters with national security. Now the United States could "follow the money," a phrase from Watergate being applied to international criminality: Washington aimed to undercut the roughly 80 percent of Soviet hard currency income derived from selling oil, gas, and guns. America was coolly and comprehensively playing to its strengths. He also rallied the nation to an intensified struggle of ideas first, territory and weapons mastery second.

From the outset, five deliberate steps were mapped out and implemented. [61]

First, and for the first time, Soviet power was assessed from the perspective of cash flow, and the cash curtailed by methods such as exposing Soviet double-dipping schemes in Western financial markets (for instance, using the same oil projects to secure multiple loans) and imposing a highly effective embargo on pipeline equipment.[62] Second, the eastward flow of legal as well as stolen Western technology was cauterized; some forty specific sales protocols signed during the Nixon/Kissinger détente were revoked. Third, U.S. news and cultural broadcasts to the East received the same priority that Kennedy had placed in putting a man on the moon. Through them the very legitimacy of Moscow's regime was challenged. Fourth, Soviet resources were bled deliberately in the world's backwaters, as in Afghanistan, where Soviet manpower too was consumed by U.S. support of the mujahideen, the loosely aligned Afghan freedom fighters. Meanwhile, the United States avoided its own third-world snares, which easily could have become major traps. The administration refused to be lured into war by the terrorist outrages of Libya's Colonel Muammar Gaddafi. Nor did it get entangled further in the Lebanon snake pit even after 241 Marines were killed in 1983 by a truck bomb from Hezbollah, the militia group formed to resist the 1982 Israeli invasion; Reagan's aim was to win the Cold War, and no vital U.S. interests were being affected by Lebanon's own sufferings.[63] Finally, the promise was quietly conveyed to Moscow that an all-out, inconceivably expensive high-tech arms race would only accelerate as America armed mightily to parley.

By the time Mikhail Gorbachev came to power in March 1985, halfway through this administration, the most that the new general secretary could do was to put a better face on the mounting changes that he was forced to accept. Contrary to today's myths about his cooperativeness, he boosted by 45 percent the Soviet military budget—likely already larger than America's—to consume one-third of the Soviet Union's entire gross domestic product.[64] He personally signed off on a Five Year Plan to expand the twenty-ton arsenal of pathogens (plague, brucellosis, tulare-mia, anthrax, smallpox), a cache utterly unknown to U.S. intel-ligence.[65] And he intensified Soviet violence in Afghanistan while vowing to maintain a firm grip on the subject nations of Eastern Europe. But while the Soviet capacity for violence grew, there was not much room for maneuver. And Gorbachev's attempt to reenergize Communist Party rule by conceding what he thought would be a harmless degree of freedom of speech spun exuber-antly out of the Kremlin's control.

Of course, Washington's emergency men kept working their mischief. A deputy undersecretary of defense—T. K. Jones, pre-viously a program manager at Boeing—created a global propa-ganda debacle by insisting that "with enough shovels" America could easily recover from all-out nuclear war. Fantasts such as Lieutenant Colonel Oliver North of the NSC staff believed them-selves global operators rather than policy coordinators. Trying to rid Central America of communism led to would-be secret CIA mine-laying in Nicaraguan harbors, about which the Sen-ate Intelligence Committee claimed it had been informed, at best, only obliquely by the Agency. And the usual sordid com-promises of supposed necessity flourished. Saddam Hussein, for example, raked in billions of dollars in Agriculture Department and Export-Import Bank loans while being styled, and supported, essentially as an ally in his war against the Islamic Republic of Iran. He received high-resolution U.S. satellite images of Iranian military positions and, from Special Envoy Donald Rumsfeld, a pair of golden cowboy spurs. He was pleased to show official U.S. visitors his videos of the stacks of Iranian dead slaughtered by Iraq's chemical weapons; Washington rationalized that the crucial thing was to save Saddam from Tehran's mullahs.[66]

And there were dreams enough right at the top of this admin-istration. No one but the president imagined the "Star Wars" mis-sile defense system to be a bulletproof shield—except the shaken Red Army chief of staff, and the head of analysis in the Soviet defense ministry. Along the way, Reagan's profoundly serious talk of complete worldwide nuclear disarmament made his "realist" admirers shake their heads and smile. But the point would be revived twenty years later, in 2007, by establishment figures such as his former secretary of state George Shultz and then advanced in 2010 by President Obama, whose Nuclear Posture Review for the first time seeks a world free of nuclear weapons.

In 1989, Reagan passed the final tasks of victory to a competent successor—the only case of a two-term president handing the White House over to a member of his own party since Ulysses Grant in 1877. That was no accident, as Leninists say, because what occurred in international affairs, as in launching the eighteen-year economic boom that began in 1983, was not a triumph of the passing intensities of magic, but of sustained upbeat patience, working to live through emergency, not to live in it. Basically pragmatic, America understood.

George H. W. Bush—former Texas congressman, ambassador, CIA director, and Reagan's vice president—deftly handled the central emergency of his own time in office, though he ended the Persian Gulf War in 1991 by disastrously encouraging thousands of Iraqi Shiites to their deaths in a general rebellion against Saddam while the tyrant was still in power. Bush nonetheless stuck to the focused, deliberately restrained mission for which 697,000 Americans led an authentic partnership—including French foreign legionnaires and an armored division, 14,500 Syrian troops, and fighting men from Saudi Arabia and Pakistan—to rescue Kuwait.

With so quick a victory, it was tempting to push farther into Iraq, on to Baghdad, and to get rid of Saddam—with almost certain similar ease, some argued. But an internationally savvy, combat-tested president recognized that objective as a different war and foresaw the prospect of America's becoming an occupying power for years. He had a veteran's scornful view of war hawks, whose wizardly vaporings he had dismissed as those of "a lot of macho guys out there that want me to send somebody else's kid into battle." His national security adviser, retired air force lieutenant general Scowcroft, a former fighter pilot and 1947 graduate of West Point, also remembered how alluringly simple it had looked in September 1950 when sudden success had beckoned American fighting men into North Korea.[67]

Thereafter, from 1993 through 2000, numerous U.S. military actions occurred that President Bill Clinton described as humanitarian or peacekeeping. The Pentagon called them "Operations Other Than War," such as the entanglement in Somalia, which began in 1992 under President Bush, to culminate tragically in 1993, and the next year's deployment of 22,394 troops to Haiti in order to return, for the time being, a legitimately elected president three years after a military coup; nothing that lasted was accomplished in Haiti—the four dead American soldiers now forgotten. Then, in 1996, there followed the dispatch of 16,500 U.S. troops as part of a NATO Stabilization Force to separate warring Bosnia, Serbia, and Croatia. And the U.S.-led NATO intervention during 1999 to compel Yugoslavia to withdraw its military and paramilitary forces from Kosovo nonetheless was also a success, to be followed by an effective UN peacekeeping mission and by internationally conducted war crimes trials in The Hague. There might have been emergency men in Washington ready to conjure up vaster, more ambitious U.S. involvements out of the existential implications of these Balkan hatreds, but no one was listening in bull market, high-tech, White House–sex-scandal-preoccupied America.

Emergency predilections, however, are always somewhere at hand. Soon after 9/11, former President Clinton mentioned in an interview that he still wished he had been president during an epic global crisis: an admission that gives us insight into the darker aspects of power, and the longings for those great extremities that make ambition virtue.

• • •

One need not be an ideologue to be an emergency man. Even so arch an emergency man and as opportunistic a politician as Richard Nixon had been too canny a customer to put himself in the hands of ideologues, being cordial but uncommitted toward true believers like conservative thinker/activists William Buckley and James Burnham. But ideology has a way of making up for any gaps in the everyday sense of menace: there's got to be a righteous mission somewhere.

In the decade between the Soviet dissolution of 1991 and the atrocity of 9/11, ideologues ruminated over different emergencies and solutions: finishing off Saddam, checkmating the looming threat of Beijing, and remaking the armed services through a high-tech "Revolution in Military Affairs," a term that oddly parroted an obsolete doctrine for gearing up the Red Army to invade Western Europe.[68] Out of office and energetic, such men and women, many of whom would enter the George W. Bush administration, eyed the revamping of the Arab world, a place that has never proven malleable to outside wisdoms. It was an explosive combination of the likeminded, should a flame come too near.

Years ago the Yale psychologist Irving Janis wrote *Groupthink*, highlighting the dangers of that refuge for the intellectually weary. He examined "collective rationalizations of shared illusions generally believed," "shared belief in the group's inherent morality," "illusions of invulnerability to a risky course of action," and naturally, of "negative stereotypes of out-groups," meaning those of us who might disagree. He took as a prize example "the best and the brightest" advisers to Presidents Kennedy and Johnson.[69] This classic work could now be updated to include the latest wave of individuals who had all the answers for Iraq and Afghanistan, for renditions and interrogations, for "Old Europe" and new adventures.

Many books and articles describe the emergency men of the post-9/11 era who declared victory too soon in Afghanistan and then helped induce the Iraq war. Kaplan's *Daydream Believers: How a Few Grand Ideas Wrecked American Power* captures a common theme: the work of the men and women involved wasn't based "on a grasp of technology, history or foreign cultures but rather on fantasy, faith and willful indifference toward those affected by their consequences."[70]

Their names and temperaments may be familiar, and we'll get to know them as well as their predecessors and successors in the chapters ahead. But it is still barely understood how they were able to take such colossal, uninformed action. Josef Joffe is publisher-editor of the German weekly *Die Zeit,* with a second career as a Harvard-trained professor of political science at Stanford. He asks flat out: "Why a free and boisterous polity fell for the notion that the United States could just wade into the hellhole of Iraq?"[71] He's doing us the kindness of looking for rationality in a foreign policymaking arena where magic often intrudes.

But let me offer an answer. A perfect storm of folly had been gathering as ill winds blew from four points of the compass. A burst of high pressure was going to set it off.

First, in September 2001, the core belief ended—and in a supremely disorienting way—that the world was running rather well for America; that history itself had halted in our favor. Second, villains who looked and sounded right out of central casting surged onto the world stage. Third, Osama bin Laden and Taliban leader Mullah Omar—even the secular Saddam Hussein—underscored a dimension of religious conflict that resonated in America, the most observantly religious of great powers. And fourth, the country had a president who was the least interested in foreign affairs since Lyndon Johnson—and the least exposed to the world since Warren G. Harding—whether by travel or military service. Moreover, George W. Bush yearned for a moral story with a decisive outcome. Thanks to the U.S. government appointment processes, like-minded enthusiasts populated the national security offices around him in depth.

The last observation is significant. By this point the American

system of patronage politics was interlocked with a highly cultivated national security establishment. Generations were succeeding each other among the cadres of talented people who had first
been deployed in bulk on Washington during the Kennedy years.
The staffing problems were becoming not too different from
those of the European Commission, that empire of paper in Brus-
sels, where actual parent-child dynasties are to be found.[72] "People
matter" in policymaking.[73] They matter particularly at the level
where policy is shaped and directed from day to day. That's why
it's illuminating to consider one sequence of recent appointees in
the Department of Defense. We get an insight into the way the
system functions, and how one cadre of emergency men, at least,
were able to put their energies to work.

Backed by the eminent Democratic senator Henry Jackson,
whom he had served as a defense policy staffer, Richard Perle had
been appointed in 1981 as an assistant secretary of defense during
the Reagan years, working well with Wolfowitz, who became an
undersecretary. Perle recruited twenty-nine-year-old Douglas
Feith as an aide; then in two years Feith became a deputy assistant secretary, the bureaucratic equivalent of a four-star general.
Twenty years later, during another transition of appointees in
2001, Perle let it be known that he would serve at the Pentagon
only as an ostensible outsider, chairing the Defense Policy Board,
a group of civilian advisers to the secretary—but, he added quietly, "I'll have all the influence I need."[74] His defense-related
business interests had become too lucrative, said he, to return to
government full time. Perle effectively pressed the claims of Feith,
a business partner while on the outside during the Clinton years.
Feith became the Pentagon's undersecretary for policy, Wolfowitz's former post in the Reagan years. In the musical chairs of
executive branch appointments, Wolfowitz now returned as
deputy secretary, Mr. Rumsfeld's number two. Feith's new role,
however, entailed "managing the Defense Department's international relations" (as the job description then was phrased at

the Pentagon) and, this time, it included creating and executing policy for Iraq.

And from the six-person lawyer/lobbyist firm that he had created during the Clinton years, Feith in turn proposed a candidate for the subordinate slot of assistant secretary for special operations and low-intensity conflict. But Michele Van Cleve's absence of qualifications for the role denied her the support of the Republican chairman of the Senate Armed Services Committee, backed by the entire Special Operations Forces community, which is why that key Pentagon post was vacant on 9/11. Yet as consolation to her patrons, and due to some experience as a Senate staffer—as well as to Republican ties that included a spouse who had directed the Pentagon's 1980–81 transition—she ended up as head of U.S. counterintelligence, an office not requiring Senate confirmation.

Such friendships and alliances are to be found in every administration. Yet the arbitrary quality of significant appointments is the most risky in senior positions tasked with national security. In Iraq itself, the Coalition Provisional Authority, established by the United States and its allies following the invasion, existed as a transitional government for eighteen months. It was headquartered in the Green Zone, as the 3.8-square mile international tract in the middle of Baghdad, previously the Baath party's administrative center, was called. The CPA was run by Paul Bremer, who returned to government from a directorship at Kissinger Associates, the business consultancy created by the former Secretary in 1982—Bremer's own cause pushed forward by the boss. The circus atmosphere amid Saddam's ornate, chandelier-studded Republican Palace has been well conveyed in Rajiv Chandrasekaran's *Imperial Life in the Emerald City*. There was little room in this show for the experienced Arab hands from State and the armed forces. They were sidelined by Bush loyalists, abetted by the above friends at court, with remarkably many new arrivals, as Chandrasekaran explains, who included children of campaign contributors and of previous Republican appointees.

72

Few of the players in Washington or in the occupation of Baghdad knew anything more about the Middle East than their predecessors in the 1960s had about Southeast Asia. But part of being an emergency man is wading into action with cheerful confidence, with that valor of ignorance. Afghanistan, it was assumed, had essentially been won. Thereafter, an undertaking as vast as transforming Iraq, let alone the other Middle Eastern regimes that were expected to fall in line, would surely succeed in the limited time that an impatient American democracy accords its overseas ventures. So too in South Vietnam: the defense and recasting of that long-ago ally, a member of the United Nations and of the World Bank, was believed literally in some business-magazine way to be *manageable*, given U.S. resources, skills, goodwill, and, of course, magic effort.

3.

THE MYSTIQUE OF AMERICAN MANAGEMENT

ANTHROPOLOGIST MARGARET MEAD OFFERED AN ACUTE OB-
servation in her analysis of American culture, *And Keep Your Powder
Dry*, written during World War II. Americans work hard to fix
problems, she said, while the English, and so many other peoples,
take pride in putting up with theirs. America's faith in its systematic capacity to fix things has energized the U.S. pursuit of success
since well before the world's first business school was founded at
Harvard a century ago. America is all about solving difficulties,
and management is the quintessential American science. It boasts
specialized academies, a rigorous literature, and radiates an aura
of civilian-driven power and decision. It is the logical next step up
from that traditional "Yankee know-how" with which America
had overleaped the early worldwide impact of English industrial
practicality. Many citizens encounter at firsthand the effectiveness
of pragmatic, collegial American management in the 26 million
small enterprises in which most of us are employed. *The Millionaire
Next Door*, after all, is not about the neighboring corporate big-
wig but the determined entrepreneurs of dry-cleaning chains or
franchisees who have prospered in a culture of enterprise like no
other. We know from experience that it works for us.

• • •

Yet why do emergency men, and so many other Americans besides, speak confidently of our power to "manage Iraq," "manage the rise of China," even to "manage the world"—and then attempt to put this hands-on authority into practice?[1] Why are the qualities of actual business management, which have built a $14 trillion economy, poor guides for what can be achieved when trying to untangle other nations' ethnic, ideological, or political troubles? How do emergency men expect to spread the risks of their overseas ventures among America's allies and clients when the going gets tough? And why do they presume that even our sternest opponents, glaring across a negotiating table, are subject to managerial direction?

To "manage" a global enterprise such as Exxon or Merck is to run it ably and according to tested good sense. In theory, reasonably well-identified problems such as market share and cost of sales are broken down into their constituent parts and the answers worked out step by step, often quantitatively. Methods tend to be rational, replicable, teachable, and formed by experience. Surprise is to be minimized. The definition of management assumes a final, responsible authority over the people and processes that one manages. Of course, big, established, apparently solidly run companies self-destruct periodically amid America's cycles of boom-bubble-bust. Management consultant Jim Collins has just brought out another bestseller, *How the Mighty Fall*, which discerns among the fatal flaws "hubris born of success" and "denial of risk and peril." Yet, thankfully, such illusions don't permeate American enterprise to the extent they do the country's national security arena—nor have the deadly consequences.

In the decades after World War II, Americans increasingly canonized managerial science and the well-schooled professional executives who practiced it. As a generation of aging entrepreneurial *founders* of corporations such as Ford, Martin Marietta, and Kerr-McGee were displaced by business *administrators*, esteem reached the level of deference to these polished young men's "businesslike" methods of practical, unemotional accomplishment. By the time Robert McNamara arrived in Washington to reshape the Defense Department in 1961, his belief that "every problem can be solved" did not seem preposterous. A good manager could manage anything, whether Ford or Frito-Lay or a disintegrating jungle nation like Laos. The promise of managerial omnicompetence played to the country's can-do instincts.[2]

Against the continuous backdrop of industrial achievement, Americans unsurprisingly believe that the attitudes and techniques of managerial success can be applied to politico-military problems abroad. Numbers may be used to make the case for action. There are always some lying around, such as the happy reckoning that earnings from Iraqi oil revenues would underwrite the American invasion and occupation.

Believing that any problem can be methodically broken down to be triumphantly reassembled convinces emergency men that they have an empirical grasp of its details. Concerns about sects or demographics or visualizing an opponent's motivations come second, or third, to emphasizing the procedures. Gary Bald, who had served in the FBI for twenty-eight years before taking over the Bureau's National Security Branch in 2005, concluded that to know distinctions between Shia and Sunni wasn't as important to his responsibilities of global counterterrorism as being a good manager.[3] It's a comforting frame of mind, as upbeat, positive, and go-getting as a Tony Robbins motivational speech at a corporate retreat. Get the formula right and you can't lose.

Today lots of Americans do mean "manage" or "run" when they discuss getting various millions of people in Europe, Asia, and the Middle East to share the wisdom of our ways. All great powers wield hefty influence. It is another story, and a very American one, to leap from that often exaggerated degree of influence to the conviction that Washington can usefully assert open, direct control over what others might or might not do. In no other country do politicians, diplomats, and intellectuals use *management* as a commonplace term to denote international aspirations. No one in Brazil speaks of "managing" Argentina; no one at the Quai d'Orsay sends memoranda or inspires articles in *Le Monde* about "managing" the European Union; Japan doesn't speak of "managing China"; nor did the Soviet Union talk of "running" Eastern Europe, even when those captive nations were dominated by the Red Army.

Yet notions of managerial effectiveness are a daily part of intelligent American conversation. Consider the *Atlantic,* a sparkling barometer of informed opinion. Several years ago, the cover featured an article titled "Ten Rules for Managing the World," by Robert D. Kaplan, a national correspondent fascinated by military culture and technologies. This thinker has since been appointed to the Obama administration's Defense Policy Board. *Foreign Policy* magazine, for its part, offers the views of a former Clinton undersecretary, David J. Rothkopf, about the "the Committee that Runs the World." That committee is said to be the NSC staff. But to fancy that you're "running the world" along with your office colleagues, no matter how well positioned you all are in the Old Executive Office Building, means clearly that you're misconstruing the world altogether.

Such fantasy twines dangerously over the most problematic place of all: China. The *Atlantic*'s literary editor, Benjamin Schwarz, previously a foreign policy analyst at RAND, writes specifically of "Managing China's Rise." (Douglas MacArthur sought to do just that, sixty years ago.) Norah O'Donnell, chief Washington correspondent for MSNBC, asks "Why don't we corral China?"; and Richard Haass, president of the Council on Foreign Relations (a private organization despite its official sounding name) reflects, as if eager to wrangle the economic heft of Guangzhou into an America dude ranch, whether Asia's "dynamism can be effectively and peacefully harnessed." [4]

At a policy conclave in Washington, Nicholas Burns, former undersecretary of state and recently the nation's highest-ranking career diplomat, also spoke about the need to "manage China's rise." Treasury Secretary Henry Paulson offered a speech on China titled "Managing Complexity and Establishing New Habits of Cooperation"—a title, observed *Fortune* magazine's Nina Easton, "that a therapist might borrow for a parents' lecture on coping with defiant adolescents."[5] Such discourse presumes that China and its future are subject not just to appropriate pressure, but to direction from the West Wing, the seventh floor at State and at Langley, think-tank seminar rooms, or just possibly from the chairman's office at Goldman Sachs. More moderate words such as speaking judiciously of "Coming to Terms with China's Rise" or of just "handling" it seem not to suggest themselves.

Crisis management is another expression that parachuted in during the Kennedy years, like *defense intellectual*. It appears in conference titles, such as UCLA's intriguing "Crisis Management and U.S.-China Relations" symposium with the Shanghai Institute of International Studies. NATO handbooks similarly use the phrase, defining it as one of "rapid decision-making."[6] The mix of "crisis" and "management," however, can be a dizzying cocktail, and "rapid decision-making" is a talent usually quite opposed to what prudent effectiveness requires. "Crisis management" recalls that encapsulation of the Kennedy White House as the place where men were in a constant hurry to implement their last-minute decisions about last-minute events. It's an adrenaline-charged ritual that many practitioners proudly believe to be a skill, and it has found a place in many administrations since. The trouble is that speed energizes emergency-oriented decision makers, and there are always plenty of "crises" toward which they can surge, whether in South Vietnam or in South Waziristan.

Even if merely the shorthand for a robust foreign policy, all these words say a lot about deeper desires and how Americans think about international affairs. The belief that other peoples and distant places can be smoothly administered foments delusions about what is achievable, over what time horizons, and with what resources. By attempting to control the inherently uncontrollable, emergency men inevitably distance themselves from the truly valuable businesslike habits of routine, accountability, gathering feedback, and charting realistic timelines over which to accomplish focused objectives.

At forty-four, Robert McNamara became the star of the Fortune 500 as president of Ford Motor Company. An excellent statistician with a Harvard MBA and two years of teaching at the B-School, he had then joined the original group of nine whiz kids who so efficiently ran statistical analyses during World War II for the U.S. Army air forces. At war's end they sold themselves en masse to Ford, where McNamara raced on as the most formidable of the company's high command. A futurist of safety and fuel-efficient engines, he nevertheless rarely dimmed his brilliant headlights as he dominated decision making less by reason than by his position and personality in a near-authoritarian corporate culture.

Kennedy appointed this nominally Republican business magnate to rein in the Pentagon's bureaucracy, which, as Eisenhower had grimly understood, clearly included the military. No matter that McNamara's international concerns until the month before had extended little further than Ford's European market share. He brought with him that "gift of certainty," as Barbara Tuchman dryly puts it in *The March of Folly*, that made him indispensable to Kennedy and Johnson. Donald Rumsfeld possessed the same "gift" during George W. Bush's presidency. The apparently indispensable qualities of each man may explain why McNamara is the longest-serving defense secretary to date, and Rumsfeld the second longest.

McNamara was seen to have "all the best qualities of a professional manager" because "he doesn't worry over details or the possibility of making mistakes." That bouquet from a RAND acolyte was, of course, offered before Vietnam hit full force.[7] Kennedy called him the smartest man he had ever met; and indeed one of McNamara's most seriously smart moves was when he stood by the president to resist the Joint Chiefs' recommendation to invade Cuba, which would have risked nuclear war, during the 1962 missile crisis.

McNamara surrounded himself with a disciplined, superbly organized successor generation of whiz kids, few if any of whom avowed any ideology beyond corporate imperatives. They adopted the business-magazine magic of the moment: "systems analysis," a method that can make sense of big problems by studying every facet to find the critical path forward through all the complexity. But they applied systems analysis to much more than the functions where it can be legitimately useful, such as scrutinizing budget lines and assessing bombing sorties. The modeling behind the fateful decisions of Vietnam—whether, for instance, to send more troops or to bomb the North in the first place—was akin to the calculations of risk that spawned the banking debacle of 2008. The math could be spun out to several decimal places, yet would serve no useful purpose because it had not been set to account for the human factors. On Wall Street, decisions rested on lots of wishful assumptions that buyers would keep pushing up housing prices forever. In McNamara's Pentagon, the infinite digits beyond the decimal points represented delusions about an enemy that had trampled Foreign Legion machine-gunners into the mud of Dien Bien Phu. And that was too emotionally charged a fact to be figured into McNamara's equations.

To Kennedy's national security cohort, concludes Bruce Kuklick in his incisive study of intellectuals and war, *Blind Oracles*, "the main problem was undermanaging reality."[8] They refused to believe that some other force, such as the single-minded commitment of hard men in Hanoi, acting through extraordinarily brave warriors in the South, might compromise their supremely rational structure for making decisions.

A generation after Vietnam, Donald Rumsfeld also set out to assure the country that victory stretched out before America like a shimmering highway. Nearly word for word in speaking of Iraq, he invoked one of McNamara's most magical guarantees: "Every quantitative measurement we have shows we're winning." He also echoed his predecessor's business jargon of "metrics" and "quantifying progress," of provinces measurably pacified, and of megawattage generated.[9] Of course when McNamara and then Rumsfeld uttered those lines, Vietnam and Iraq were spiraling downward.

One big difference separated them, however—not that it would make much difference to what befell America in either war. Rumsfeld had never compiled an actual managerial track record remotely comparable to that of Robert McNamara. He had instead made his name in politics, rising from Congress into the Nixon and Ford administrations, maneuvering Vice President Nelson Rockefeller off the Republican ticket in 1976, and deflecting George H. W. Bush from filling the slot. After working the levers as President Ford's chief of staff, he had then moved himself to the Pentagon to serve adequately as secretary for thirteen months while the administration dwindled; Rumsfeld returned to his home state of Illinois in 1977 to become a businessman, the CEO of the ailing G. D. Searle pharmaceutical company.

Undertaking a corporate turnaround is a peculiar executive function. The common practice of slashing the workforce and selling assets to boost stock price, which Rumsfeld adopted, does not resemble the creativeness and teamwork required to build, say, a solid enterprise that produces cars and trucks or, for that matter, delivers breakthroughs in life science. As a former member of Searle's Big Six accountancy relates, Rumsfeld was an "erratic CEO."[10] But he brought value as a Washington insider, making sure that NutraSweet, the aspartame additive cooked up before his arrival, broke through to Food and Drug Administration approval. Once Searle was downsized and its miracle product loose on the shelves, the company finally attained a sale price serious enough to make any chieftain's fortune. Thereafter, backed by a private equity fund, he conducted a second turnaround of cuts and asset sales at General Instrument, another company heavily invested in a Washington-regulation-thick environment, this time within high-definition television technology.

Kennedy had acclaimed McNamara as "tough" and "ruthless." Nixon said exactly the same about Rumsfeld when bringing him into the White House. Each had a technique of rapid-fire questioning designed to intimidate. Once Rumsfeld got into business, *Fortune* placed him among America's "Ten Toughest Bosses" for his performance at Searle. In the George W. Bush administration, he showed "toughness" in spades whether in turf fights with State or in punishing subordinates.

U.S. Army Chief of Staff General Eric Shinseki, for example, disagreed with the secretary that a relatively small U.S. invasion force could constructively be in and out of Iraq in three months or so. Shinseki was, of course, right. Having been grievously wounded in Vietnam, he also knew combat and occupation firsthand. He too warned the emergency men against illusions of easy pickings. "Something in the order of several hundred thousand soldiers" would probably be required to occupy postwar Iraq, he testified to the Senate Armed Services Committee.[11] With echoes of McNamara's rebuke of General Decker on the slide into Southeast Asia, Shinseki would be ridiculed by Rumsfeld and Wolfowitz—to retire, yet to return to Washington in 2009 as an esteemed secretary of veterans affairs.

Such supposed toughness and ruthlessness are enemies of proportion. They hold us back from being able to recognize the bad news while we still can learn from it. And those who rely on these sterling abilities end up running an organization only on the strength of their uninstructed will.

Sloganized forms of conduct tend to follow. At first, leaders who are deemed "tough" can be admired in policy circles as decisive. "We will impose our reality on them," Rumsfeld said of the Iraqis.[12] But under scrutiny, such assertions prove to be little more than the self-impressed promise that one will overcome problems through the superiority of one's own temperament. "Unflinching confidence has an almost mystical power," author Ron Suskind observed about Rumsfeld's last boss in the Oval Office. "It can all but create reality."[13] That is emphatically magical thinking. It is also likely to be a blustering form of self-comfort, like whistling past a graveyard.

There are different styles of management. In contrast to McNamara's exactitude, Rumsfeld's approach featured a narcissistic form of micromanagement. From his office there blew a "blizzard" of "drop-everything-and-get-me-an-answer-immediately" memos that "on a typical day could be two dozen; some days it topped one hundred," one of his deputies recalls admiringly. Recipients, however, soon learned that they could ignore such snowflakes because neither the secretary nor his staff had the attention span to follow up.[14] At the same time, the secretary's relationships with his peers in the cabinet fizzled. The Department of Defense trusted neither the CIA nor the State Department. "It was like Shia and Sunni in Washington," recalls Charles Duelfer, President Bush's choice in 2004 to continue the search for Iraq's nonexistent weapons of mass destruction: "If you can't organize Washington around our common mission, how on earth are you going to do that in Baghdad?"[15]

There are certainly many examples of sound leadership in government; otherwise Washington would collapse on itself. In government as in industry, change at the top can deliver an effective new direction in short order. Louis Gerstner, arriving at IBM as CEO in 1993, resuscitated and by 2002 had turbocharged a foundering giant. In a similar redirection of an enormous organization, Robert Gates arrived to replace Rumsfeld in 2006. He encouraged Rumsfeld's remaining aides to leave. He took steps that, however their merit proves out, were different from staying the despairing course in Iraq. And he became the only defense secretary to be asked to stay in office by a new president, let alone one of the opposite party. He'd lower the heat further in 2010 by directing his military staff to return to wearing dress uniforms at the Pentagon, with jackets and ties, rather than the combat fatigues that soldiers had symbolically worn since 9/11.

The magic of such leadership is that it draws on no magic. It merges steadiness with the ability to change when change is necessary. It involves asking the right questions and not expecting to know the answers in advance. It means also granting authority while insisting on accountability, having a sense of proportion and good judgment, and relishing no Oz-like claim to see the future.

Like McNamara, Secretary Rumsfeld came to personify the emergency man as supermanager. The spectacle played out all too intensely right down to his final memorandum for victory: "21 Illustrative New Courses of Action." Those twenty-one new courses included social engineering for young Iraqis—that is, jobs programs and reconstruction funds to "start rewarding good behavior" in order to "stop rewarding bad behavior." Always the micromanager, even after his fall from grace he mapped out the steps of his departure. There would be ceremonies at the Pentagon with bands and a parade, a last flight to Baghdad, and a new item on the Pentagon website celebrating "Six Years of Accomplishment with Secretary of Defense Donald H. Rumsfeld." His efforts, the site declared, had "liberated 50 million people in Afghanistan and Iraq." More specifically, they had "liberated 31 million Afghans from Taliban control" as well as "27 million Iraqis from a brutal dictatorship."[16] But there were more serious problems than the math. Uncannily like McNamara, he had not understood how to overcome a dispersed, fluid, and poorly defined enemy whose terror tactics and devastating low-tech innovation didn't fit into American concepts of how an enemy should fight.

Larry Bossidy, the legendary chairman of Honeywell, offers a straightforward three-step course of action for getting things done in business.[17] Effective execution comes down to "aligning people, operations, and strategy" upon a seriously formulated objective. These linkages tend to break apart when applied to grand forms of foreign policy—as, for example, the determination expressed by Secretary of State Rice to "realign" the Middle East.[18]

Questions about the relative benefits of procuring the F-22 fighter jet or how most efficiently to preposition combat cargo at sea are problems perfectly suited to savvy public policy management. The more meticulous, the better. Those are the types of problems at which Secretary McNamara had excelled. His methods of planning, programming, and budgeting (PPBS) are still used at the Pentagon to allocate resources among competing projects. But that type of systematic control is less and less effective as the problems to be solved become more abstract. This is understood in business, rarely so in foreign policy. Anyone who spoke of trying to "realign" a competing corporation or of "managing" an industrial sector, let alone composing "rules" to do so, would be laughed out of the boardroom.

Let's look at the three components in Bossidy's prescription to see why they don't relate to effective execution in foreign policy. First, consider the "people." Of course, getting things done in business is often crippled by confident, well-credentialed men and women who prove inept at particular tasks. It's a fact just recently restated among partners of elite private equity firms such as THL, Quadrangle, and Apollo in episodes that mimicked the subprime mortgage debacle. Expert financial engineering turned out to have been based on easy money and the confidence that one could always flip companies, in industries from mattresses to magazines, to yet greater fools. The end of the boom years exposed the delusions.[19] In foreign policy making, however, the mismatch between talent and task shows itself more often, because the extent of political appointments randomizes abilities and temperaments.

In a Pentagon directed erratically from the top, it could not be assumed that the men and women whom Rumsfeld brought with him into the building—as senior officials with enormous responsibilities—were up to administering their own inboxes. Tom Ricks's horrifying account of the American military adventure in Iraq, *Fiasco*, observes that "the owlish Feith was a management disaster" whose "office was managed worse" even than elsewhere in this unevenly administered hive.[20] And Deputy Secretary Wolfowitz's priorities were sufficiently askew as for him to lose count of the American dead in Iraq. The correct number was 51 searing percent higher than what he reported to the House Appropriations Subcommittee on Foreign Operations in 2004.[21] Eighteen months before Rumsfeld's own exit, Wolfowitz left the Pentagon to be dispatched by the White House as president of the World Bank. But the managerial style that he transferred to the bank led to his departure after two tumultuous years.

It's not unfair to single out such appointees for their managerial shortcomings. Business magazines do so all the time in profiles of corporate bosses. Nor were management gaps limited to the Pentagon. George Tenet, a former Senate Intelligence Committee staffer who directed the CIA from 1997 to 2004, couldn't read a balance sheet, according to the chief operating officer of In-Q-Tel, the Agency's technology investment arm. Within the Coalition Provisional Authority in Iraq, observed Lieutenant Colonel Brad Jackson, U.S. Army, "There were a lot of people who, being political science majors, didn't know what an income statement was. . . . That was giving us ulcers."[22] Since a core mission of the CPA was to reconstruct Iraq's economy, this was unhelpful.

"Operations" is the second place where the link breaks down when sound managerial execution in business is compared to the procedures in foreign policy. In business, "operations" embraces the day-to-day handling of accounts, supply chains, and sales channels. It's knowing and quantifying the details, as fine-tuned adjustments to a production line. But attempts to apply this degree of deeply informed managerial exactness and hands-on control to foreign affairs have, by and large, been counterproductive for decades. A faith in the pipe dreams of political engineering nonetheless persists among "global architects" at the Pentagon, the "world-order men" in Langley, and the professors and think-tankers who concern themselves with national security. The left, right, and center are afflicted with resemblant strains of the virus. Consider just one unhappy neighborhood: the results in Pakistan, Afghanistan, and Iran of the nipping and tucking that emergency men believe make the world safer.

In 1958, the Eisenhower administration gave a nod to Pakistan's first military coup. Martial law was imposed to ensure that center-left secularists couldn't win upcoming elections; the Pakistani military became the praetorian arbiter of the country's politics, and Washington began its long lament that U.S. aid sent to Pakistan should be used against communists (think Al Qaeda and the Taliban today), not against India. U.S. fine-tuning—including sanctions as punishment for Pakistan's nuclear program—continued through to the support lavished on the regime of General Pervez Musharraf during 1999–2008, followed by an attempt to rig some power-sharing arrangement between him and a new favorite, former prime minister Benazir Bhutto. "They need a reality check," says retired lieutenant general Talat Masood, a commentator in Islamabad, about U.S. policymakers whose maneuverings have resulted in no more than 10 percent of his countrymen feeling well disposed to America. His advice was followed promptly by a bipartisan echo as Foreign Minister Shah Mehmood Qureshi scolded the Obama White House: "Pakistan [will] not stand for being micromanaged." [23]

Across the western frontier in Iran, U.S. efforts to whittle that country's destiny into shape have been ceaseless. They became apparent early on when they replaced the spineless Shah on his Peacock Throne in 1953 and continued through the self-described policy of "carrots and sticks" offered to Tehran by the George W. Bush administration, the "sticks" to include commando reconnaissance missions out of Iraq. In dealing with other nations, Washington always holds to the faith that it can effortlessly adjust for the better. Even the shrewd former NSC counter-terrorism adviser Richard Clarke, who served in both the Clinton and George W. Bush White House, believes in such tweaking. He writes matter-of-factly about "Jimmy Carter's abandonment of the Shah of Iran"—as if the fate of Iran, and of that country's furiously mobilized population of 50 million, could by then have been channeled into decisions out of Washington.[24]

Afghanistan, in turn, has been chronically nipped and tucked. Not long after 9/11, Milt Bearden, a former CIA station chief in Islamabad, summed up the U.S. effort as having gotten "too fancy" and "too cute by half."[25] In that case, delusions of exactness were growing fast out of the ever-expanding mission not just to destroy Al Qaeda's base network and to punish the Taliban, but to try to build a democratic political order.

Of course, opportunities emerge to apply focused, well-informed U.S. pressure—as the Obama administration is doing today in seeking to align Russia, China, and Europe to wrestle with Tehran's corrupt, threatening regime, and as the Bush administration succeeded in tandem with Egypt, in maneuvering Syrian troops out of Lebanon in 2006 after the assassination of former prime minister Rafik Hariri. Nearly always, however, these applications of "carrots and sticks" cannot be done by oneself alone.

Nonetheless, American policymakers' belief in the steadiness of their fine-tuning can be found at work just about anywhere. For example, Thomas Barnett, recently professor at the U.S. Naval War College and author of *Great Powers: America and the World After Bush*, speaks in a single breath of simultaneously engineering both sides of Asia. He applauds the decision to invade Iraq as the "right to lay a Big Bang on the Middle East's calcified political landscape" while urging Washington to "lock in China as soon as possible as the land-power anchor of an East Asian NATO."[26] Such miracles could supply the entire soundtrack of *Groundhog Day*. It might be recalled that the last "East Asian NATO," to cite John Foster Dulles's description, was SEATO, the alliance that helped pull the country into Vietnam. And as always, details get overlooked amid geopolitical charm-selling—such as how China, let alone Japan, might react to this idea.

Another obstacle arises in effectively managing the day-to-day operational details of a troubled world. To execute successfully in business, a manager can't blink at reality. A money-losing factory must be shuttered; a fading product line has to be replaced. When such decisions are avoided, a declining corporation ends up as a data point in Jim Collins's *How the Mighty Fall*. But in the game of nations, a lot of resistance boils up against adjustments that require a prudent step or two backward.

When Ronald Reagan pulled U.S. forces out of Lebanon, for example, even his supporters offered ritual denunciations of "retreat" and of the president as "irresolute." To step back might even be immoral, emergency men believe, since the hands-on exercise of American authority is surely synonymous with peaceful world order.[27] Once there, we're there, as Americans heard from a retired U.S. Army vice chief of staff, General Jack Keane, who championed "the surge" in Iraq: "We're going to be here for 50 years minimum," along with America's "forward industrial bases." Thankfully, withdrawals are nonetheless being made, but in the direction of Afghanistan, where Keane had instructed the incoming commander of U.S. forces in the spring of 2002, "We are in and out of here in a hurry."[28]

The third critical component of Bossidy's model—strategy—entails the longer-term deployment of resources and the ability to make choices while there is still opportunity to choose without duress. It seeks to lay out objectives over time with clarity, a dependable resource base, and relative predictability. In business, America has pioneered the rigorous analysis and practice of strategy. An entire industry composed of such global consulting firms as McKinsey, BCG, and Bain assists companies to make long-term decisions along lines that can lessen risks and heighten opportunities. In U.S. defense, however, such rational coherence keeps proving elusive.

Two sharp scholars from a respected think tank, the Center for Strategic and Budgetary Assessments, welcomed President Obama's appointment of a more or less bipartisan national security team. But they cautioned that "US political and military elites no longer exhibit competence at formulating, much less implementing, good long-term strategies." Their benchmarks include the years of Marshall, Acheson, and Eisenhower, when relative dispassion and a dour settling in for the long haul were paramount. The cause of the decline in performance, they conclude, "is an intellectual one."

In U.S. national security planning, strategy tends to be equated with a list of desirable outcomes. There is little specific discussion of how obstacles are to be surmounted, or of the appropriate resources to be committed. During the Clinton years, they argue, policymakers seemed to believe that "strategy is an illusion." The problems of the day were to be worried about during the day, and tomorrow's tomorrow. For a description of the ensuing Bush years, they cite the president's famous dictum: "Our strategy can be summed up this way, as the Iraqis stand up, we will stand down."[29] What he announced, of course, is not strategy but the outline of a desired end. He said nothing about how to get there. The results are now apparent in abysmal logistics and maintenance of the Iraqi Security Forces, and of hospitals, as the state slides back toward the corruption familiar from the days of Baathist rule.

Whether in operations or in strategy, business commitments

usually vector in on closer timelines than do ventures in foreign policy. It is difficult for a CEO to avoid very public failure when he or she stumbles. Mistakes quickly show up in stock collapse, sputtering sales, and rivals' gloatings as they snatch market share. If he can, the CEO must revamp costs, personnel, advertising, and objectives at warp speed. Any self-deceptions about "staying the course"—as had been voiced at IBM before Gerstner arrived and at the Pentagon before Gates—would generate unflattering profiles in *Forbes*. Yet in the foreign policy arena, even a "CEO president" can adhere year after year to a demonstrably ruinous pathway, as in Iraq from fall 2003 through 2007, and amass kudos for being bold.

A final break in the link of effective execution is the emergency man's obliviousness to a classic paradox of management: the contradiction of "scaling down." Immense, evidently complex issues can, in fact, be the easiest to settle, while those that appear to be minor and a good bit simpler can't be untangled.

Eight years after Americans walked on the moon, evolutionary economist Richard R. Nelson wrote one of those enduring commentaries on public policy that illuminate multiple topics. Underneath its examination of technocratic hopes of social betterment, *The Moon and the Ghetto* asks straightforwardly: How can stunning accomplishments exist side by side with inner-city blight smack in the middle of this most achieving of all societies? "If we can put a man on the Moon," the saying went, "why can't we [insert type of problem]?"

This paradox becomes stark in global conflict. For example, Soviet SS-18 ICBMs were kept in their silos by the Politburo's knowledge that at least some U.S. Minutemen and Trident nuclear missiles would survive to bring vengeance on the motherland. Yet unremarkable civilians could hit the Pentagon with a jet-fueled missile, using no more than box cutters. The capacity to pull off one or another immense achievement such as deterring the Kremlin for decades is no guarantee that we can bring off ostensibly easier tasks such as protecting the Pentagon itself from fanatics. Eisenhower's insistence that because America could win big wars it could win small ones illustrates this paradox. Oftentimes, the sensational problems just require the money and energy that America has in abundance. But to address seemingly humdrum difficulties can open a Pandora's box of intricate details.

The year astronauts landed on the moon was the same year that 11,775 Americans fell in Vietnam. As that war had roared into high gear in the mid-1960s, six new deepwater harbors were created along the coast, through which rumbled giant tractors, bulldozers, and cranes of the Army Corps of Engineers, amply supported by contractors such as Bechtel and Halliburton (as Brown & Root), which toiled around the clock to carve out roads, build bridges, dredge rivers, and erect prisons. U.S. military headquarters in Saigon grew so large that the sprawl was named "Pentagon East." More than one-third of the U.S. Army was deployed in Vietnam. The South was turned upside down; the boom times brought to Saigon's bars and brothels a septic culture alien to all parties, neither Western nor Vietnamese. It was an excellent way to undermine the goal of uplifting a government, one effective and sovereign over its own people.

In Vietnam—as in Iraq and in Afghanistan—Washington believed for a fateful amount of time that America could do it all. At least at the start. Saigon's army was brushed aside, not adequately to be trained or equipped for years. In Iraq, what remained of Saddam's army was indiscriminately disbanded soon after the invasion, not that the JCS were consulted. The U.S. military, in the opinion of Bremer at the Coalition Provisional Authority, could handle "stability operations." But then, right at the beginning of his memoirs, he admits that he didn't know anything about Iraq when stepping down from Kissinger Associates to become America's proconsul.

Provoking an enemy to rush into war and then committing more resources until his very numbers work against him materially in the field—and politically at home—is a common strategy of insurgent warfare. And it's used regularly against those swift-moving, open, impatient cultures, which America epitomizes. "I *want* them to send more troops," North Vietnam's president, Ho Chi Minh, remarked to an astonished Aleksei Kosygin when the Soviet premier warned in 1965 about the consequences of not settling with the Americans.[30] Having boasted of spending no more than five hundred thousand dollars in bringing off 9/11, bin Laden could not have put it better about the U.S. plunge into Iraq—or, for that matter, its further steps into Afghanistan.

Five years after the Iraq invasion, the State Department designated a full-time researcher just to determine how many contractors, advisers, technical specialists, and Foreign Service officers were reporting to Foggy Bottom from the theater of war, and to attempt to clarify what each of them might be doing. It had simply lost all track among the high-energy activity—and so had the Pentagon.

At least by that time, the more outrageous escapades depicted in Chandrasekaran's account of the Green Zone had been left behind. "It isn't any longer like Oz," observed the newly arrived head of Iraqi reconstruction, Ambassador Marc Wall, "but we've now got so many Americans injected into Iraq's ministries that they're in the way of the Iraqis just doing their jobs."[31] (In Vietnam, the estimate had been that Saigon's officials had to spend half their day dealing with the Americans, leaving little time for their own work. We had been warned.)[32] Each week during the final months of the Bush administration, Wall joined Ambassador Ryan Crocker, a career Middle East envoy, and the U.S. commanding general in Iraq for a secure videoconference of up to an hour with President Bush and Vice President Cheney, the latter "sitting like a Buddha" and rarely uttering a word. "They were throwing more and more money, advisers, and just plain *stuff* into Iraq, maybe to save some sort of legacy," Wall concludes. American wealth and intensity were again generating problems for America.

The enormous U.S. military installations so familiar from Vietnam—Long Binh, Tan Son Nhut, Cam Ranh Bay having been among the largest bases in the world of any power—had blossomed again like a desert rose. Four enormities that the Pentagon initially called "enduring bases," such as one of 16.4 square miles adjacent to Baghdad, kept growing while Iraq's electricity grid was worse than under Saddam. Those heavily over-air-conditioned cities in the sand with their Taco Bells and Cinnabons were a few yards and a world apart. The fortresslike U.S. Embassy compound the size of ten football fields that has been dropped into central Baghdad is so large that erecting it diverted money targeted for Iraqi reconstruction, as well as for Afghanistan. The result—with all its guard towers, gates, and bunkers—is an unwelcoming architectural symbol of America's outreach to the Middle East. "We're throwing people and money at something without estimating what the culture demands," reflected former secretary of state Lawrence Eagleburger. "It's hubris."[33] True, but it's also magical deference to an older ideal of management gone with the giant steel mills along the Monongahela. So much, it is hoped, may be accomplished through all that plain massing of size, strength, and well-intentioned effort.

Recall how Americans think differently about risk, especially so from our major allies as seen in our incessant boom-bubble-busts. The Dutch may have distended the first speculative balloon during 1636's tulip craze, but Americans do this nearly all the time. Obsession with canals in the 1830s was followed by an obsession with land rushes, railroads, radio, "plastics," conglomerates, dot-com, and telecom, to name only the more memorable. This roller coaster of hopeful excitement doesn't stop until the bolts fly off. "Recession-Plagued Nation Demands New Bubble to Invest In," ran a headline in the satirical paper the *Onion* during the Crash of 2008, and by 2010, observed the *Wall Street Journal's* Jason Zweig, the faith of American investors in fantastically high long-term stock market returns was "like a fairytale." "What are we smoking and when will we stop?" he asks.[34] Presuming risks to be easily overcome, and suspecting that this time trees just might grow up to the sky, however, is also part of the mind-set that propels America "where no man has gone before."

The spirit can deliver spectacular achievements, such as going into space. But its underside can be a one-way ticket to those crumbling border defenses on the Mekong or Euphrates about which President Kennedy rhapsodized. And it's a trip we usually end up taking nearly alone.

There is an odd contradiction in the way America has dealt with allies during its wars in Korea, Vietnam, Iraq, and now Afghanistan. Early on, Washington is confident that other developed democracies will share the burden of a cause so obviously right. Yet at the same time emergency men persuade themselves that America will do just fine if it has to proceed by itself. "At some point," President George W. Bush noted of Iraq, "we may be the only ones left. That's okay with me. We are America."[35] In either case, Americans soon discover that all the importuning and threats of "alliance management," as dealing with European ministries has long been called, will by no means necessarily bring about the full-throated engagement of America's closest partners when the country goes to war.[36]

A look at the headlines over the years is telling: "U.S. Prods Nations: Suggests U.N. Members Send More Troops to Fight in

Korea"; "[Secretary of State] Rusk Urges Allies to Help U.S. Counter Reds in Cuba and Asia"; "America to Press Europe for Broader Security Help" in Afghanistan.[37] No matter the bravado about going it alone, each quiet negation is met with anguished disappointment in Washington. The same disappointments blighted the alliance manager's day when the Soviet Union was lapping against the edges of the North Atlantic Alliance; America could never extract an amount of defense spending proportionate to its own from the allies. Decades in and decades out, conferences and documents speak of "NATO in Disarray," as if it had ever been in array. U.S. emissaries keep shuttling back and forth, as in 1973 to declare a "Year of Europe" (to meet the supposed "new realities" of détente) or in 2003 (to line up allies against Iraq). The same false certainties prevail; Richard Perle, as chair of the Defense Policy Board during the latter quest, insisted until two weeks before the invasion that "just before the war starts France will jump on our side," and then "we shall have plenty of allies."[38] France chose not to jump.

When America finds itself with few significant partners, foreign policy pundits offer the same refrain: "The United States cannot dominate, much less dictate and expect others to follow."[39] Well, yes. Except the hesitancy of allies might have little to do with U.S. decorum. There are sufficiently sound reasons for an ally not to throw itself into Iraq or Vietnam or North Korea, or into combat in Helmand Province during the ninth year of an Afghan war.

"America is from Mars, Europe is from Venus" imagery became a think-tank staple after the 2002–2003 split over how to bring down Saddam.[40] Different "strategic cultures," it was intoned, mean that impatient Americans are quick to use force while world-weary Europeans prefer to retreat behind diplomacy, call for international law to be applied, and believe that most apparently desperate "crises" usually resolve themselves. But the differences are neither that complicated or new. For at least fifty years they have come down to a simple point: following two devastating world wars and many bloody, protracted colonial exits, whether in Kenya or Malaya, Indochina or Algeria, most Europeans have grown cool toward seeking to impose grand solutions abroad, to say nothing of backing American dreams.

Yet, starting with Korea and the war with China, Washington convinces itself that it can spread the risks when embarking on world-revising politico-military projects. In Korea, the British only agreed to send troops in summer 1950 after what the Foreign Office concluded was an "obscurely worded menace" from Secretary Acheson, which meant not so subtle threats to their economy.[41] Like France, the British cited other global peacekeeping duties, conveniently to be found in their colonies and protectorates. American opinion was outraged at what it saw as footdragging. In time, two British brigades arrived, to be followed by a French battalion. Both allies fought gallantly, but within eighteen months began severely to redirect their troops to colonial wars in Malaya and Indochina.

There were other contributions from thirteen additional allies to the UN undertaking in Korea, although the minimal size of such commitments made it easy for Americans to forget them. Turkey, ancient enemy of Russia, had been the first to send its soldiers to Korea; Colombian Indians would die on Old Baldy in west central Korea, as would Brazilians and Ethiopians near the Yalu. But these were "tokens" indeed. General MacArthur could never work out why the Europeans were "not fully supportive" about liberating North Korea. So much of the public fury over the Korean War came from realizing that America, except for a feeble South Korean army, was in the fight essentially alone. "Never again" became the U.S. slogan. Not only would America "never again" engage in grinding combat on the ground, but never again would it find itself abandoned in a war for "other people's freedom."[42]

"Where are Britain, Japan, and Germany?" Lyndon Johnson nonetheless groaned just twelve years after the Korean armistice, shaken that London refused to dispatch even a symbolic battalion to Vietnam.[43] Britain, along with France, was a member of SEATO. But nobody at the Elysée believed any longer that their country's frontiers were on the Mekong, nor, at that stage of imperial retreat, did Downing Street believe that any equivalent to Britain's own borders might still exist along the Tigris and Euphrates. The days of Washington threatening the pound sterling as a means of "alliance management" were gone, and such strong-arming was not even to be tried on France's imperious president, Charles de Gaulle.

In Vietnam, Washington eventually hammered together a 68,889-man mosaic of Free World Military Assistance Forces. It was larger than the coalition that had been assembled in the Korean War and larger too than the Iraq War's Multinational Force would be. Yet like those combinations, it was less than the sum of its parts. There would be no "SEATO force boasting British and French contingents" in Vietnam, as Washington had hoped. Instead, America ended up with fighting men from the more easily pressured Republic of South Korea, and detachments from the successively less easy to persuade Philippines, Thailand, Australia, and New Zealand. Once again the eager-to-help Chinese Nationalists on Taiwan offered their troops, but no one else even wanted to think about courting another war with Beijing.

Washington also hoped to rope in soldiers from Argentina and Brazil, perhaps a valued few from pliable Honduras and Nicaragua, maybe "military observers" from the Netherlands and Greece, and ideally even the British-led Gurkha mercenaries who had excelled in Korea, as they would in Iraq. But no dice. For its part, a still-divided Germany knew in 1965 that some kind of Bundeswehr expeditionary force would chill a lot more people than just its own electorate, including the Russians. So the Federal Republic offered medical aid. France agreed to provide credits to Saigon to import French industrial equipment. Denmark trained twelve South Vietnamese nurses. Britain supplied a typesetting machine for Saigon's Government Printing Office, while maintaining a lively trade until 1969 with Hanoi.

In Iraq, the latest vision of alliance husbandry in another American-led war went the way of its predecessors. It began with a previously unreported episode that highlights U.S. hopes, manipulations, and self-deception.

Perle, Feith, and Wolfowitz insisted until days before the invasion that Turkey, a Muslim democracy and NATO ally, would permit a U.S. infantry division to pass through its territory to strike Iraq from the north. That step was central to the U.S. war plan; so the 4th Infantry Division's equipment was kept afloat in the Mediterranean and 2,200 soldiers were working pointlessly in Turkey itself to prepare for the division's arrival from the United States, while U.S. officials frantically "tried to bully" the Turks into agreement, according to Major Ian Palmer, U.S. Army, who was on the scene.[44]

Yet it had been clear for eleven long months that Turkey would never agree to open its borders to an invasion force—despite the insistence in 2010 by former chief political adviser Karl Rove, on the occasion of publishing his memoirs that "We had a plan," though "Turkey den[ied] at the last minute the entry of the 4th ID into western Iraq."

Ankara had helped immediately against the Taliban during fall 2001 by granting a U.S. request to overfly Turkish territory. But public opinion had turned vehemently against the U.S. intention of invading Iraq. The State Department knew this, as did the CIA, which had a perfectly placed agent within the power-juggling Turkish General Staff. The generals' word on this was final, the agent reported, and Turkey's ever more confident civilian authorities wouldn't budge, no matter what Washington's financial inducements. Moreover, the General Staff had conveyed that message face-to-face to the CIA's head of European operations in March 2002.

Nevertheless, enthusiasm at the White House and in the Pentagon for war with Iraq was mounting. Wolfowitz also appeared in Ankara that spring, having already stated his approach to alliance management: "Those who refuse to support you will live to regret having done so."[45] Unimpressed, the generals emphasized their refusal. They used the same straightforward words offered to the CIA operations chief—as is known from the agent's inside reporting of the Wolfowitz meeting. Yet the deputy secretary of defense raced home to insist that his mission was accomplished; Turkey had yielded to his compelling advocacy. He had worked his magic. Outside the Pentagon, no one could make sense of this account. In fact, Wolfowitz had heard what he wanted to hear. And his certainties were ratified by Feith and Perle, who believed they knew Turkey intimately. Ankara, after all, had been a lobbying client of Feith's law firm in the 1990s, and Perle had been part of the effort.[46] The men and equipment of the 4th ID would eventually be rerouted to enter the war via Kuwait.

Then the administration scrambled all the more to show the breadth of global support for its endeavors. "The population of Coalition countries is approximately 1.23 billion people," trumpeted a White House press release one week after the invasion. "Every major race, religion, ethnicity in the world is represented. The Coalition includes nations from every continent on the globe."[47] But what did that mean on the front lines? It was a "jerry-rigged series of deals," explains Tom Ricks; Iraq was invaded by U.S. and British troops, though fifty-four nations would sign on in some fashion.[48] Good people all, except what was offered by the Marshall Islands and Micronesia and Estonia proved, as General MacArthur had said during Korea, to be "tokens" indeed. And the coalition began to crumble within months as members faced political strife over an unpopular war that had neither UN nor NATO nor regional endorsement.

As for Afghanistan, NATO had responded magnificently right after 9/11 in the alliance's first major operation outside Europe.[49] Within weeks, commandos from Britain's elite Special Air Service and France's marine parachutists were collaborating with U.S. special operators to rout Al Qaeda and the Taliban. Yet in the glory of the truly rapid capture of Kabul, the White House decided to reject NATO's fuller support, insisting that the international military presence in Afghanistan need not be expanded beyond the capital. Americans would do the mopping up. Now nine years into the fight against a resurgent Taliban, NATO's twenty-eight members are at the core of a UN-created International Security Assistance Force embracing some forty-two nations. Except that NATO undercuts itself through national caveats; countries provide forces but then restrict how they can be deployed. Meanwhile an "Americanization" of the mission increases with the latest buildup. But then the United States itself has been experiencing a familiar problem, according to Defense Secretary Gates: Washington has had no "overarching strategy." [50]

During the Kennedy "crisis years," the president had received a memo from one of his key foreign policy aides, Walt Rostow, previously a professor at MIT and eventually to succeed McGeorge Bundy as national security adviser. "We should prepare ourselves for what you might call a High Noon stance," Rostow argued romantically. "You recall Gary Cooper dealt with the bandits alone." [51] And nearly alone America would be in Southeast Asia, just as today she still finds it pretty lonely in Afghanistan, and perhaps tomorrow in Yemen or Kashmir.

Another compelling belief often accompanies the illusion that America as Lone Ranger can set the world right: emergency men regard themselves as personally wearing the badge. Policymakers of that disposition become seduced by the magic of their own centrality. As they manage a summit or topple a regime, they may believe in their unruffled certitude that they're playing with the cat, while in fact the cat all too likely is playing with them.

In the election year of 1972, President Nixon staged successive breathtaking Beijing and Moscow summits less than three months apart. Americans came to believe that a few great men in Washington were bringing about some sort of geopolitically instructed reworking of the world's whole system of power and suspicion. Delusion, instead, followed, offering a supreme example of the obliviousness of emergency men to the players on the other side.

First up was China, during what Nixon called the "Week that Changed the World" in February. This production in Beijing did nothing to "forever change the Cold War by reconfiguring the communist bloc," as is now conventional wisdom.[52] To reinforce the lesser of one's two main enemies is instead a tactically sound response to the logic of a world in deep conflict. While China had grown real again in American eyes after twenty years of no U.S. contact, the fact barely registered in Washington that Beijing's overtures represented the most seasoned judgment of Soviet malevolence. Deadly border skirmishes had made Moscow more than ready to launch a nuclear attack on China, and Beijing's leadership knew it. They had just enough of their own nuclear weapons to terrify their recent patron.

The Sino-Soviet "bloc" had dissolved at least ten years earlier, and evidence of China's desperation was there to see— it was vividly apparent to me as a student talking to junior People's Republic diplomats in France a year before. Equally clear was the extent of Russian fear and outrage during the winter of 1970–71, grimly visible both in Moscow and along the Amur River border with northeastern China.[53] Washington was not driving the new relationship with China. Yet in America's hurry to stage-manage the drama, there was again a failure to recognize the *agency* of other countries. Americans convinced themselves that all was unfolding because of what they were doing, with little thought to China's frantic motivation. Mao's prime minister, Chou En-lai, derisively remarked that Nixon too "eagerly" grasped out for an invitation to Beijing.[54]

Of course it was wise to respond. The timely formation of U.S. and Chinese politico-military ties may have prevented an Asian nuclear war. And there would be disadvantages for Moscow on the global chessboard. U.S. technicians in Xinjiang, for example, were eventually able to monitor Red Army missile testing at Kapustin Yar. But blunders were inevitable in the excitement of trying to "change the world," or at least to appear to be doing so. To name just one, the White House essentially countenanced the extermination of at least half a million Bengalis by Pakistan. After all, Islamabad had been helpful the year before in the high drama of the gratuitously secret preparations that surrounded Nixon's visit to China. "We had to demonstrate to China we were a reliable government to deal with," remarked Kissinger's chief aide on the NSC. "We had to show China we respect a mutual friend." [55] So in this searing instance no attempt was made to bring U.S. influence to bear. America repudiated its tradition of being a human voice in a harsh world, which had a formative influence on the successor generation of Pakistani military leaders who saw firsthand how Washington could be played.

No matter who was president, rapprochement with China was in the cards. Given the actual circumstances, however, a better sense of proportion would have been to schedule Mao Tse-tung—or, if he was too frail, Premier Chou En-lai—for a breakfast at the White House. Instead, the sudden "opening" got deliriously out of hand. Along with the Moscow summit to come, Americans could deceive themselves that "the Cold War is over," as *Newsweek* proclaimed. And Pakistan's American-countenanced slaughters of 1971 will be remembered in South Asia long after the last clink of glasses in the Great Hall of the People has faded from memory.

At the far end of self-deception, emergency men convince themselves that they know how their opponent actually thinks. General MacArthur insisted that no one understood the "Oriental mind" better than he, whether those "minds" were Japanese or Filipino or those of Chinese revolutionaries. In contending with Moscow, Robert McNamara shared a similar conceit. "As a Red Army marshal, I would . . . ," he shouted furiously at perceptive U.S. intelligence analysts who were trying to convince him that Soviet bargaining about ICBMs, in contrast to UAW negotiations over labor contracts, might be governed by a zero-sum definition of success.[56] (In the stunned silence that followed, no one said, "Well, Mr. Secretary, but you're *not* a Red Army marshal.") Henry Kissinger had similar illusions that he knew how the Soviets thought. "What in the name of God is strategic superiority?" he famously asked his critics in exasperation. The marshals and party bosses in fact had a precise, well-calculated, and cold-blooded answer, which they felt no reason to hide.

In a rare misunderstanding of the past, Michael Howard, most eminent of living military historians, lauds the Nixon era's extraordinary "success in managing the Soviets."[57] His use of the term, however, is deliberate. "Management was the watchword of our delegation," recalled Gerard C. Smith, the capable Washington lawyer and political appointee who oversaw preparation for the summitry wonderments in Moscow. U.S. negotiators, he adds, "expended a great deal of intellectual capital to educate the Soviet leadership" about what America at that juncture regarded as appropriate nuclear policy.[58] No longer would deterrence rest on the United States' power to destroy Soviet military targets incrementally, as McNamara had originally reasoned. Now that the Soviet Union had achieved rough nuclear parity, deterrence would depend on the promise that, even after a Soviet attack, the U.S. riposte would obliterate Soviet *cities* from the start—with enough megatonnage left over, to be sure, to scupper Soviet armanent.

Mutual assured destruction, as Americans called their latest doctrine, was a geopolitical suicide pact. But the Soviet ruling caste looked at an altogether different outcome, in which the motherland could fight a nuclear war to victory, at least as victory was reckoned by veterans of Stalingrad and Kursk. "While rejecting nuclear war and waging a struggle to avert it," summarized the Central Committee's V. V. Zagladin in the empire's final days, "we nonetheless proceeded from the possibility of winning it." [59]

No U.S. instruction about proper arms control management was needed. To the Soviets, destruction was not a theory. Should attack seem imminent, the Kremlin intended to strike first, and to have sufficient firepower to cripple at first blow America's retaliatory capacities. Damage to the Soviets' own country from those U.S. missiles and bombers that remained would be limited by a combination of extensive civil defense works as well as a crude but likely effective and operational antiballistic missile system. (The United States eschewed both capacities.) After all, the men across the table from U.S. negotiators had just a quarter century earlier fought and won at the sacrifice of some 27 million dead. The United States, they could persuade themselves, was not too dissimilar a foe. Yet prevailing opinion in America exulted at make-believe arms control, creating an extremely dangerous setup for the decade to follow.

Like any other overbearing tyranny, Moscow was happy to sign deals and then to proceed as it saw fit. One barely remembered detail underscores the depths of U.S. self-deception. In these encounters, the Americans were left to provide *all* information and data—for the Soviet negotiators as well as for their own side—concerning *all* the weapons to be discussed in the meetings. The Russians simply let the eager Americans lay out Washington's idea of Soviet weapon numbers, types, capabilities, and locations. They would then indicate their assent to U.S. assessments of their own forces, often misleadingly, by remaining silent. Moreover, the Nixon/Kissinger fantasies of arms pacts were lubricated by one-sided trade deals and, most delusional of all, given who was dealing with whom, by a thousand-word code of conduct in which America and the Soviet Union each renounced efforts to obtain unilateral advantage at the expense of the other.

Wishful thinking has a way of flourishing where good-hearted, confident people prefer not to look closely at authentic, ruthless power—the power enjoyed, for instance, by the KGB and Red Army orchestrators of the arms negotiations, not the milder Soviet diplomats who served as front men.[60] A negotiator comes to believe that hard, brutally practical apparatchiks of the sort who then and now have hacked their way into the Kremlin are somehow disposed to being converted to a managerial give-and-take by the latest American revelation of how the world is supposed to work.

The self-deceptions herein are not ancient history. They are used regularly as instruction for today. The "opening to Mao's China," which the distinguished British historian Alistair Horne sees as "engineered by Nixon and Kissinger," is routinely acclaimed as "one of the greatest feats of U.S. statecraft, ever," as by the *National Journal*; the one in Moscow is simply an accomplished fact of "genius," adds Leslie Gelb, president emeritus of the Council on Foreign Relations.[61] Delusions recur whenever policies are affected by hopes as ethereal as those of corralling China or when Americans believe they are fashioning the conducts of Pakistan, Iran, or, for that matter, Russia—the informed speculation of the moment addressing itself to "how Obama aims to play Russia."[62] Bismarck, however, said gloomily that Russia is like the weather: you can't change it; you have to live with it. A persistent influence over time was about as much as could be expected.

There are exceptions. America succeeded in the 1980s in fatally undercutting Soviet power. But there are two points to remember. One, the U.S. effort was phenomenally dangerous. The Reagan administration was walking far closer to the edge than it realized, as the Soviet Union swayed on the brink of initiating nuclear war. The Kremlin had come to believe, from the combination of changes in U.S. strategy and some routine NATO maneuvers, that the West was preparing to attack. The months of fall 1983 dwarf the peril that we self-referentially attribute to the Cuban Missile Crisis.[63] Second, the end of that Soviet tyranny was enabled by unique timing. America was steadily becoming "the country of tomorrow" with its high-tech boom-time attainments, while the Soviet Union was essentially the same rigid monolith as in the 1930s.

Today Soviet communism is gone, but Russia exerts itself in familiar ways, from political murder to threatening to devour a neighbor or two, such as Ukraine. And we live with that behavior. Now arise other great lands that can also be said to be like the weather, certainly China and India. America's attempts to manage them won't go far, either. In fact, in a twenty-first-century networked world of free-flowing technologies and ideas, that might be said about most every other state, nation, church, or multinational corporation as well.

The conviction nevertheless persists that every problem has a solution. There was no significant discussion in the Bush White House whether just to live with a boxed-in Saddam Hussein in Baghdad, and forgo invasion. Even our elegantly uniformed but uncooperative allies in Ankara were supposed to agree. Sooner or later, however, our magical manipulations are ground down by reality whereupon emergency men insist that they, at least, have done everything right. They really did think through the next steps; they of course scrutinized every intelligence source; and allies have made personal commitments to them. So what can have gone wrong? All the figures of the dance have been performed correctly.

When visions insist upon falling apart, the visionaries are embarrassed. But they can always blame others. With their faith in elaborate solutions, whether the summits of 1972 or the invasion of 2003, one can always demonstrate how subsection (3a) of this particular rule-based grand plan was regrettably mishandled by "some poor son of a bitch who doesn't get the word."[64] An emergency man can then retain the guise of a coolly calculating crisis manager. He becomes available to analyze the latest "crisis" to a public that has better things to do than to recall who was saying what concerning victorious action or world-recasting treaties only four or five years earlier. The *Atlantic*, for instance, solicits Feith's thoughts on, of all things, the future of Vladimir Putin. *Vanity Fair* asks a former Defense Policy Board member, Kenneth Adelman, known for promising a "cakewalk" in Iraq, for a critique of the Pentagon. And by the fifth anniversary of that minuet along the Tigris, the *New York Times* enquired of "experts on military and foreign affairs," such as Perle and Bremer—who today is an adviser to RAND's Middle East center—about what had most surprised them since the invasion.[65] Why would anyone care?

The way that Vietnam has come to be explained is a telling example of how to rationalize failure when illusions evaporate. That's because the war was so articulately chronicled. Consider Arthur Schlesinger, Jr. This first-rate scholar of the times of FDR and Andrew Jackson served not only as Kennedy's biographer-designate but as a special assistant on foreign policy. No less than McNamara and Bundy, Schlesinger was convinced that it was possible for America to manage that maelstrom, and that it was deeply in America's interest to do so. Even four years after Kennedy's assassination, as the war's promises evaporated, he advanced in *The Bitter Heritage* unhesitant arguments against abandoning the Saigon regime—going far to indict those who disagreed as enemies of American security. The war was still raging a chastening five years thereafter. He then wrote in his journals that America's entanglement was "not a record of wickedness or criminality; it is a record of glibness, illusion and intellectual mediocrity."[66] So true, but an observation made without a shred of self-reproach. The illusion-ridden men who had impaled their country were faceless, except for Lyndon Johnson; how strangely cool and uninvolved remained Schlesinger's heroes. Similarly with McNamara, who remained active nearly until his death in 2009.

He'd speak about the war and intone ghostly regrets. But more often than not he would talk of the Kennedy and Johnson decision makers as "they."[67]

"What I tell you three times is true," declares a hunter of the Snark in Lewis Carroll's poem of the impossible quest of an unlikely crew to find an inconceivable creature. If you say something ridiculous often enough, people come to believe it. Perhaps even the blame for Iraq can be made to fall on unnamed others: it must have been a doppelganger sitting in your chair at that meeting in the Pentagon E-ring, or who composed the *Times* op-ed to which your name was forged.

One of the sharper advisers to serve on the Defense Policy Board during the run-up to the 2003 invasion was Elliot Cohen, professor at the Johns Hopkins School of Advanced International Studies (SAIS). Just before being appointed counselor to the secretary of state in 2007, he explained his disillusionment about the war he had so adamantly endorsed at the start: "What I didn't know then that I know now is just how incompetent we would be in carrying out the task."[68] It was a common enough lament among the war hawks of the latest venture, including journalist Christopher Hitchens, former undersecretary Feith, as well as a professor of politics at Princeton who had been Vice President Cheney's national security adviser during 2003–2005. All condemned "mismanagement," with Feith writing a memoir unsurpassed in its recriminations at failures by people at State, the CIA, and the Coalition Provisional Authority. Former Defense Policy Board chairman Richard Perle also identifies ineptitude in those high offices and decries people "whose knowledge of Iraq is often recent, shallow and wrong."[69] He came to insist that he had little to do with any part of the mess. Listening to him expound at a Washington think tank in 2009, the *Washington Post*'s Dana Milbank "had a sense of falling down the rabbit hole."[70]

And note the "we" in Cohen's observation—at first glance a generous assumption of responsibility, but which on closer look proves to distribute blame everywhere but on the speaker and his fellow enthusiasts for war. Instead, the "incompetence" imputed is that of the *implementers* of emergency policies—U.S. infantry colonels in Fallujah, Agency for International Development (AID) specialists struggling with Iraq's electrical grid, GS-15 auditors coping with Halliburton.

In their shock at their country's "incompetence," emergency men as diverse as these seem never to have studied that melancholy procession of approximations, of lungings forward and homeward by fits and starts, that all together compose Cold War History 101. Blood-drenched retreat and painful concessions in Korea, tens of thousands of American dead in Vietnam, and scores of covert and public blunders and just-in-time recoveries, might have given some warning of what lay ahead in Iraq. And having sat on the Defense Policy Board, Cohen knew of the Pentagon/ CIA mistakes in December 2001 at Tora Bora, the cavern complex in the White Mountains of eastern Afghanistan, which left open Bin Laden's path to freedom. A more routine blunder, still closely held in Langley, may not have come to the board's attention: lost somewhere in the huge, phenomenally detailed Map Library at CIA headquarters that autumn were maps of the caves, tunnels, and dugouts that bin Laden had helped to engineer at Tora Bora long before, passed on fifteen years earlier by the Afghan guerrillas America was then backing.[71]

These have been the standards of performance in U.S. national security policymaking. Yet during the "crisis management" excitements of 2002–2003 that prefaced the invasion of Iraq, all worrying precedent was easy to brush aside in the belief that "any problem can be solved." And anyway, who really wanted to second-guess such commanding abilities as those of Rumsfeld, or indeed those of Kissinger, back in action as a valued adviser with his own perch on the Defense Policy Board, as well as direct lines to the White House?

4.

STAR POWER

A French journalist asked the great impresario Charles Frohman why one saw nothing but actors' names on Broadway's theater marquees, whereas in Paris the names in lights were those of playwrights. "That's because in America," Frohman explained, "the emphasis is always on the doer, not upon the thing done. There are stars in all walks of American life. It has always been so in democracies"—from Alcibiades onward, he might have added. This disposition to create a hero for every moment is not unique to America, but Americans take it to unrivaled heights. As the most individualistic of all democracies, America embraces stars and champions because our culture most intensely extols personal success.

But why are well-informed Americans starstruck by reputed wizards of national security? Why do they go way too far in placing their faith in the most dubious of experts and "expertise," and even give benefit of the doubt to outright frauds when "terror" and "national security" are invoked? How come convenient third-world dictators, strongmen, and the occasional psychopath are turned into client "heroes" as routinely as tyrants and terrorists are elevated to the world-shattering capacities of a "Hitler"? Finally, what does it tell us about the state of the nation on those occasions when we make celebrities out of our own brave, dutifully serving generals for anything short of defeating the Wehrmacht?

The degree to which America celebrates its stars is visible on the $2.4 billion-a-year speaker circuit. Yes, other countries often pay celebrity speakers handsomely. Ironically, these are usually visiting Americans: former presidents Clinton and George W. Bush each received $150,000 in 2009 to talk at an event organized by a Toronto-based company affiliated with motivational guru Tony Robbins. But by and large the big-money circuit is a U.S. phenomenon. Sensible, achieving Americans want to press the flesh of a star. They seek inspiration or guidance from an hour's encounter with a former president or cabinet secretary, a retired general or a bestselling journalist, a national security expert or a self-help philosopher. They shell out exorbitantly for these encounters, including the imputed cost of the hours lost that could have been spent reading a good book at home.

Former CEOs can also be found on the speaker circuit. In America, corporate giants are heroized and compensated as nowhere else, and the aura lingers—at least until a smash comes along. *Tycoon* is a term of Japanese origin meaning "great lord," but now applied primarily in America to powerful business leaders. "The key step" to better corporate performance, observes Jim Collins about the men and women atop the Fortune 500, "is to stop looking for outsized personalities and egocentric celebrities, and instead to scrutinize for results."[1] It's a telling point about the culture of American business that this needs to be said aloud. It should make us similarly alert in national security policymaking. A culture publicity mad like no other, and in which everyone indeed gets their magical fifteen minutes of fame, opens the door further for emergency men.

Any serious endeavor that relies so heavily on personalization is in big trouble. To cast leaders into the stratosphere of celebrity catapults them above reality. Who are we to challenge such master spirits? Those seeking stars in business or in politics tend to look for a superman waving a wand, relieving them from having to think, to learn, or to change their minds by their own efforts.

In Washington, an awe uncharacteristic of America greets accomplished men and women with certainties to sell. Henry Kissinger was widely hailed as a "miracle worker" and as a "magician." The White House press corps burst into applause when Gerald Ford announced, immediately on Nixon's resignation, that he would be retaining Kissinger in the joint position of both secretary of state and national security adviser, a combination unique to the Watergate era. Closer to today's events, Americans were also all too deferential toward the concentrated brilliance of the so-called War Cabinet "dream team" that led the country into Iraq.[2] That same awed reverence, though far more deserved, led to General MacArthur's being dubbed the "sorcerer" of Inchon. We Americans repeat ourselves, especially here.

The hypnotism of fame took hold, as did much else, during the Kennedy years. Under Eisenhower, few well-informed Americans had any idea who the president's national security assistant might be, or who was serving as undersecretary of defense. But stars filled the sky when "the best and the brightest" arrived in power—beginning with the Pulitzer Prize–winning, rich and witty PT-boat commander president. In his administration, even deputy assistant secretaries of state came to be addressed as "Mr. Secretary." And at the Pentagon was Robert McNamara: news footage of the time shows case-hardened senators on the Armed Services Committee visibly dazzled by his fluent testimony on budget and procurement issues of the utmost complexity. Meanwhile, McGeorge Bundy ran the NSC. He was "a man of sharp—even acid—brilliance, lean and trim of body and mind . . . agile, combative and confident, on the tennis court and in intellectual volley," glowed the *New York Times*.[3] And *Time* magazine had him on its cover, beneath the title "U.S. Foreign Policy in Action."

The structure of the NSC itself exhibits a telling detail in the ascendancy of celebrity under the public eye. Its staff is directed by an appointed official formally titled "assistant to the president for national security," but who has become known just about exclusively by the grander designation "National Security Advisor," replete with British spelling, as it stands on the White House website today. With the Kennedy administration, the desk of the NSC director moved from the Old Executive Office Building to the West Wing, declaring to the world that there was a star closer to the sun than the dutiful secretary of state slogging through papers six blocks away at Foggy Bottom.

Several characteristics of magical thinking keep popping up around our national security celebrities. Secretaries of Defense McNamara and Rumsfeld were not only applauded as supermanagers but also elevated to stardom. Each was the face of a magically reassuring belief that war could be fought with nearly painless high-tech efficiency. Each man was even considered right for the Oval Office. LBJ privately asked McNamara in June 1964 to be his running mate. *Time* speculated that he could succeed Johnson in 1968. (Still a registered Republican, McNamara declined.)

Twenty years later, Republican politicos gave Rumsfeld a credible chance for the 1988 nomination. Few voters agreed. But after 9/11 back in Washington, he was extolled as no defense secretary had been since McNamara. That astute military historian John Keegan gushed in a *Vanity Fair* profile that Rumsfeld was obviously "the right man at the right time . . . schooled at that most military of great ivy league universities." (That would be Princeton, for some reason.)[4] Nothing imparts a faster drumbeat to the march of folly than the enthusiasm of those who've thrown themselves under the spell.

The stars of national security policy such as McNamara and Rumsfeld—and those men and women undoubtedly to come— are defined largely by ongoing activities that lend themselves to media dramatization. They spring surprise visits on Saigon or Baghdad, shake hands with Saddam, while counterparts at State exchange toasts with Mao and deliver peace plans to the Middle East. Eminent scientists have also been seen glowing at the heights of the nation's defense apparat, such as the two preeminent "wizards of Armageddon," physicists Robert Oppenheimer and Edward Teller. They too were cast as stars and widely known from their own covers of *Time* in an era when that conferred global recognition. But unlike the stars of policymaking, each had contributed hugely to the core of his discipline. And no one challenged the power of their reasoning, however bitterly their wider views were disputed.

Henry Kissinger is the rare emergency man whose wisdoms are still sought decades after he carved his niche in the national imagination. He is remembered as a "fabled negotiator," and his miracle-working reputation from the 1970s continues strong, implying that his actions were of helpful consequence.[5] Kissinger's lengthy essays appear nearly monthly in the *Washington Post*. The George W. Bush White House and the Rumsfeld Pentagon consistently sought his advice, and today he remains on the Obama administration's own Defense Policy Board. But the reason Kissinger's aura has never been eclipsed isn't because of a lack of ability among his successors; it's due to a happy lack of occasion. The pinnacle of diplomatic theatrics since 1945 was the back-to-back summitry of 1972 in Beijing and in Moscow. Such exalted moments have never come round again. Nor has there been another moment when a president has resigned—with the secretary of state, as the senior cabinet officer (and, when not foreign-born, fourth in the line of succession), being somberly at hand to emphasize continuity.

Theodore Draper, the preeminent freelance social critic of the last fifty years, observed that Henry Kissinger, whom he had known since they were GIs together in World War II, will likely belong to the history of publicity rather than to the history of diplomacy.[6] Kissinger appeared on the American stage at the moment when TV cameras were able to chronicle live the excitements of diplomatic appearances in cinematic capitals. At a time when Americans still were inclined to defer to words like *Harvard* and *summit conference*, Kissinger arrived as the premier wise man of foreign policy. He possessed the Hollywood-Teutonic accent of a mitteleuropa geostrategist as well as a riveting personal story of escaping the oncoming horror of Nazism to serve the land that took him in. He was also the first, and the last, central figure in public policy making to profit from the title of "Doctor," a label that implied deep understanding of global turmoil. Americans had never heard of a "Dr. Wilson" as that uniquely Ph.D. president wrestled with the 1919 peace settlement. Nor would they hear about a "Dr. Shultz" as Ronald Reagan's capable secretary of state helped to guide the country through the perilous Soviet endgame. And in the years since Dr. Kissinger was in office, it has become ever less remarkable to have a secretary of state or a national security adviser who holds a Ph.D. Altogether these factors cast a mystique around him. And this mystique generated plenty of illusions as star power penetrated U.S. foreign affairs.

Dr. Kissinger's career began as a young chaplain to the establishment. He earned his doctorate in government at Harvard and proceeded to become the entrepreneurial director of the university's Summer International Seminar, bringing up-and-coming European and Asian leaders to Cambridge for U.S. foreign policy studies. Along the way he became the adviser to New York's glamorous Governor Nelson Rockefeller on national security matters. Like George Kennan, Kissinger's standing has also been enhanced by his own lucid writings over a long career and by a formidable ability to assimilate reams of forbidding material. Unlike Kennan, he has a wry sense of humor first cultivated for a welcoming public while serving as a foil to the likes of H. R. Haldeman, Nixon's chief of staff and self-described "chief executioner."

The Doctor's first book, *A World Restored: Metternich, Castlereagh, and the Problems of Peace 1812–1822,* was a blaze on the tree for the public life to come. It examines the astuteness of traditional European diplomacy, centering on Prince Metternich, ultimately chancellor to the emperor of Austria—Metternich now being a presence to whom Kissinger is compared for his fame, his guile, his lofty offices, and above all for insights so much profounder than those of his principals. But as a historian might note about the book's confusing title, nothing had truly been restored after the flood of revolutionary and Napoleonic power had been swept from Europe. What resulted from all the congressing and treaty-signing in Vienna was a working approximation of order that the Industrial Revolution was about to blow away. During that decade, people's minds were not turned back like clocks to 1789. The world of Louis XVI and the impatiently reforming Emperor Joseph had not been reclaimed; it had been moved back momentarily just like a stage set. *A World Restored* is instead valuable as a metaphor for what can be seen some 150 years later: the great figures of world power at the summit equally oblivious to the changes circling around them while they try to construct a spurious top-down "stability"—just as the most changeful age in history crashes in.

But the book that would make Dr. Kissinger's name as a defense thinker was *Nuclear Weapons and Foreign Policy.* Also published in 1957, it became a surprise bestseller in a nation rattled by Sputnik. It addressed prospects of "limited nuclear war" to argue that low-yield weaponry and a disciplined adherence to escalation could confine a superpower nuclear exchange to the traditional killing fields of Europe. Like Kennan, Kissinger excelled at putting an intellectual twist on bad ideas. He additionally argued in this book that "we could have achieved a substantial military victory" in Korea had America just committed but four more divisions against China's limitless People's Liberation Army.[7]

Nuclear Weapons, like *A World Restored*, is essentially a management text. In both books, the reader encounters eminent men, historically continuous with their predecessors, who are supremely confident in their abilities to direct from on high epochal political change and even military devastation. In *Nuclear Weapons*, those certainties included laying out the moves "to strike the balance between the desire for posing the maximum threat [to an aggressor] and the need for a strategy which does not paralyze the will."[8] It sounded effective. The book was respectfully received in the press and at the Council on Foreign Relations. It took a master of the game to focus unwelcome professional attention on *Nuclear Weapons*.

Paul Nitze was an able Wall Streeter who had been vice chairman of the U.S. Strategic Bombing Survey in 1945, an organization that investigated the effectiveness of Allied bombardment of Germany; he had then served under Acheson as director of policy planning and would eventually be a prime arms negotiator for President Reagan. Now he matter-of-factly exposed the flaws of math and mere geography, always the weak points of emergency men and of this one in particular: the Doctor had miscalculated the blast effects of twenty-kiloton bombs by an order of magnitude of one hundred to one, and in proposing a Rube Goldberg system of open cities free from nuclear strikes, he had overlooked that few cities in Western Europe are more than sixty miles apart.[9]

Into the 1960 presidential election, Kissinger was among the adamant critics proclaiming that Eisenhower had neglectfully allowed a "missile gap" to develop with Moscow. The assertion benefited Governor Rockefeller's quest for the Republican nomination, by making the Eisenhower administration appear weak, though Vice President Nixon still won it. Eight years later, Kissinger shifted his political future away from Rockefeller as Nixon stood on the cusp of finally winning the presidency. It was a few years thereafter, toward the end of Nixon's first term, that Kissinger first became renowned as a miracle worker—thanks to Soviet and Chinese totalitarian manipulators and to Hanoi's delegation at the Paris peace talks. In all three contexts, he was the prime negotiator. In 1972, he appeared to effectively orchestrate a simultaneous détente with Moscow and civil relations with Maoist China, as well as a January 1973 deal with Hanoi that ended direct U.S. military involvement in Vietnam. "Peace is at hand," he announced.

Miracle No. 1 was China. When a change occurs that impacts American life, we reflexively ask, "*Who* made it happen?" The Sino-Soviet quarrel had been gnawing away with increasing malignancy since 1958, as Kissinger understood. Yet only when a U.S. emissary responded to Beijing's initiative did a bedazzled nation assume that the wondrous breakthrough had suddenly been brought off by some star performer. To believe in such personalized agency is to reverse cause and effect.

Miracle No. 2 was the Soviet Union. "Détente," concludes his biographer, historian Alistair Horne, "remains a triumph for Kissinger's personal role," including "his wooing of Dobrynin, the Soviet Ambassador in Washington." Here is a grave misunderstanding of détente, and particularly of the "wooing" that Draper concludes led to "tragicomic confusion and cross-purposes" in Washington.[10]

This was an administration at war with itself from the start. The Kremlin knew early on that the Nixon White House was lying repeatedly to its own secretary of state—Kissinger's predecessor, William Rogers—and occasionally to its secretary of defense, on Soviet-American policy. That cagey ambassador—who never reciprocated these intimacies—was the instrument for enabling Kissinger to use all the back-channeling that the Doctor pleased. Amid the infighting that followed, the Joint Chiefs resorted to placing a spy within Kissinger's NSC staff to find out what was going on—as, in a similarly dysfunctional administration thirty years later, the NSC staff would place one at the Pentagon when it was kept in the dark by the bureaucratically manipulative Rumsfeld. In the Nixon years, however, such Machiavellian amateurism further set up the country for foolishly solipsistic arms control and trade deals, as well as the dreamy one that affirmed no more international rivalry with the Soviet Union.

Dr. Kissinger's personal, or "shuttle," diplomacy between the world's belligerents was tireless. Being televised, it was welcomed by an American public growing disillusioned with "the burden and the glory" of planetary struggle, now eager to seek a way out of arms-racing, nation-building, of being "watchmen on the walls of freedom" and of all the accompanying hours of maximum danger. The public thirst for disengagement was burnished by journalists who refused to believe that a man as dislikable as Richard Nixon could of his own accord have been able to launch these sparkling overtures. Kissinger became the focus of celebration.

In the Middle East, the Doctor appeared pivotal to separating the mutually dazed antagonists of the 1973 Arab-Israeli war. "Henry Kissinger turned Egypt from a Soviet client into an American ally," writes columnist Charles Krauthammer, who then compares what he believes had been accomplished in Egypt with the flourishing, American-created democracy that he sees today in Iraq.[11] But neither Kissinger, nor Nixon, nor some other American superstar had "turned" Egypt any more than they had "turned" China.

Kissinger had never visited the Arab world before 1973. The previous year, Egypt's President Anwar Sadat had expelled thousands of Soviet advisers. But the White House wouldn't risk a high stakes peace initiative in the midst of Watergate—one risk being the danger of alienating key Nixon supporters in the Senate. While Nixon and Kissinger refused to engage, three warnings arrived from Moscow that Sadat would otherwise try to change his fortune through war. Veteran *New York Times* and *Washington Post* correspondent Patrick Tyler offers a less enthralled account of Kissinger's magic after war indeed occurred, along with a devastating oil embargo: "The course he pursued reinforced the diplomatic paralysis. It perpetuated Israel's hold on the territories it had occupied in 1967," Tyler writes in *A World of Trouble*, because Dr. Kissinger "found it impossible to advocate a course of action that ran counter to the prevailing consensus of Israeli leaders." [12] But then, as today, there had to be a star.

Reminiscing about his years in office, Kissinger insists that there was "no alternative" to anxious propitiation of Moscow, to opening the American armory to the egomaniacal Shah, to backing a murderous Chilean military regime so glaringly contrary to U.S. interests, or to feeding carnivorous dictators to uphold an "African balance of power," as if such an otherworldly state of affairs ever could or would exist. [13] But alternatives of course there were. To argue "no choice" is a classic excuse of the emergency man recoiling from the scrutiny of his heated decisions. These years were also the last point in public discourse where third-world peoples such as the Bangladeshi and Timorese, Kurds and Hmong, and Palestinians, too, were virtually invisible in a less technologically connected world. In those parts of the planet, Kissinger was a hard enough player, and not to America's long-term advantage.

Nonetheless his reputation as a "miracle worker" blossomed. He received the 1973 Nobel Prize, for bringing peace to Vietnam. His North Vietnamese opposite number at the peace talks, with whom he shared the prize, refused it.

In April 1975, remnants of South Vietnam's army continued to fight as that country stumbled to the graveyard—overrun by an enormous Soviet-backed conventional invasion from the North. "Why don't these people die fast?" White House Press Secretary Ron Nessen records Kissinger as saying. "The worst thing that could happen would be for them to linger on." Given that emergency men rarely recognize their illusions even when those evaporate, it took Gerald Ford's midwestern candor to recall that "Henry Kissinger had urged me to tell the American people that Congress was solely to blame for the debacle in Southeast Asia"—

as if a merely representative body could serve as the oafish fall guy for deeds the elite no longer cared to remember.[14]

On leaving government nearly two years later at the end of the Ford presidency, the Doctor began to flourish as a business consultant. Along with David Rockefeller, chairman of the Chase Manhattan Bank, which had a huge undisclosed financial stake in the decision, he urged the Carter administration to give refuge to the ousted and ailing Shah of Iran. Jimmy Carter grudgingly yielded to these pressures and, quid pro quo two weeks later, ended up with the 444-day-long agony in Tehran, where fifty-two U.S. diplomats were taken hostage.[15]

For an emergency man to stay in the limelight when out of office, like Kissinger, requires an even more humbling sort of industriousness than is needed to get appointed in the first place. Come the Reagan administration in 1981, the White House had to designate a member of its own NSC staff to field Kissinger's letters to the president. "They were written as to a dull high school student," recalls Norman Bailey, who was then the NSC's Senior Director for International Economics. "The president had no interest in them. I was tasked with writing detailed replies under Reagan's signature—which unfortunately meant that for two years these long, ponderous letters kept arriving about every three weeks. Henry was dying to be appointed to something."[16] (He finally got an advisory role involving Central America.)

By the time George H. W. Bush came to office, the former cabinet secretary could share his thoughts with the White House through his former deputy, General Scowcroft, who had again become National Security Adviser. The Doctor's legend was safe: in 1996, the Council on Foreign Relations honored one of its prominent members by creating the Henry A. Kissinger Study Group on Exit Strategies and American Foreign Policy.

It would take the combination of another fraught presidency, like Nixon's, along with a 9/11, to bring Dr. Kissinger back to center stage, or as close as was practical for an enthusiast soon to be in his eighties. To him, "Afghanistan was not enough." The guidance he provided George W. Bush, once America got stuck in Iraq, had its similarities. The "salted peanuts" memo arguing against withdrawing troops from Southeast Asia was repurposed and given to a president bewildered by a disastrous commitment.[17]

Kissinger's prime contribution to American diplomatic practice may be the production of an immortal image—the emergency man in the mode of audacious New Frontiersman. He described himself to the crafty interviewer Oriana Fallaci as "the cowboy who leads the wagon train by riding ahead alone on his horse, the cowboy who rides all alone into the town."[18] Although he regretted this revelation, Kissinger's is the emergency man's daydream of uncanny powers—the faultlessly quick and accurate draw, a keen eye to read the land, endless stamina. Above all, such a character does not have a career, but rather a role. Careers may be derailed; roles maintain strength in their mythic endurance. Nixon had to resign and Gerald Ford was voted out of office. But Gary Cooper's Marshal Will Kane is invulnerable over the years to all the troublemakers loosed on a Technicolor world.

The eagerness of Americans to find stars in every walk of national life extends to a passion for specializations and specialists. Americans are the world's busiest of people. They work more hours, change jobs more often, consume more, and devote more time to volunteering. They also change residences more frequently and spend more time in church. It makes sense to delegate avoidable responsibility and strain to someone apparently able to solve a worrisome new predicament—an expert with specialized insights. And busy Americans have never been fussy about the qualifications of even the most exotic panjandrum. Historian Walter McDougall chronicles this astonishing inattentiveness at least as far back as the mid-nineteenth century's hucksters of land development schemes and medicine shows.[19]

Americans defer to the latest surge of expert authority until it is debunked. Then they search for the next unburdening slogan and latest sage. Millions welcomed the pretensions of Werner Hans Erhard's est, or have committed their souls to L. Ron Hubbard's religion of Scientology. Millions more bought into the prediction that the Dow Jones Industrial Average would leap to stratospheric heights, as argued in the book *Dow 36,000*, published right before the dot-com crash by an economic commentator, James Glassman, who would go on to become undersecretary of state for public affairs in 2008. It is part of the American metaphysic to believe that anything can be accomplished, whether in spiritual fulfillment, in investments, or in global affairs, should the appropriate expert be called in. Given the country's achievements in science, technology, and industry, the belief has its points. But when it goes wrong, it can go really, really wrong.

The canonization of an "expert" can anesthetize reason. The expert will settle the problem for us. No need to worry about how. This response usually makes sense, given our lack of time or information for independent judgments. Experts who are plainly qualified deliver unequivocal value, as do nuclear physicists interpreting the source of stellar energies, or plumbers who unclog the drain. But the value of national security policy "experts" has a much more checkered history.

Economists point out the dilemma of "expert service": the same expert who diagnoses the flaw in a product is the one who will be called on to help fix it. Similarly, the same policy expert who detects a "crisis" will make darn sure that he or she is part of the effort to solve it. It's the problem that Nixon referenced when he observed that Kissinger would be ready to spark a crisis over Ecuador did Vietnam not exist. Emergency men identify a calamity—whether in Georgia, Iran, Venezuela—then sound the tocsin, offer quick verdicts, and jump forth with action-oriented remedies. It's an unhelpful progression because, in decision making of such consequence, the distance from discerned "trouble" to legitimized "action" should be as wide as safely possible.

Many people in the national security arena would be unlikely to count as experts were Americans not forever crying out for expertise. Who, after all, is an "expert" on terror? There are some superb ones, such as Brian Jenkins, a former Special Forces captain and RAND analyst who has mastered the continuities and disruptions of this subject for thirty years. So too is CNN analyst Peter Berger, who is known for conducting the first television interview with Osama bin Laden in 1997. But legal scholars dealing with terrorism cases are skeptical about what constitutes a qualified expert witness on the subject.[20] Alleged experts still prosper in think tanks and consultancies years after the fantastic links they drew between Saddam and Al Qaeda have crumbled into the sand. But many of these experts also saw their perceived links between "Islam" and the all-American Oklahoma City bombing in 1995, with its 168 dead, go up in smoke.[21]

In sprawling, innovation-hungry America, the bar for being considered an "expert" is particularly low when the subject is "national security." To be an expert on Saudi Arabia would at least require knowing Arabic. It would also entail an ability to expound the demography, perhaps derived from experiences of trekking the Rub' al-Khali and of sitting through dinners over the years with princelings in Ta'if. Or such an expert might even have garnered insights from having talked privately in Europe with certain politically influential wives. Those sorts of requirements go out the window when a commentator pushes himself forward as an expert on Saudi Arabia *and* its significance for U.S. national security, let alone an expert on Saudi Arabia *and* terror. This lowering of standards was to be seen during the Cold War as well. There were deeply schooled specialists on the Soviet Union, and then there were widely cited authorities of various abilities on national security. Authentic experts on the Soviet Union *and*

U.S. national security, such as RAND's Nathan Leites and Fritz Ermarth or Brookings's Raymond Garthoff, were few.

Today Danielle Pletka is vice president for foreign policy and defense policy studies at the American Enterprise Institute (AEI); she speaks barely a word of Arabic, but is presented repeatedly without demurral as "a Middle East expert."[22] In discussing U.S. Middle East policy, she can condemn "casualty-averse" U.S. military commanders who, in her view, do not know "anything about the politics of the region," and not a peep emerges about what this critic herself might know of Baath and Tudeh, let alone of deadly combat.[23] In government, Elliott Abrams, the last administration's NSC senior director for Near East, Southwest Asian, and North African affairs during 2002–2005, had no serious background on these regions—other than activities resulting in two years' probation for his involvement in the Western Hemisphere end of the Reagan administration's Iran-Contra foul-up when handling inter-American affairs as an appointee at the State Department. Vice President Cheney's chief adviser on the Middle East—a political scientist previously responsible for monitoring the Arabic press for the Pentagon's Feith—had made no contributions that anyone can recall other than moral theorizing. Nor does President Obama's top dedicated Pentagon official for the Middle East—a competent generalist of national security studies who had been an assistant political science professor and a fellow at the Council on Foreign Relations—speak Arabic or Farsi.

The problem of sketchy qualifications goes beyond that of language. However, not to know a language of world standing common to the region for which one has responsibility, and on which one even claims to be an expert, might indicate that a high official has not prepared for the basics of his or her subject.

The extent to which Americans take expertise on faith highlights a rare passivity in national life. Even outright frauds can win captive audiences in the alarm-ridden domain of national security—all the more so when the subject is *terror*, rather than say, NATO relations. Hunger for national security experts can be intense. In 2007, one charlatan was "Dr." Alexis Debat, senior consultant on terrorism to ABC News since 2001, a senior fellow at the Nixon Center (a think tank created by Nixon during his effortful rehabilitation after Watergate), and recipient of an academic appointment at George Washington University's hastily created Homeland Security Policy Institute. Besides his more scholarly pronouncements, this much-quoted Middle East authority was a tireless proponent of bombing Iran—until his Ph.D. proved to be as bogus as his interviews with Bill Clinton, Michael Bloomberg, Bill Gates, and Barack Obama, let alone his news sources among "terrorists" worldwide.

"It's hard to know what's real and what's not," observes Laura Rozen, now foreign policy reporter at Politico, who broke the story about the additional work that Debat was doing for the Pentagon concerning "Islamic warfare." "In this small world," she concluded, credentials are taken on face value.[24] As if to underline her point, the elaborately fabricated "Harding Institute for Freedom and Democracy," named for the inept twenty-ninth president, opened its doors in Washington during 2008. An apparently well-credentialed senior fellow at the institute, "Martin Eisenstadt," offered articulate absurdities during interviews. In fact, an imaginative filmmaker named Eitan Gorlin had cast himself as "one of the neocons in the Bush administration" and his "Dr. Eisenstadt" proved convincing enough to be quoted by MSNBC, by the *New Republic*, and in the blogs, until the *New York Times* took a closer look.[25] Today, there's the customary Washington memoir: *I Am Martin Eisenstadt* (2009).

In Britain, France, Russia, or Japan, professional scrutiny, tighter alumni networks, and inherent jealousies over others' success would make it impossible for a would-be Oz to command such issues from behind the curtain for more than a day. Yet this prominence taps into the very American practice of reinventing one's life story. In no other country, for instance, do so many citizens find reason to legally change their full names, like Werner Hans Erhard, that cultural icon of the 1970s, who was born John Rosenberg in Norristown, Pennsylvania. However, the make-believe expertise enjoyed professionally "in this community," to cite Rozen, may be unprecedented. Even amid the terrible dangers and urgencies of World War II, no imposter was able to invoke special knowledge and dire emergency to bring off such effronteries in Washington.

Shamefully, this fraud, combined with way too much citizen deference toward insider expertise after 9/11, ran interference for the black magic of so-called enhanced interrogations of scores of terror suspects. The U.S. armed services have had to examine themselves over systematic use of brutally coercive techniques in every major detention facility in Iraq where interrogation took place, as well as in Afghanistan. But it was within CIA that a pattern of torture got under way at widely touted expert hands. By the spring of 2002, an increasingly queasy nation began to learn of just a fraction of these torments.

The White House, the Office of the Secretary of Defense, and likely enough key members of Congress's intelligence committees assumed after 9/11 that savvy interrogators at the CIA knew what they were doing, and that their specialized techniques had value. But methods condemned by the United States as torture in World War II were being surreally recast as an "alternative set of procedures." Consulting psychologists who designed the waterboarding and other harsh applications would be fired—but only in 2009, rather late in the game for scrutinizing skills, qualifications, and global political consequences.

A compelling reason presents itself, I believe, as to why decent, law-abiding Americans—children of the nation that first codified the laws of war in 1861, long before the Geneva Conventions, to restrain excesses against prisoners and civilians—chose to tolerate what got under way. It was not merely out of a panicked post-

9/11 acceptance that anything goes on the "dark side" of war, as is generally believed. No, it derived from sensible, solution-seeking Americans being repeatedly assured that expert hands were justly and effectively educing information from figures of darkness. White House, Pentagon, and Justice Department decision makers who made the case for "enhanced interrogation" seem further to have convinced themselves that expertise, of a sort, was being applied. The psychiatrists, psychologists, and interrogators toiling away, President Bush vouched to the nation, were "professionals who are trained in this kind of work."[26] And to limit those techniques, said the believers, would constrain "highly trained CIA interrogators."[27]

Illusion No. 1 was that any of these CIA "professionals" had a clue as to what they were doing with their simulated drownings, the extreme sleep deprival that Stalin's torturers had dubbed "one-hundred-hour conveyor" interrogations, and sensory deprivation techniques gleaned from Chinese practices on American POWs in Korea.[28] Other experts were deployed: CIA physicians and psychiatrists monitored waterboarding, among the tortures, while keeping data on the subject's reactions; and personnel from the Agency's medical services office were dispatched to each of the CIA's secret "ghost prisons" overseas.

In fact, the Agency was flailing blindly. Despite lurid myths out of the Cold War, it really knows little about interrogation beyond a heavy dependence on the polygraph—that most shamanic of instruments—for the occasional Q&A of the foreign agents with whom it works. The cluelessness before and after 9/11 is noted by the Intelligence Science Board, the advisory panel on key scientific and technical issues to the government's senior leaders responsible for intelligence. "There had been little or no development of sustained capacity for interrogation practice, training or research" before 9/11, or thereafter, concludes a Harvard Medical School instructor who served on the board. "Interrogators were forced to 'make it up' on the fly."[29]

The architects of Langley's approach to systematic torment—"the docs," as the CIA calls its credentialed mind readers—featured two military retirees and psychologists, Bruce Jessen and his partner Jim Mitchell. Neither could claim any relevant scholarship, or language skills, or any experience on anything to do with terror, let alone with Al Qaeda. One had written his Ph.D. thesis on high blood pressure, the other on family therapy. But they were *experts*, and for a moment they were stars as well. Their consulting firm—Mitchell, Jessen & Associates—raked in millions of dollars by selling "interrogation and training services" to the Agency.[30] No one at Langley or in the White House had the time or interest to look deeper.

The quackery that passed for expert professionalism came largely from various attempts to reverse-engineer the methods used by the military since the late 1950s to train commandos to resist savage questioning by enemies not abiding by the Geneva Conventions. These methods were intended to induce "learned helplessness" and were shaped by the psychologists. U.S. Army Special Forces seemed to have done the most realistic work in this realm. Spending an hour inside their simulated enemy stockade, located deep in the North Carolina piney woods of Camp Mackall, is enough to make a visitor confess to having planned Pearl Harbor. But "it was the only other game in town," concludes Colonel Steven Kleinman, an analyst for the Intelligence Science Board and previously the Pentagon's senior officer for special survival training. Using those methods was "the proverbial attempt to place the square peg in the round hole," he adds, because such "defensive interrogation operations" differ intractably from "offensive" attempts to carve out information.[31]

Illusion No. 2 was the belief by alleged experts and their supervisors at Langley that these brutally coercive techniques led to action-producible results. They did not hear what they did not want to hear. To have considered opposing arguments, moreover, would have risked discrediting the Agency's "psychiatrists, psychologists . . . and interrogators"—those supposedly expert "docs" who, for the time being, were the not-so-unsung heroes of counterterrorism.

Kleinman reminds us that "the scientific community has never established that coercive interrogation methods are an effective means of obtaining reliable intelligence information." Arguments that it is indeed effective nonetheless resurfaced in 2010, accompanied by new claimants to expertise, by anecdote substituting for evidence, by Langley's defensive bureaucracy, and by assertions that there was no alternative. Yet the FBI, as is well-known, deploys actual experts on the subject. Its trained and knowledgeable interrogators apply the savvier methods of "rapport building," as well as deceptive psychological tricks. The Bureau establishes affinities with even the vilest of subjects through this so-called "Magic of Rapport."[32] Saddam Hussein is an example. He spoke openly about Osama bin Laden, Iran, whatever else was asked once he was in the hands of George L. Piro, a Lebanese born agent fluent in Arabic. Like the "magic" of effective leadership, the FBI's unparalleled successes in interrogation derive not from anything uncanny but from extraordinary skill and experience. Dismayed at the CIA's amateur brutalities, FBI experts backed away fast from the Agency's undertakings at Guantánamo and at its arc of "ghost" or "black site" prisons stretching from Romania to Thailand.

The CIA's overnight professionals of mind-opening did not shun only the FBI. Amid all the urgency, excitement, and latitude for experiments, they avoided any systematic examination of how other advanced democracies have acted when menaced by terror. There was no focused, dedicated effort to learn from Israeli officials facing conflict on multiple fronts, from British interrogators unpleasantly familiar with the hammer blows of the IRA, or from the internal security agencies of Germany and Italy that not so long ago had battled Soviet-backed urban atrocity. No advice was asked even from France's coldly capable Interior Ministry.

Not until more than five years after the twin towers fell, and in the absence of any comparative analyses by Langley, did the Intelligence Science Board undertake its first steps toward a still-classified, slow-moving study of all this previously untapped experience. The study's outlines would be reported soon after the change of administration in 2009, including the work of Intelligence Board member Philip Heymann, Harvard's Ames Professor of Law, whose task force began to compile comparative data on what our allies' interrogators do. What hasn't been disclosed are the telling first steps of the earlier initiative, and the response. As part of that secret effort, senior veterans of Israel's internal security arm, Shin Bet, were interviewed by legitimately specialist U.S. civilian researchers. The initial findings were presented in a discomforting top-level briefing in the Virginia suburbs in 2007, again rather late in the game.

"They might as well go to the beach," one Israeli veteran declared, scoffing at U.S. "professionals" and would-be experts who speak only English and know essentially nothing about the places, clans, and motivations inspiring the captives who were then in American custody.[33] Israel's own recourse to torture had been halted, more or less, by its supreme court in 1999. But the very able Shin Bet veterans acknowledged that few of the sufferings they had helped to inflict had ever proved effective anyway. Their message: the CIA was deceiving itself, and the country, about the value of terrorist statements exacted in fear, rage, and near madness.

Why was such homework not done at the start? Why were the simplest of inquiries eschewed that could have prepared allegedly expert U.S. personnel to elicit critical information in ways both more rewarding and more decent? "The reasons for this omission remain unknown," concludes Kleinman.[34] But let me offer one here: it is magical thinking to believe that the square peg can be fitted into the round hole through sheer exertion. Self-deception to this degree comes from ignoring experience and substituting

angry passion backed by frantic improvisation. True to commonplace emergency behaviors, the most senior administration
officials displayed neither second thoughts nor any indication of
soul-searching. There wasn't *any time* for unpoliticized reasoning
as administration decision makers and CIA implementers took
the "plunge"—in the words of the Intelligence Science Board—
into what, in the real world, is unambiguously torture.[35] Plus experts were at hand, with Ph.D.s.

But who even knew if the right people were being hurt? In
2008, the chief judge of the Court of Appeals for the District of
Columbia Circuit, David Sentelle, known as one of the most
conservative jurists in the country, compared the government's
argument in *Parhat v. Gates* to Lewis Carroll's nonsense poem about
the Snark. The prosecutors claimed that flimsy evidence against
a supposed terrorist was to be deemed reliable because it was
mentioned in three different classified documents. The rendition
of another suspect, a German car salesman, was thought by his
abductors to be mistaken identity from the start. But the CIA flew
him to Afghanistan and kept him in a dungeon for five months.
"She just looked in her crystal ball and it said that he was bad,"
said an Agency colleague of the officer in charge of that case at
Langley.[36]

Celebrity, expertise, and bold individual lawbreaking ultimately combine in a bottomless, dangerous muck. It's hard to
think of another country where a cabinet secretary responsible
for homeland security would say of a brutal TV action series full
of fictional national security crises like *24*, "Frankly, it reflects real
life."[37] "Everybody breaks eventually" was the explicit, yet uninstructed, premise of *24* as evildoers fell into the expert hands of
secret agent Jack Bauer. For him, torture magically works. Washington succumbed in unique ways to L.A. celebrity as the wish-
fulfilling drama aired from late 2001 through spring 2010. This did
not go unnoticed. Making clear reference to *24*, the Intelligence
Science Board went on the record to caution that people "even

within professional circles have unfortunately been influenced by the media's colorful (and artificial) view of interrogation as almost always involving hostility." Colonel Kleinman saw fit to add that "a likely factor driving the progressive 'dumbing down' of interrogation and interrogation training in the United States has been the ubiquitous treatment of the craft in movies and Hollywood." [38]

Star-obsessed America romanticizes beyond reason the sort of third-world supermen who don't bat an eyelash over any such "alternative methods." Syngman Rhee, South Korea's strongman from 1948 to 1960, was held up to a not closely informed nation as a "beacon of democracy." Lyndon Johnson described Ngo Dinh Diem, South Vietnam's heavy-handed premier from 1955 to 1963, as the "Churchill of Asia." In the Iraq War, the hero on whom victory was to rest was that shadowy banker Ahmed Chalabi, "the George Washington of Iraq," according to Feith's deputy at the Pentagon, William Luti. [39] President Bush called Chalabi a "defender of freedom" and sat him next to the first lady at the 2004 State of the Union address, an honor unlikely to be bestowed in front of Russia's Duma or Japan's Diet, or before Parliament or the Assemblée Nationale.

All these leaders have been packaged as figures of preternatural virtue rather than as momentarily convenient business partners of the state. Each fantasy rationalizes imprudent attachments. They appeared to be so much like us. Their allure included American education and Western tailoring. Each possessed that reassuringly civilized quality of speaking excellent English. It is likely that rougher, less articulate—though perhaps more effective—characters were available with whom to collaborate in these and other instances. But choosing among such men would have required deeper understandings of these beleaguered societies, as well as more American time, attention, and awareness of difficult choices.

The allure of each of these clients also stemmed from their years spent in America, as well as from their knowledge of how to game the boisterous U.S. political system. Americans are uniquely susceptible to being swayed by exiles, especially ones with compelling personal stories and a reassuring presence—a vulnerability connected to being a nation of immigrants. Wide-open, welcoming, America is a natural friend to the courteous stranger, like each of these men who spent significant parts of their lives in America. On politico-military matters, exiles become valued for their alleged special knowledge about what's happening in their native lands. As apparent experts on such matters themselves, they can develop potent social and political connections while in America, and do so more easily than anywhere else on the planet. They claim universal political support at home, and their unique means of delivering democracy (or, at least, "stability") thereto. The most practical of U.S. leaderships can take such claims seriously, and these upwardly mobile exiles become heroes.

Rhee, for his part, was a Methodist with Ivy League degrees and, once in power, an accumulating record of civilian massacres. Though this record did not compare with the "Great Leader" in Pyongyang, South Korea's Truth and Reconciliation Commission continues to uncover its scope. Yet still the United States placed its dreams of a democratic unified Korea on Rhee. Having converted to Christianity, he got himself to America at the beginning of the last century to earn a B.A. from George Washington University, an M.A. from Harvard, and a Ph.D. in international law from Princeton—returning to teach at Seoul's YMCA at the same time that Japan openly annexed that unhappy peninsula. Fleeing Korea, he fought against the occupation first from China (still run by Rhee's fellow Methodist Chiang Kai-shek) and then from Hawaii and Washington.[40]

Aided by his radiant Austrian wife, he grew close to a large contingent of the earnestly proselytizing, anti-imperialist American elites of the mid-twentieth century. In due course becoming a shrewd and merciless ruler of South Korea, he drew part of his power from offering a new Asian stereotype: the admittedly stern, but surely anticommunist and perhaps eventually democratic chieftain on whom Americans could project their own qualities and visions. Before the Korean War, Rhee's ancient civilization had been just about invisible. But he developed solid contacts in Congress and in the press—along with a lobbying arm in Washington. By the time the armistice was struck in 1953, he held a "psychological whammy" on America, said the U.S. commander in Korea, as Rhee obstructed a cease-fire and thereafter cemented his strong-arm sovereignty under U.S. protection.[41] The military-fueled economy he helped to create would boom, but one South Korean despotism or another held on until 1988.

In Vietnam, the hero was the aristocratic authoritarian Ngo Dinh Diem, a brave nationalist and faithful Catholic in a largely Buddhist land. He was hated by the French and by the communist leader Ho Chi Minh alike, which helped to turn Diem into America's prototype of a postwar Christian anticolonial champion. While in exile, he had spent 1951–53 at the Maryknoll Seminary in Lakewood, New Jersey, returning to conduct an increasingly nepotistic regime under American auspices. Despite the crucifix in his office and the Western sharkskin business suits in his closet, that backing began to fray as he proved increasingly unhelpful to American nation-building. Films of Buddhist priests immolating themselves in protest against his government sickened the American public. Staff at the NSC and officials at State abetted a coup in Saigon that segued into Diem's murder in November 1963—to no one's surprise but its U.S. instigators'. And the "Pottery Barn Rule"—"you break it, you own it"—grabbed America by the throat, with a succession of seven coups and countercoups in just the following year.

As for Chalabi, American journalists would recall his round face, incessant gossip, and "wizardly smile."[42] Despite his being trailed by accusations of bank fraud, no previous power-brokering exile, nor any foreigner without official status, has so manipulated Washington. Interacting directly with the emergency men behind the Iraq invasion, particularly at the Pentagon, he was central to the U.S. decision to go to war. This exiled leader of the Iraqi National Congress helped convince them of what they wanted to believe: that with their help he would be welcomed as president of an Iraq cleansed of Saddam. Chalabi provided much of the false information used by the Pentagon to establish Saddam's supposed ties to Al Qaeda, as well as Iraq's make-believe stash of weapons of mass destruction.

In this manner, Chalabi built critical connections within the U.S. government; there had been no such constituency for Rhee or Diem. They had enjoyed powerful supporters in their day such as Time, Inc.'s, publisher Henry Luce. But no group had then existed as focused, energetic, and as well-connected throughout the bureaucracy as that composed of Wolfowitz, Perle, Feith, Cheney's assistant "Scooter" Libby, let alone their principals. He proved more adept at arranging receptions for himself in Washington than among his fellow Shia back in his native land. His B.S. from MIT and Ph.D. in math from Chicago were evidence of impressive skills indeed, but ones no more relevant to what lay ahead than the Savile Row suits that equally impressed his admirers along the Potomac. When in 2007 a recent Iraqi defense minister judged that the Bush administration had invaded an "imagined country," a lot of that make-believe could be traced back to Chalabi.[43]

Chalabi had spent much of his life in Britain as well, but he never made a splash. Some telling reasons are offered by Peter Galbraith, who was the highest-ranking American official working for the UN in Afghanistan until he was forced out for revealing the extent of the 2009 election fraud. He had dealt with

Chalabi while on the staff of the Senate Foreign Relations Committee, and thereafter in the Clinton administration. "You can't blame him," he laughs, hoping the worst is over in Iraq. "He knew us cold. His money, manners, charisma and bluff let him push every button in Washington." [44] Today Chalabi spends much of his time in Iran. U.S. intelligence regards him as essentially an agent of Tehran who has created a pivotal role for himself to manipulate sectarian politics while zooming in and out of Baghdad as a member of parliament.

The problem, of course, is that once America builds up its overseas client-heroes as stars, it can find itself with no choice but to keep working with them even after they no longer appear indispensable.

Americans keep reposing their hopes in illusory assets that offer such eloquence and flair. The hero-making goes way beyond these three examples, and it is hard to say who is using whom. Pick any year. In 1975, when Kissinger worried about a tilt in what he also called "the African equilibrium," America began playing favorites among postcolonial factions in Angola. [45] By the time the Reagan administration arrived, each of these would be hiring Washington lobbyists to help argue its case. One warlord favored battle fatigues when visiting the White House. Representatives of another murderous movement were dressed for success by their K Street handlers in Brooks Brothers suits and horn-rimmed glasses to impress Capitol Hill. Seductive advocacy mingled with promises of imminent democracy. U.S. checks as well as Angolan bodies piled up to no purpose.

Nor has this changed much. Lots of generally attentive Americans, including on Capitol Hill, in the White House, and in the press, become boosters of overseas paragons who pay us the compliment of trying to look and sound the way we like. They feed American appetites for inspiring narratives as they speak of a shared security.

Afghan president Hamid Karzai, with his Western-style technocrats and talk of democracy, was immensely appealing to Washington after the Taliban was ousted. For more than seven years, reports the *Times*' Dexter Filkins, Karzai was "a White House favorite—a celebrity in flowing cape and dark gray fez," a dramatic outfit that he had designed himself, but that had no origin in Afghani dress. Every two weeks Karzai held a videoconference with President George W. Bush. "We thought we had found a miracle man," moaned one diplomat.[46] On closer inspection, the sorcerer proved unconvincing as the opium trade and corruption flourished. By the time the Obama administration took power, Americans were hearing about the vicious Afghan warlord General Abdul Rashid Dostum—who in 2002 had quickly adopted a business suit and new political links with Karzai to avoid prosecution for war crimes—as open to "reform," the general then working to shape Karzai's cabinet in 2010, after Afghanistan's tainted presidential election. The accusation that Dostum stuffed his prisoners into closed metal shipping containers to starve and suffocate them was "unimaginable," retorted the general, "to the extent that has been claimed."[47] Enchantments continue.

For years, the flaws of redoubtable U.S. client-heroes have been paid no heed. Like the Shah, such men are persuasively reassuring—until the stage collapses beneath them. "Where's the leader?" President Bush had asked in dismay when Iraq ineffectively struggled to sort out its future once a legislature had been established under U.S. occupation. "Where's George Washington? Where's Thomas Jefferson? Where's John Adams, for crying out loud?"[48] There was a rather short answer: "Not in twenty-first century Baghdad, sir." But that was too painfully obvious for even his political opponents to take pleasure in delivering.

Fascination with boldface names also undermines America's engagement with its enemies, and with terrorists in particular. When the country confronts a seriously hostile power, such as the

Soviet Union or a nuclear-armed North Korea, the opponent's makeup is more or less easy to identify. Dangers are tangible. Newsreels and then television used to relay chilling footage of Red Army divisions marching past Lenin's tomb on Victory Day, ICBMs rolling behind them, while the Politburo massed itself atop the mausoleum looking heavy, hard, and brutally in charge. Today, North Korean missile tests can be followed on Google and Kim Jong Il's underground nuclear detonations monitored by the local university geology department. Terrorism, however, is a relatively anonymous phenomenon, and its practitioners are far less visible. No parades. Terrorists instead make themselves known by their atrocities. We witness the blood-soaked marketplace, the burning towers. Americans, always eager to personalize, rush to slap a name and face on the "terrorist mastermind."[49] So a bin Laden or an al-Zarqawi today, an Arafat or a George Habash in decades past, get raised into a daimonion of recognizable evildoers. But forces of outrage are at work upon the world more ominously weighty than such unshaven menaces.

These threats nonetheless become larger than life, as do America's more visible enemies. No one sees a resemblance to Hitler so indiscriminately as do we—President Johnson, for instance, equated Hitler and Ho Chi Minh.[50] It's unusual for the British to compare an enemy to Hitler, though there are exceptions: for example, an unthinking remark by Prime Minister Tony Blair about Saddam and a famous denunciation by an earlier premier about Egypt's strongman, Gamal Abdel Nasser, during Britain's Suez intervention in 1956. The French do it rarely and the Russians even less so, being 27 million dead the wiser—though Russian premier Vladimir Putin has muttered about the Third Reich in reference to America, and Russia's deputy interior minister places Georgia's president among "neo-Nazis and neo-Fuhrers."[51] But only China has been as frenzied in its comparisons of an opponent to a "dictatorship of the Hitler type"—and that was in 1976–77 as Beijing railed against the Soviet Union once more.

Many influential Americans compared Saddam to Hitler before the 2003 invasion. The first President Bush began making the case in 1990, though to him Saddam was "worse than Hitler." The most frantic of emergency men go even further. As deputy secretary of defense in the run-up to invasion, Wolfowitz made few appearances on Capitol Hill in which he did not boost Saddam's henchmen to the evil, let alone the mighty efficiency, of the Waffen SS. Perle then took the logical next step. In his co-authored book, *An End to Evil*, which he describes as "a manual for victory," he urges the usual "new audacity in our strategy abroad" but goes on to insist "There is no middle way for Americans: It is victory or holocaust." [52] All sense of proportion evaporates. Alarms in the 1950s about falling dominoes sound quaint, as they do today when we hear about "Hitler marching into the Rhineland" to describe Iran's ambitions for nuclear weapons. [53]

Such a degree of star personalization makes it easy to imagine that knocking off just one or another undoubted evildoer could be like killing Hitler circa 1941, or at least throwing a bucket of water on the Wicked Witch. If we can just get rid of that bad guy, then all those millions of basically decent little people on the other side will change their minds overnight. It's an illusion to be found on the front lines as well. "A lot of us thought that it was going to be a real milestone in our progress against Al Qaeda," a senior U.S. intelligence officer remarked in 2006 about the well-informed, well-targeted killing by two U.S. Air Force F-16s of Abu Musab-al-Zarqawi, head of Al Qaeda in Iraq. His death only served to encourage Rumsfeld to stick with a failing strategy, reports one of the secretary's biographers. [54] But Zarqawi's death made no more difference to curbing the violence than had the capture of Saddam two and a half years earlier. The administration had treated that previous scuffle with a cadence that echoed General Eisenhower declaring the end of World War II in Europe: a sudden presidential address to the nation announced the momentous occurrence of "December the 13th, at around 8:30 p.m.

Baghdad time."[55] Yet 4,200 Americans who were alive on that triumphant Washington afternoon were yet to die, as well as more than 90,000 Iraqi civilians.

America traditionally has not made celebrities out of its top commanders for winning anything much short of world wars. The reasons include the existence of a true gold standard—Washington, Scott, Grant, Sherman, Lee, Pershing, MacArthur, Ike. When the spotlights otherwise begin to shine on shoulders full of stars, however, that's a sign that something is wrong.

Militarist societies romanticize generals, weaponry, and armed power. They find spiritual rewards in sacrificial bloodshed for its own sake, and organize themselves for violence as they extol authority. Unless one turns the definition of militarism inside out, as is done frequently in public policy writings, this description emphatically does not fit America.[56] Individualistic, moneymaking America has never had much patience for uniforms or hierarchies. In fact, militarism idealizes a determinedly backward stage of life, and there has never been a high-tech, basically decent militarized society. To that end the U.S. armed forces are a true extension of American civil society, rather than a world apart of regimental silver and insular tradition as found among the militaries of older great powers. Our officers' messes have the atmosphere of Elks or Rotary clubs or of a state university faculty lounge, especially now that each service in our self-improvement-obsessed nation places a priority on graduate degrees.

So for the country at large to carve a general into an equestrian statue has, ever since the epic achievements of 1945, been outside American custom: such stardom "bought at the jeopardy of men's lives," and for the world's greatest nation, had better be extraordinary indeed. Otherwise the fevered acclaim is more likely to reflect the nation's desperate hopes and wishful thoughts—

and the more worth examining for the recurring examples of American self-deception.

Consider the phenomenon of General David Petraeus, regularly described in the press as "the celebrity commander" and a "military superstar."[57] He is a smart, capable officer of proven courage, with the grad school degrees now deemed to authenticate exceptional ability among flag officers. His forty-minute briefing on quelling violence in Iraq during 2007–2008 displays the strong, modest disposition of the citizen-soldier. But beginning with his January 2007 appointment to command the Multi-National Force–Iraq, he was built up by Washington into a startling presence for an American general. No other serving U.S. officer has ever had his good name pulled so thoroughly into a presidential campaign, invoked by the 2008 candidates like a *Good Housekeeping* seal on their respective defense platforms. He became known as "one of the greatest generals in American history" and among his many admirers there is reflexive talk of a presidential run in 2012, at which he convincingly scoffs.[58] Why?

Adoration this fervent doesn't indicate sober praise for duty well done so much as it amplifies a desperate wishing that all will somehow, someday, turn out right in the uncalculated ventures of Iraq and Afghanistan. Thus General Petraeus's arrival in Baghdad at the start of 2007 was compared on Capitol Hill to Truman's replacing MacArthur in Korea by the gifted General Matthew Ridgway, whose steadying command halted the long retreat. "Petraeus is going to lead us to victory in Iraq," sighed the editor of the *Weekly Standard.* But by then *victory* was a word used only by starry-eyed civilians and not by Petraeus, who spoke only of "buying time"—"winning" to be done in Afghanistan.[59]

Something was also seriously askew after the first war with Iraq in 1991. In this instance, the problem spotlighted by all the heroizing wasn't a desperate and likely unrealistic hopefulness, but an equally self-deceiving catharsis.

General Norman Schwarzkopf hadn't sought applause; quite the contrary, as with Petraeus. Yet $5.1 million was paid for his autobiography, *It Doesn't Take a Hero*, and he garnered huge fees as a speaker.[60] Both revenue streams had become unremarkable for American celebrities, though no general had received such a sizable book advance since Eisenhower, for *Crusade in Europe*. America elevated Schwarzkopf as well to the ranks of Marshall and MacArthur. A ticker-tape parade up lower Broadway's Canyon of Heroes lauded him and his homecoming troops three months after the guns fell silent in the Gulf. Confetti fell in blizzards; the clamor and glare of bands, floats, and evening fireworks filled the streets and sky. The over-the-top excitement reflected not the rather modest nature of the victory, but the fact that the Gulf War was America's first significant combat since Vietnam, the expeditions to Grenada (1983) and Panama (1989) having been just a few steps up from police work. President George H. W. Bush claimed that America had finally shaken off its post-Vietnam despair. Big, burly, profane, and victorious, General Schwarzkopf—with three Silver Stars from the Vietnam War—personified this release. But on that June day on Broadway, America's tactical success in Kuwait was being misread as strategic triumph. Saddam had not been toppled by then, as the president and CIA had fully expected back at war's end in March. The Shia uprising that America had encouraged was being wiped out.

General Schwarzkopf was hardly the first of the post–World War II commanders to be extolled before the public, nor the most acclaimed. In the three major wars since 1945, General William Westmoreland had been celebrated the longest and perhaps the loudest. Given what occurred in Vietnam, this third example of celebrity-making is especially telling. We blind ourselves to what is under way.

The six-foot-two, sinewy artilleryman commanding U.S. military operations in Vietnam from 1964 to 1968 was *Time*'s Man of the Year for 1965 and President Johnson's "our beloved Westy." Kennedy had wanted him for army chief of staff in 1962, but was advised by the brass that, as a forty-eight-year-old major general, Westmoreland was much too junior. By 1967, while still directing the war, he returned from the field at President Johnson's request to address a joint session of Congress, a singular honor bestowed on MacArthur and later on Schwarzkopf, who like Westmoreland appeared in full uniform. Hailed as the "personification of the American fighting man," Westmoreland embarked on what he called a war of attrition.[61] Hence the "body counts" of supposed enemy slain as he deployed large-scale forces through the deep jungles. Young Americans were sent out to kill as many Viet Cong guerrillas and North Vietnamese regulars as possible until Hanoi eventually lost heart. "We have more guts" was Westmoreland's mantra as Washington granted him uncritical latitude for four worsening years.

Like MacArthur, Westmoreland had been First Captain at West Point, the highest position in the cadet chain of command. He had fought in Europe and had led a regimental combat team in Korea. But his press clippings emphasized management training at Harvard Business School at a time when such attainment was both rare for an officer and, in the McNamara Pentagon, highly prized. "Westy was a corporation executive in uniform," concludes Stanley Karnow, one of the best historians of the war.[62] He was also known to be considerably more cautious about the task at hand than were the civilian war leaders in Washington. Ultimately, however, Americans lost faith, not just in "Westy" but in Saigon's latest shaky regime. It cut little ice to read, again in *Time*, that "the U.S. last week announced a major shift in strategy . . . and named a new commander to carry it out."[63] This triumphant-looking commander without a triumph was kicked upstairs to be the U.S. Army chief of staff, and even came to consider a run for president. He had his backers, but his country's sustained judgment is ultimately too steady and practical to let the nation be led by military élan; Westmoreland faded away faster than any other old soldier.

One more hero—certainly an authentic one, as are perhaps the others above—remains to be considered for his significance about how even practical, businesslike, thoroughly civilian America can be dazzled by stars in uniform. He was an officer of startling achievement and ultimately terrible myopia whose aura ensured that bad advice was taken deadly seriously.

He is the most celebrated of all U.S. generals serving between MacArthur and Petraeus. Westmoreland was a protégé. During that half century, no name in uniform acquired the resonance of General Maxwell Taylor's. This tall, ramrod-straight paratrooper was said to have been observed reading Aeschylus, in the original, before jumping into Normandy with his 101st Airborne "Screaming Eagles" an hour before D-Day. One of the youngest and smartest generals to emerge from World War II, he became superintendent of West Point, commander of the Eighth Army during the Korean War's final static months, and then army chief of staff. He retired from service in summer 1959 to write *The Uncertain Trumpet*, a book of brilliant discontent, then worked a half year as president of the Lincoln Center for the Performing Arts in New York before President Kennedy made him his personal military adviser and ultimately chairman of the JCS: "somewhere between Virgil and Clausewitz," a *New York Times* "Man in the News" profile described him.[64] In 1965, after Lyndon Johnson appointed Taylor ambassador to Saigon, Bobby Kennedy would name one of his boys after this politically attuned warrior-scholar. Taylor spoke fluent French and Spanish, competent Japanese, and some Russian—which in later life he'd use to check out the linguistic abilities of any young academic presuming to discuss defense policy with him.[65]

The empirical soundness of this fighting man's guidance went unquestioned, except by Eisenhower, who in his last year of office was furious over Taylor's demand for "heroic measures" to offset the Republicans' alleged neglect of U.S. ground forces. But Kennedy embraced Taylor's recommendations.

As America then took its first major steps into Southeast Asia, Taylor saw fit to conclude that Vietnam's jungle hill country and swampy paddies were "not . . . an unpleasant place to operate for American soldiers." Vietnam could never turn into something as terrible as Korea, he vouched; besides, even on that bitter northeast Asian peninsula, U.S. troops had "learned to live and work without too much effort." [66] This steely, larger-than-life figure brushed off warnings from less well-connected officers who argued that only the use of overwhelming U.S. force could preserve South Vietnam. Instead he endorsed the McNamara/Bundy formula of graduated pressure to demonstrate American resolve. He also endorsed another one of that era's high-tech illusions: a plan for electronic surveillance of South Vietnam's borders with the North and with Laos and Cambodia—essentially a fence to nowhere, an idea eventually deep-sixed by its multibillion-dollar price tag. [67] His other views could be equally fantastic: for instance, his glowing reports to the White House about the Shah of Iran's "armies of freedom" after he and that besotted autocrat had stood atop a hill near Tehran observing troop maneuvers below. [68]

Like most everyone who encountered General Taylor, I came to admire his mind and rectitude as we worked together on U.S.-Soviet defense issues in the year after Saigon's fall. But I was puzzled how a man of this capacity—scholar, soldier, policymaker—could have gotten so much so wrong only a dozen years earlier. *The Best and the Brightest* had been published in the interval, and Taylor featured as the central military figure who rationalized the civilians' step-by-step intervention in Vietnam into something eminently manageable. Halberstam posed the core question that I quietly harbored: "Why men who were said to be the ablest to serve the government in this century had been the architects of what struck me as likely to be the worst tragedy since the Civil War." [69]

This irony extends beyond the best and the brightest of any one era. We can see it in the civilian chain of command in Washington during autumn 1950, as U.S. soldiers and marines were ordered into the deadfall of North Korea. We find it in the "dream team" of smart, bureaucratically savvy men and women who helped smooth the United States's slide into Iraq. And we are seeing it again today in Afghanistan. Most of all, it's a question that has defied logical answers during decades of self-delusion among foreign policy intellectuals—and occasional top officers—who with frightening repetition point a great and good nation in the direction of folly. Let's try to discover why.

5.

A WORLD TO BE LABELED,
NOT UNDERSTOOD

A FEW YEARS AGO, I ASKED HISTORIAN ROBERT DALLEK, WHO had just published his lively *Nixon and Kissinger: Partners in Power,* to explain why Americans allow leaders such as these to misguide them in international affairs. "The business of America is business," he answered, citing President Coolidge's aphorism about a nation simultaneously smart about its internal affairs and inclined to shrug off all the confusing alarms on its attention *out there.* "People don't want to think of public affairs."[1] True, and it's likely one reason that we take intellectual shortcuts, and even retreat to plain laziness, in foreign policy. Indeed, that's how two definitive accounts of the Iraq War, Tom Ricks's *Fiasco* and *Cobra II* by Michael Gordon and General Bernard Trainor, describe Washington's decision making at the time. But there are other reasons.

Why are educated Americans less curious about world affairs than the professional classes of other nations? How to explain such remoteness punctuated by intense emotion, and the poor choices that result, as displayed by "men of superior ability, sound training, and high ideals" in the run-ups to wars in Iraq, Vietnam, and North Korea?[2] Given America's unparalleled abundance of schools, think tanks, and government research institutes devoted to national security, why, then, do foreign policy savants evince so much lower a horizon of wisdom than might be expected—to judge, most recent, by the herd-mentality readiness with which they supported the invasion of Iraq? And why, decade after decade, are these failures of insight not offset by a more effective CIA, the nation's premier intelligence organization?

More than the citizens of any other advanced society, Americans have traditionally economized on their involvement with national politics, let alone with foreign affairs. In the United States, only half the electorate bothers to vote anyway, the lowest of turnouts among any democracy besides Switzerland and Poland. Otherwise well-informed citizens—doctors, businessmen, lawyers, teachers—demonstrate significantly less knowledge about the world than their counterparts in Germany, Britain, France, Scandinavia, Japan, Brazil, or Argentina.[3] Already in 1831, after much travel through the United States, Alexis de Tocqueville was struck by the lack of Americans' interest in other cultures. The trait has grown up, and endured, with the Republic.

One of the reasons for this indifference may be the country's immigrant past and present. Assimilating to American life—and repudiating what one is putting behind oneself—can be an all-consuming, even disorienting multigenerational experience. A lifetime ago, Marcus Hansen, the Pulitzer Prize–winning historian of immigration, laid out this argument. Entering America's whirlwind of change can diminish one's awareness of distant lands. The new arrival may be eager to shake off the attitudes of the old country, while perhaps retaining a general interest in the well-being of those left behind. However, the second generation wants essentially nothing to do with the continents which its parents fled. By the third generation and thereafter, the now thoroughly assimilated American—to the extent he or she takes the time—comes to look at these ancestral countries through the misty lens of caricature: dancing peasants, a forelock-tugging proletariat, decadent urbanites smoking Gauloises around the zinc café tables of "Old Europe." [4]

Activists of ever more varied ethnic backgrounds may revive or maintain attachments to ancestral nations: Greeks and Macedonians, Indians and Pakistanis, Armenians and Turks, Jews and Arabs. In no other country is there such a tangle of well-organized and financed communities wrestling in the domestic politics of foreign affairs. In Britain, for instance, the Indian community is not remotely as involved in Anglo-Indian issues as is its counterpart in America, whose members weigh in on Kashmir, the Pakistani menace, and increasingly on China. Here is that great high school virtue of pluralism in action. Dozens of different interests compete for attention. Sentimental concerns often linger. But though an Irish-American may enjoy a wedding reception at the local Hibernian Club and petition his congressman to denounce the British presence in Belfast, his passions tend to focus on this one distant place, which eclipses just about all the rest of the world. Moreover, the political activists are themselves prone to self-deception: they're convinced that America's interests are synonymous with those of the foreign lands for which they're passionate.

Overall uninterest about details of different cultures and peoples is a natural response in a continent-sized, entrepreneurially driven, immigrant-rich democracy. Much of the developed world is judged to be not only different but hidebound, and the extent of our understanding of others often doesn't reach much further than disparaging them for not being like us. This, too, is a deep-going perspective, as in the simple certainty that America is Columbia the Gem of the Ocean, "the world offers homage to thee." Even as recently as 1942, GIs shipped to Europe were incredulous that the *Queen Elizabeth* was not American; what other nation could build on such a scale? Today, radio hosts with audiences of millions yap about impoverished, sickly Europe, while a senior economic adviser to one of the two presidential candidates in 2008 claimed that France and Germany's vibrant social democracies "have a third world standard of living," and went uncontradicted.[5] This attitude creates a fertile environment for magical assumptions.

Other intellectual and cultural obstacles impede a better grasp of the world. Americans have so much else to do in "the pursuit of happiness." They believe, with good cause, that they live in the most fascinating of all countries. Bright, outgoing people find more than enough to occupy them right here. George W. Bush is the paramount example. By age fifty-five, he had left American shores only a few times, and then just for the briefest of trips. Despite the vital excursions that legislators take to Rio for an economic conference or to Paris for the biennial air show, probably half of our congressmen still do not hold passports. This was also true, well into the 1990s, of the management teams of such huge corporations as AT&T. So it shouldn't be surprising that McGeorge Bundy had never ventured to Asia before he helped push his country into Vietnam; or Henry Kissinger had never seen the Middle East before he "reinforced the diplomatic paralysis" among the belligerents; or, a generation later, that Douglas Feith, when number three at the Pentagon and responsible for "managing the Department of Defense's international relations," had never been to China or Japan, either; or that half the U.S. civilian personnel in the "Emerald City" fantasyland of Baghdad's Green Zone had never previously been outside the United States.[6]

More than three years into the Iraq War, Jeff Stein of *Congressional Quarterly* exposed this narrowness of vision among U.S. intelligence and law enforcement officials, as well as among members of Congress directly responsible for overseeing national security.

"Do you know the difference between a Sunni and a Shiite?" he asked, and followed up by inquiring whether Iran and Al Qaeda might be Sunni or Shia. These were not unfair questions, as he rightly said: "Wouldn't British counterterrorism officials responsible for Northern Ireland know the difference between Catholics and Protestants?" But most everyone he interviewed had no idea about these deep distinctions of armed faith in Iraq.[7]

A few years earlier, during the last cycle of Balkan miseries, several alert Capitol Hill staffers made a point similar to Stein's. Deeper U.S. engagement appeared imminent, and congressional testimony was required from top people at State and Defense. Were those decision makers able to distinguish between the Ghegs and the Tosks? This time congressmen asked the question, and drove home the fact that knowing the principal ethnic divisions of the Albanian people might just be required to make U.S. military intervention effective. A hapless official took a stab at an answer, having a fifty-fifty chance to get it right, and guessed wrong.

This is where intellectual shortcuts begin to enter decision making, while at the same time we expect wondrous returns from efforts that are little more than enthusiasms. We simplify and mislabel while sallying forth with a "cartoonish" view of the people and countries we intend to set straight. And "cartoonish" is just what Charles Duelfer, the savvy UN weapons inspector whom President Bush chose to search for Saddam's nonexistent WMD, called the U.S. understanding of Iraq.[8]

The same had happened, only with even worse consequences, in Vietnam less than a generation before. "The Kennedy people," observes Halberstam, "were always sloppy in their homework."[9]

Essentially no single American on the ground knew much about the place. The one authentic U.S. expert on Vietnam was the heroic Austrian-born socialist refugee Nazi-fighter and self-taught scholar Joseph Buttinger, then living in New York. He understood Vietnam's culture and politics, owned a uniquely comprehensive research library on that nation of thousands of books and articles in various languages, and would himself write the seminal two-volume work *Vietnam: A Dragon Embattled*. But his lucid interpretations of what was likely to occur should American military action escalate were of no interest to Bundy, McNamara, and their colleagues. Nor did anyone have time to hear from George W. Allen, a midlevel civilian intelligence analyst at the Pentagon—and the only one specializing in Vietnam—who was already warning about Washington's unwillingness to sweep illusions aside: U.S. officials "were in thrall to a self-induced image of a mythical country that was hardly ever the real Vietnam." [10] (The legendary CIA operative Lucien Conein was also just one man— little heard in policymaking councils—though he had been conducting covert operations in Vietnam since 1954.) And nobody in power wanted to hear what the French, known to be colonialists and losers, might have winnowed from earlier disaster in Vietnam. With one exception, it was only in 1983, a decade after U.S. ground forces had been withdrawn from Vietnam, that France would be asked to share some markedly valuable experience. By that time, the problem was how to track down and account for the 2,646 Americans missing in action. [11]

Korea was every bit as misunderstood, as were the risks of marching toward China: potentially helpful sources of guidance were ignored, alternatives went unscrutinized, yet wondrous results just had to occur.

The United States had only one American in its employ who knew anything useful about the nation and its people: Donald Nichols, "Lawrence of Korea," as he was known with real respect by the British. The Chinese and North Koreans gave him another nickname, the "Man of Disguises," and placed a quarter-million-dollar bounty on his head, an honor not granted to Generals MacArthur or Ridgway. This thirty-six-year-old motor-pool sergeant with a sixth-grade education from Bayonne, New Jersey, had taught himself Korean while stationed at Kimpo air base. He had been entrepreneurial enough to springboard an assignment

with a security detail into an entire network of shadowy contacts throughout the peninsula, thereby gaining the confidence
of President Rhee. He had then unsuccessfully tried to warn
MacArthur's staff as to the very week in which Pyongyang would
strike. Given all the improvising that followed, Nichols soon had
at his disposal much of the Fifth U.S. Air Force, Royal Navy warships, and whatever troops he required. Since the rank of sergeant
hardly carried sufficient clout, he operated as "Mr. Nichols," by
which name he is known to legend, from his headquarters compound deep in a mountain valley. But Nichols was essentially just
one American alone in his knowledge of Korea, had no input on
the high-level decisions as to whether to head north, and didn't
know much more than most anyone else about Maoist China,
with which the United States soon found itself at war.

Big gaps in understanding don't inhibit emergency men. Long
after Saigon fell, McNamara could observe that a major lesson
for America was to "know your opponent." To emphasize a point
so blindingly obvious, indeed the most basic rule of war, shows
a disdain for reality. Impossible dreams ensue. As Bundy concluded by 1965, "this damn war is much tougher" than had been
anticipated.[12] Repeatedly the men and women who confidently
make the original decisions are surprised. "I thought it would be
tough," Secretary of State Rice remarked about Iraq during her
last year in office. "I didn't think it would be *this* tough."[13]

Backup plans are rare. If not easy, the problem at least appears manageable. "You work with Plan A," said Rice. "I don't
think you go to Plan B." (President Bush had explained simply
that "Plan B is to make Plan A work.")[14] Secretary Rice and other
decision makers as well as advisers from the think tanks were
following a well-worn path. "We can't assume what we don't
believe," Bundy had scoffed to one of Eisenhower's former aides
who inquired about the chances of failure in Southeast Asia.[15] An
unwillingness to contemplate the possibility of being mistaken is
a crucial ingredient of magical thought. Pilots do not *believe* they

will crash. They know, however, that they can, and they drill for it. The more they drill, the less they crash.

By the time America got around to the troop "surge" in Iraq, a civilian think-tanker who had pushed for reinforcements as the decisive means to lower violence—the presence of more U.S. troops was among a half-dozen factors that brought such results—came up with a piece of truly intellectualized nonsense: having any Plan B, said the AEI's Frederick Kagan, would be "antithetical to the dynamic nature of war." [16] After three thousand years of armies getting lost in the fog, astute commanders always contemplate worst cases and the alternatives arising from them. Intellectual shortcuts, or "laziness," help to drag the country into these predicaments in the first place; then more shortcuts are hacked as we try to get out. But it all looks easy at the start: Bundy argued early in the experience that casualties from an expanding U.S. involvement in Vietnam would be no more painful than the annual traffic-related toll in Washington, D.C. [17]

Governor George W. Bush was spot-on during PBS's 2000 presidential debate when he argued that America is most globally effective if it proceeds in the world as "a humble nation, but strong." [18] Humility stems, in part, from being aware of what we don't know, and then from recognizing how flawed our decision making can be in any event, given the subject's complexity. There's all the more reason for humility when an organization such as the Pentagon or State, or the NSC staff gears itself into perpetual crisis mode. Corners truly get cut; misunderstandings multiply. Humility might also be called for in the light of our characteristic lack of preparation in foreign affairs: after three years of occupying Iraq, only six out of a thousand U.S. professional staff in Baghdad spoke fluent Arabic, reported a U.S. government study. The British Embassy in Baghdad's International Zone and France's training and reconstruction missions in Kabul boast a far higher proportion of professionals who've mastered local languages and dialects.[19]

The science of decision making keeps revealing new layers of the extent to which we're all prone to deceiving ourselves—the multilingual Foreign Service officer Arabist as much as the Washington lawyer-lobbyist suddenly atop the Pentagon. Emergency men, however, are unlikely to have the forbearance to slow down, which is why corners are sliced through and labels like "communist" and "terrorist" pasted over genuine ignorance. Yet emergency men can excel at getting their way.

In their *Foreign Policy* essay "Why Hawks Win," psychologists Daniel Kahneman and Jonathan Renshon lay out the unconscious reasons why emergency men, so often synonymous with war hawks, tend to prevail in policy arguments. In the best of circumstances, these scholars demonstrate, we are all prone to exaggerating our strengths, to assuming the worst from our adversaries, and to embellishing the amount of control we have over outcomes. These influences make the emergency man's readiness for a forceful *solution* all the more pronounced, with the expediencies to follow. He or she exemplifies another problem that psychologists study; that of "action bias" in decision making. Individuals feel compelled to "do something," anything, when confronting a challenge, as in a soccer match, where the goalie darts to the left or to the right rather than just standing at the midpoint of his twenty-four-foot domain. The results often prove the same. So too in foreign affairs, one might argue. Like staying in place, leaving a "crisis" alone can be a better means of handling a problem.

Other behavioral impulses compromise sound understanding. An "optimism bias," as psychologists call it, can induce even someone so tested by war as Senator John McCain to anticipate that a U.S. invasion and occupation in the Middle East would be "fairly easy." Decision makers can also find themselves seduced, more quickly than has been recognized, by a fixed idea, under whose spell they will adhere to a course of action originally chosen at a time when all, indeed, did seem easy. Change is conceded only with agonizing delay. Men and women responsible for creating the mess also conceal from each other the despair they truly feel. Thus it took four years for Washington to abandon "attrition warfare" in 1968 and replace the much-diminished Westmoreland with a commander who emphasized smaller-unit operations while deploying more forces to protect population centers. It took another four years for Washington to respond to the heightening violence in Iraq that began in late 2003. Just as before, a desperate administration finally replaced the top U.S. general with a commander who emphasized smaller-unit operations while deploying more forces in and around cities, towns, and villages to protect the population. But those four years were gone, on the ground and at home—and many good people, too.

Magical thinking isn't demonstrated just by wrong choices, bad decisions, or failure to anticipate events. The savviest Foreign Service officers and reliable journalists make misjudgments all the time.[20] Predictions by defense analysts and policymakers are likely to work out no better or worse than those of diplomats and journalists, or of economists, political scientists, editorialists, or manufacturers as concern their own specialties.[21]

But while there's no way to predict the future, there are some surefire signs to show that disaster is being courted. For example, to make decisions "by gut," as George W. Bush described his preferred approach, tends to countenance extreme corner-cutting. To be a "gut player," as he called himself, rarely enables one to digest information that gives stomachaches. Wishful compulsions too easily replace hard evidence.[22] That occurs too with decisions made by hunch, as in Perle's "hunch" ten days before the Iraq invasion that "we can wrap the whole thing in 30 days."[23] In *The Last One Left*, John D. MacDonald offers the best assessment of men who rely on hunch and gut: they drift "at half efficiency through a haze of myth, superstition, and self approval; shrewder than most, perhaps, but capable of fatal mistakes if too many things started to go wrong at the same time."

"This was foretold," says Brent Scowcroft, the national security adviser during the Persian Gulf War and, in 2003, chairman of the President's Foreign Intelligence Advisory Board, recalling what he believed was likely to result from the invasion.[24] No prescience was required. It was enough to hear glib talk about "wrapping up," a promised "cakewalk," and the supposedly learned arguments that Shia and Sunni hatreds would lead to nothing worse than neighborhood spats. Like Scowcroft, who had also served as a calming presence as Kissinger's deputy on the NSC staff, there were unflappable players on Wall Street who detected irrationality at large before the 2008 financial meltdown. And among them was Traxis Partners, the hedge fund run by Barton Biggs, investment strategist and author of *Wealth, War, and Wisdom*. The firm's motto is "Doubt All Before Believing Anything"—an excellent antidote to magical thinking, because it compels reflection.

Decade in and decade out, an absence of understanding seeps through the bureaucratic system. Everyone believes they are doing good and that they are closely informed. But emergency men by definition are in a rush. They brook no interference. "They didn't know how ignorant they were," says Charles Duelfer, the Bush administration weapons inspector, about decision makers at Defense, State, CIA, and the White House. "They spent more time trying to sort out things in Washington than trying to understand where the crux of the issue was" in Iraq.[25] The same obtuseness could be tagged to the Nixon years of "détente," and the Kennedy and Johnson ones of Vietnam.

By 1966, the carnage in Vietnam had gone way beyond traffic fatalities in Washington, to recall Bundy's comparison from three years earlier. James C. Thomson, Jr., was a thirty-five-year-old Sinologist whom Bundy had brought down from Harvard at the start of the Kennedy administration. Thomson resigned from the NSC that year, along with his increasingly disenchanted boss, to return to Harvard as an assistant professor of history. Two years later, as an average of 354 U.S. fighting men were dying each week in Vietnam, Thomson published a chilling article in the *Atlantic*, "How Could Vietnam Happen?—An Autopsy." [26]

Unnerving as it is to read, at least it breaks through the illusions of that era and, by implication, exposes the ones we encounter today. Like Halberstam, Thomson was fascinated, as he put it, by how "men of superior ability, sound training, and high ideals" could bring about such a disaster. Coming from an insider who had worked closely with Bundy, the preeminent intellectual of the Kennedy and Johnson administrations, his postmortem stands out. Though he never mentioned the national security adviser's name, Thomson's discretion didn't prevent his former dean from refusing to talk to him for years.

Thomson recounts the topics of fierce executive office disputes. They sound familiar. Was civil war under way or international aggression? (In the councils of power, the appropriate response is "aggression" in all cases.) Who was the "real enemy"? Wouldn't committing publicly to a withdrawal date "embolden" the enemy, whoever he might be? Can America build up the local forces quickly enough before chaos descends? None of the answers was sorted out as the United States got in deeper.

Thomson explains that part of the reason was "the banishment of real expertise." Again, similarities with Korea and Iraq jump out. The hotter the issue and the higher it rises in the bureaucracy, he argues, "the more completely the experts are excluded while the harassed senior generalists take over." Those harassed generalists include undersecretaries, presidential assistants, the NSC director himself. Papers are deemed "too sensitive" for wider review or, in today's argot, an official is not "read into" an ultraclassified program. Savvy career professionals and the more prudent appointees are cast as pessimists, perhaps as defeatists.

They're replaced by " 'can-do guys,' loyal and energetic fixers un-soured by experience." The mantra becomes "A test of America's national will." "Stabilizing," say, South Vietnam is defined as vital, and therefore it must be so, though one might substitute here—as throughout Thomson's inquest—the importance of "stabiliz-ing" North Korea in 1950, Iraq in 2003, or Afghanistan today.

"Those who doubted our role in Vietnam," he writes, "were said to shrink from the burdens of power, the obligations of power, the uses of power, the responsibility of power." And at the time that he wrote this in 1968, America was only halfway through the ordeal. Then as today, naysayers are pushed under Neville Chamberlain's umbrella. As war intensifies, the willful-ness of emergency men increases, as does their reputation for "toughness." A human aversion to cutting one's losses plays its part, which explains why gamblers keep betting, no matter the cost. Jim Thomson concluded that "one force—a constant in the vortex of commitment—was that of *wishful thinking*." (The em-phasis is his.) Wishful thinking prevents reasonable discourse and brings forth endless magical simplifications. It's what marches the country into North Korea, into Vietnam and into Iraq, and deeper into Afghanistan, as well as into a Wall Street crack-up.

"I want you to read something," McGeorge Bundy asked Thom-son during a private meeting in the West Wing in 1964, the year that America truly started to escalate. Thomson recalls that the document was "all about a fantastic, escalatory multiple-bombing track to force the North Vietnamese to their knees." Telling the national security adviser that he himself knew nothing about firepower, but a good bit about postcolonial Asia, Thomson ten-tatively demurred that these proud people were very unlikely to be bombed into submission. The insurgency would continue, or worse, he cautioned, until the United States went home. "Well, James," Bundy replied, "thank you so much." [27]

This insouciant style of command is all too common among emergency men. Skeptical Foreign Service officers or thoughtful scholars such as Thomson may squeak about the facts. But their superiors' synoptic understanding of how the world *truly works* is going to be so much more relevant than the mere ability to spell the names, to understand which way a country's rivers flow, to sort out the hatreds, to expound the faiths. Part of being an emergency man is never to lack for opinions. People who say "I don't know about . . ." or who respond "Yes, but . . ." are already one step removed from the genre, and the game.

Men and women like Thomson can offer only qualified conclusions. When an Oval Office decision has to be translated into orders for action, their informed lack of certitude is assuredly unhelpful. These experts argue brilliantly, no doubt, but they also have the freedom to bob and weave; they do not have to *make policy*, nor do they read *all the cables*. More and more decisions can be crafted by just a few of the best and the brightest. Fewer and fewer people really need to be *in the know*. At that particular juncture in 1961–66, discipline and direction were required—which men such as Thomson would get from Mac Bundy: Yale '40 (mathematics), an admiral's aide in World War II, the precocious coauthor of Secretary of War Henry Stimson's memoirs, a Harvard Junior Fellow, his mother a Lowell.

Kennedy wanted his inside man for foreign policy, his own mandarin and intellectual to streamline the toughest, fastest, coldest-eyed executive decisions. Bundy was one of his first appointments. Halberstam, who was then with the *New York Times*, noted that many people "thought of him as the best the country could offer . . . a legend in his time." He added that Bundy "was smarter than the average blue-blood WASP." Columnist Joseph Kraft found Bundy to be "perhaps the only candidate for the statesman's mantle to emerge in the generation that is now coming to power . . . almost alone among contemporaries [as] a figure of true consequence," and he referenced Milton to do this star justice: "A Pillar of State, And Princely Counsel in his face." [28]

Bundy's nephew Hugh Auchincloss, Jr., a surgeon who currently serves at the National Institutes of Health, advises any author to be careful about presenting his uncle as being driven by arrogance and overconfidence.[29] After all, McGeorge Bundy was regularly open to debate, especially from young up-and-comers—provided, of course, that their points were made tight, fast, and smart. Having mastered Harvard under a weak president, he was brisk but also hospitable to new ideas, and convivial with people different from himself, leaving aside a comment or two such as "the *New York Times* is run by Zionists." [30] He was an aristocrat to whom little appeared too complex. For Bundy, a favorite way to cast doubt on a counterargument was to call it "intellectually incomplete." What he displayed is not as unadorned as simple hubris. Instead he embodied a deep trust in the magic that appeared to crackle at his fingertips: his faith lay not just in his own authority and insights, but in the entire circle of supremely competent world architects who moved around him.

Observers recall that Bundy was an early hawk on Vietnam largely because of his "energy." He held to the conventional wisdom that China was a devouring incubus about to swallow the entire ancient nation at a gulp. No need to listen to Thomson's time-consuming refinements about why and how Vietnam boasted a history of maintaining its identity against the Middle Kingdom. Bundy's first trip to Asia in February 1965 coincided with a midnight Viet Cong commando attack on the U.S. air base at Pleiku that left nine Americans dead and 137 wounded. Of course, the attackers had no idea that this White House emissary was in Vietnam; most likely, they didn't even know he existed. Nonetheless Bundy seems to have regarded the incident as meticulously arranged. In Saigon that night, he took charge in the U.S. operations center. General Westmoreland, merely the commander in South Vietnam, acidly and perhaps unfairly recalled him overseeing the response with "a field marshal psycho-sis."[31] The next day Bundy went to Pleiku, where he visited the wounded. Having seen blood flow, he became "a believer," as LBJ chortled, and Bundy's own staffers were surprised by the intensity of their boss's emotions.[32]

In any event, to Bundy this was terrorism, now seen directly, against which America would stand ever more firmly. Back in Washington, the "fantastic, escalatory multiple-bombing track" began to fly: 55,000 flights with 33,000 tons of bombs over North Vietnam in 1965; 148,000 flights with 128,000 tons the next year. Bundy urged President Johnson to rally public support through an "Americans Against Terror" PR campaign.[33] If the United States got deeper into a ground war, it occurred to him, then per-haps that could be fought just by asking for volunteers. Perhaps there should also be a public relations campaign on the theme "Only Americans Who Want to Go Have to Go." He suspected the Joint Chiefs of Staff might object to this rallying cry, but he thought the idea worth sharing with the president.[34]

He would privately mock Lyndon Johnson's penchant for fantasy, amused that LBJ possessed a "really quite funny internal belief" about policymaking: "If he could get it stated *his* way in the papers, it would *be* that way. . . . [G]etting a good press [was] getting a good reality."[35] But clearly Bundy was at least equally self-deluding.

Bundy epitomizes the brilliant, supremely credentialed, action-oriented enthusiast who does not know what he does not know, and who may be somewhat out of touch with his own country. He would have been indignant at any imputation of unreason. Didn't his whole authority rest on Ivy League reflection and gentlemanly self-control? He might be willing to fence good-naturedly with qualified tyros such as Jim Thomson, as he would with a successor generation of young faculty during his visits back to Harvard in the late 1970s. But when dealing with the Joint Chiefs, or Secretary of State Dean Rusk, or his contemporaries in age or seniority, this was not a man to recognize the significance of another's thought. He could not see the world through anyone else's eyes, and that included those of the implacably ruthless men in Hanoi.

"The American role in the Vietnam War, for all its stumbles, was no accident," reflected the *Washington Post* in Bundy's 1996 obituary. "It arose from the deepest sources—the deepest and most legitimate sources—of the American desire to affirm freedom in the world." Actually, it was the commitment that was no accident; the "role" itself was far more stumble than affirmation. Before long, Americans came to regard the war as having little to do with Kennedy's original pledge to defend liberty in South Vietnam against "saboteurs, assassins, insurgents"—the phrase he intended to use in his afternoon speech in Dallas on the day he was killed.[36] There were hard, real-world American interests in upholding an ally against Soviet-backed terror. But the objective of affirming freedom in that faraway country about which we knew nothing wasn't high on the list to start with, and it slid steadily down.

At that time the Ford Foundation was America's largest philanthropy. Bundy became its president after leaving Washington, and served through 1979. McNamara joined him in 1968 as a trustee. From its coffers Bundy dispensed around $135 million in today's dollars for the study and endorsement of arms control, which underwrote Harvard University's Program for Science and International Affairs, Stanford's Center for Arms Control and Disarmament, UCLA's arms control program, and other elite defense-related university research efforts. In addition, Ford sponsored forums such as the Aspen Arms Control Seminar, an intellectual summit attended annually by defense thinkers and administration appointees, though rarely by anyone from the armed forces. The professional magazine *International Security* was launched to pull together and to publicize the findings that resulted from such cross-pollination. Here were the original intellectual bricks and mortar from which today's foreign policy leadership generation was built.

No other nation possesses this wealth of independent inquiry: international security centers at Harvard's Kennedy School, Johns Hopkins's SAIS, Princeton's Woodrow Wilson School, and Tufts's Fletcher School; plus a growing number of specialty programs in homeland security. There's an entire alphabet of government-sponsored defense policy research institutes such as RAND, MITRE, CNA, ANSER. Foundations like Carnegie and MacArthur make their own grants for national security studies. Numerous Washington-based think tanks are inhabited by foreign policy "experts ready to comment or consult on a moment's notice." [37] They include the Heritage Foundation, AEI, the Hudson Institute, the Center for Strategic and International Studies (CSIS), the Brookings Institution, plus the venerable Council on Foreign Relations, headquartered in New York. Like universities, all are ostensibly nonpartisan, as their tax-exempt status requires, whether funded by grants, endowments, individual patrons, or by direct mail. Scholars of equal quality and credentials to those in the universities address similar subjects. Many of them move back and forth between the universities and the think tanks, or hold dual affiliations; and most are eager as well to segue into NSC posts, an assistant secretaryship, or indeed an undersecretaryship when the right administration arrives. This is an altogether opulent gymnasium, not only for study but also for career-building and advocacy.

In no other country do policy research institutes and academic centers do double duty as way stations for men and women moving in and out of high office. Other countries have bodies such as the Royal Institute of International Affairs, the University of London's Department of War Studies, the Institut français des relations internationales, Germany's Gesellschaft für Auswärtige

Politik, and Moscow's Institute for USA and Canadian Studies.[38] But these are significantly smaller outfits, whose scholars will not surface after an election as a permanent secretary in Whitehall or as *directeur du cabinet* to the French defense minister. The policy recommendations their scholars might offer to government will, with few exceptions, be received at best with arched eyebrows by forbidding civil servants and mandarin career diplomats.

In contrast, America's efflorescent seedbeds of ideas are decidedly influential as well as characteristically entrepreneurial. Spin-offs and start-ups abound, such as the Center for a New American Security or the University of Connecticut's M.A. program in homeland security leadership. This freewheeling approach now passes as unremarkable among those Americans who follow foreign policy. But it's one that further perplexes even such informed overseas observers as Christopher Coker, professor of international relations at the London School of Economics. "There's no telling who's going to pop up in your defense agencies out of the 'tanks' or university policy centers," he observes, "or to guess what they're going to do."[39]

Think tanks across the ideological spectrum can provide useful allies to shrewd military commanders. It's a new development that accompanied the failing war in Afghanistan. Think-tank fellows, researchers, and advocates are respectfully consulted, and hired as advisers—as by both Generals David Petraeus and Stanley McChrystal, the former commander of the overall International Security Assistance Force in Afghanistan, who have also appeared frequently at institute conferences. An officer less "adept at working Washington," as was said of General David McKiernan, previously the top U.S. commander in Kabul (who in 2009 became the first wartime theater commander to be fired since MacArthur), risks slighting such civilian opinion leaders.[40]

All this money and brainpower, nevertheless, yields disappointing returns. Public enthusiasm for military action in Iraq, never deep in the first place, wavered up and down in the six months before invasion. Yet determined support for action was heard from the dean of Princeton's Wilson School, as well as from the president of the Council on Foreign Relations, who told the Associated Press three days before the invasion: "I'm in favor of this. . . . It's the best medicine for anti-Americanism around the world I can imagine." The liberal-centrist Brookings Institution "was AWOL" during the buildup to war, observers recall, but scholars at AEI filled the breach by offering tough-guy "Black Coffee Briefings" for the Washington policy community, including the press, over the week Iraq was invaded. AEI's purpose was to examine "U.S. efforts to fight terrorism overseas."[41] All in all, something seems amiss when Vice President Dick Cheney and Professor Joseph Nye, the calm, open-minded dean of the Kennedy School and author of *Soft Power: The Means to Success in World Politics*, agree on how to execute regime change.

National security studies has meanwhile become a distinct academic field of concentration. There are professional associations, scholarly journals, and accredited graduate degrees. Some of this work is profound, as shown by articles in *International Security*— "Motives for Martyrdom: Al-Qaida, Salafi Jihad, and the Spread of Suicide Attacks," to cite just one. The overall literature of the discipline, however, is thin when one ventures beyond monographs, case studies, and discussions of current events. Few conceptual breakthroughs in national security thinking have been made since the first seminal writings on nuclear deterrence, such as economist Thomas Schelling's *The Strategy of Conflict* (1960), and on military affairs, such as political scientist Samuel Huntington's *The Soldier and the State: The Theory and Politics of Civil-Military Relations* (1957).[42] Examining recent contributions, we find no comparison with the advances in other disciplines. There has been nothing like genome sequencing in biology or the cosmological advances opened by the discovery of quasars, much less like the reconsideration of relativity in physics or the conceptualizations of economic issues by James Tobin and Kenneth Arrow. Or, in a more cognate discipline like history, it is difficult to find a contribution to national security research that might compare to breakthrough studies on slavery.

Instead the major works of national security, and of foreign affairs in general, are high-profile meditations—think pieces, rather than rigorous analyses wrestling with awkward facts. The best-known ones include writings on the global triumph of the liberal idea, as by Francis Fukuyama in his *The End of History and the Last Man*, and thoughts on the cultural and value differences that lead to epic conflict between peoples, as in Samuel Huntington's equally well-received *The Clash of Civilizations and the Remaking of World Order*. Meditations can be astounding in their synthesis, if one thinks of Machiavelli or Montesquieu—or, indeed, of Marx. But otherwise they are unlikely to break new ground, no matter how engagingly intricate the argument. The eloquent ability of meditations to restate known issues is not the enduring scholarship needed in light of the world's prodigious increase in knowledge, interconnectedness, population, and compounding technological revolution.

Interior meditations, however subtle, are only marginally helpful as guides to useful policy. One of the most widely discussed contributions to the international security field in the last half-dozen years has been the notion of "soft power"—the cumulative weight exercised by the attractiveness of a country's ways and values, in contrast to the "hard power" of military might, economic substance, and political strength. It may prove valuable to examine the concept: perceptions that have not previously been systematized can be brought together. But an exposition of "soft power" is likely to be as frustratingly diffuse as the term itself. It's one more label that can attach itself to most anything. It evinces a total absence of quantitative approximation, even compared to the imprecise yet commonly used ways of measuring military capacity as a function of firepower, mobility, and survivability.

"Soft power" in fact has been part of America's strength in the world since 1776: the country succeeds on a dangerous planet "not only by force of arms but by the virtues of humanity," as William Livingston, governor of New Jersey, explained in 1782, while General Washington refused to respond in kind to British atrocities that dwarf those of the 9/11 attacks.[43] And soft power as well as hard was deployed fully and innovatively across the board against the Soviet Union from 1981 onward, twenty years before the term took hold in the literature. It would be helpful to hear something new.

Meditations, because they take attention away from specific facts and details, can also serve as rationales for emergency-man action. It proved easy in Washington to leap from arguing "the end of history"—as did Fukuyama when positing that the triumph of Western liberal democracy might signal the endpoint of humanity's sociocultural evolution—to Perle's insistence that "all I want is for the Arabs to have a robust open market economy so that they can have a share in the fantastic prosperity created by the new global economy."[44] And hopes of a clash or two of civilizations play straight to emergency men's deeper predilections.

Illusions burgeon as politicians, the public, and defense intellectuals themselves come to assume that surely there must be some useful return on all this abundance. Ideas get signed off on by deans, senior fellows, and august professors. Decision makers feel their confidence boosted, barely aware of the wishfulness swirling around them.

Four reasons further explain the consistent misunderstandings of the world that emerge even out of our nation's rich intellectual resources: a paradox of plenty; an effectiveness trap; faddishness; and the phenomenon of misplaced expertise.

First, the paradox. The wealth of research, position briefs, white papers, and press releases that spring from think tanks and university national security centers have a way of canceling each other out. For instance, during the Somali pirate "crisis" of April 2009, when four hijackers seized the container ship *Maersk Alabama* off the coast of Africa, policy insights included those from the Center for Strategic and Budgetary Assessments' senior fellow Martin Murphy, author of *Small Boats, Weak States, Dirty Money: Piracy and Maritime Terrorism.* ("Thinking Smarter About Defense" is the CSBA motto.) Arguments came too from the Center for Security Policy, a robust organization founded by Frank Gaffney, once an assistant to Perle and the lead author of *War Footing: Ten Steps America Must Take to Prevail in the War for the Free World.* That center's contribution included Gaffney's argument that the U.S. State Department "imports pirate-jihadist types into this country," while he drew ties between the seagoing teenage thieves and "Islamic terror." [45] Two months later, like clockwork, scholars, commentators, and politicians were debating the extent to which "the U.S. should take ownership" of turmoil in Tehran following a fraudulent election—meaning whether the White House was being "sufficiently tough" in condemning that government's violence against protesters. [46]

It's unlikely that minds were changed or much was learned amid Washington's Sturm und Drang in either case. It can be difficult even to keep the think tanks straight and to tell who is saying what at the Institute for Defense Analyses or the one for Advanced Defense Studies, at the American Security Project or the Project on National Security.

In the middle of this plentiful, bustling field of policy entrepreneurship there is an additional hitch: a think tank, or a top-flight professional school, can be persuaded to tailor its work to less reputable sources—sources even more problematic than government benefactors like the CIA. In *Turkmeniscam: How Washington Lobbyists Fought to Flack for a Stalinist Dictatorship,* Ken Silverstein of *Harper's* chronicles executives from APCO and Cassidy & Company, the capital's two preeminent lobbying firms—men and women who know every sparrow that falls in Washington—pledging in their sales pitches to deliver select think tanks at which Turkmeni delegations might conduct conferences and forums, enjoying the prestige of independent imprimaturs. Possible hosts, APCO promised, "would include the Heritage Foundation, the Center for Strategic and International Studies, or the Council on Foreign Relations." Cassidy & Company added that it would deploy pliant academics—"think tank analysts, members of the academic community"—to boost Turkmenistan's image.[47]

A second reason for the shortfall in our nation's intellectual resources is what Thomson, as good a guide as one could have along the march to folly, called "the effectiveness trap," a phrase that usefully defines the reluctance to depart further from the mainstream of discussion than is considered appropriate. This self-imposed gag order keeps men and women from speaking out when in office, lest their ties to power be severed. It can also stifle men and women in foreign policy think tanks and university centers as easily as in the corporate world.

The otherwise acute, nonideological scholars who got themselves caught up in the prevailing arguments about whether or not Iraq urgently needed invading underscore this point. But playing it safe also means skirting volatile subjects. "*Why* did you write *that*?" exclaimed Harvard University President Lawrence Summers to Kennedy School Executive Dean Stephen Walt, a renowned professor of international relations, in spring 2006. Walt had just co-authored "The Israeli Lobby" in the *London Review of Books.* "You could have become president of this university!"[48] But the risks of examining Israel's influence on U.S. foreign policy had not been unknown to Walt.

To be a player entails consulting off and on for government, maybe getting confirmed by the Senate for a job or a sinecure on a presidential commission, participating on panels at the Council on Foreign Relations along with grandees from previous administrations, identifying yourself as an "owl" rather than as a hawk or a dove, and writing books that with any luck can get blurbed by

Dr. Kissinger. This opulently carved door opens but narrowly, if at all; it can close completely on those who ask awkward questions or bring up troublesome facts.

There's a practical reason to speak out with conviction in any event, whether or not one knows if a page of Arabic is upside down or right side up. Livelihoods are on the line. It can essentially be a job requirement among faculty in the university national security programs to commit a day a week to consulting at Defense, State, or another part of the security apparatus, as well as to be a visible presence in public debate. For think-tankers themselves, their number of media appearances, which benefit both their institution's fund-raising and its influence, can be part of their annual evaluation.[49] Little of this adds to a better understanding of what's at stake.

The institutional as well as personal compromises made to uphold mainstream effectiveness have been exacted for decades. By 1981, influence on public policy particularly on national security policy—enjoyed far greater pride of place in parts of academia than did dutiful, dusty scholarship. Within months of Ronald Reagan's election, the dean at the time, Graham Allison, and some key faculty of Harvard's John F. Kennedy School of Government hastened to retain political standing by the convenient revelation that the school's title should simply contract to a tactful "Harvard School of Government." Learning of this, the outraged mayor of Cambridge promptly designated the venerably WASP-named Boylston Street, on which the school fronts, John F. Kennedy Street, as it remains today. Equally sensitive to the political winds, Stanford's Center for Arms Control and Disarmament added "International Security" to its name and dropped the romantic "Disarmament," later becoming the Center for International Security and then adding, in the more sanguine Clinton era, "and Cooperation." The Aspen Arms Control Seminar is now the no-nonsense Aspen Strategy Group.

Come the invasion of Iraq, there was no less a need to be seen as welcome in the seats of power. The then president of the Council on Foreign Relations, Leslie Gelb, offered the NSC director and her deputy the assistance of his organization to advise the occupation—a submission without precedent, even during Vietnam. It was declined.[50]

A third obstacle to sound understanding comes from intellectual fads. National security is a segment of public policy in which scholars can keep turning ideas into fleeting practice on a monumental scale before trooping on to the latest newsworthy enthusiasm. "There was something of a fad for tactical nuclear weapons" in the late 1950s, observed Halberstam.[51] Regions also come and go, such as Africa: John Kennedy had made 479 references to Africa in his presidential campaign, asserting that the United States had "lost ground" there under the Republicans; then it essentially dropped off the map except for dismal attempts at fine-tuning, until the George W. Bush administration committed unprecedented aid and also created U.S. Africa Command, which once again emphasized the continent's strategic and human potential.[52] "Energy security" has also risen and fallen and is now back on the intellectual agenda—pioneered in research, conferencing, and bestselling books between the 1973 and 1979 OPEC boycotts, only to disappear under the weight of more classic Cold War preoccupation. So too is counterinsurgency a fad, for all its soldierly toughness.

In the Vietnam era, Thomson was already observing "a new breed of military strategist and academic social scientist": professors and consultants introduced "theories of counterguerrilla warfare, to be known . . . as 'counterinsurgency.' " They were "eager to put [their theories] to the test." To them, counterinsurgency was the latest panacea for coping with third-world "instability." And it too rose and fell in fashion and favor. Indeed, counterinsurgency faddishness in the 1960s reached vertiginous political heights. Attorney General Robert Kennedy kept a green beret on his desk at the Justice Department. President Kennedy read Sun Zu and Mao and Che Guevara and added them to U.S. Army reading lists. "A sort of Joint Chiefs of Staff for the control for all agencies involved in counterinsurgency" was chaired by General Maxwell Taylor, while serving as the President's assistant.[53] Yet fascination with the subject vanished after failure in Vietnam, along with training, money, and equipment. The civilians in and out of government who are ultimately accountable for U.S. ground forces did nothing about this neglect, and the mere basics of protracted war against indistinct enemies have had to be learned anew in Iraq and Afghanistan.

One other fad stands out, which briefly pushed to the forefront of defense-intellectual attention a generation ago—the prospect of nuclear weapons falling into the hands of terrorists. John McPhee's riveting *The Curve of Binding Energy* (1974) introduced the country to the world of physicist Theodore Taylor, the most creative and imaginative of America's nuclear-bomb designers. Taylor for some odd reason worried that nihilistic cells attached to no state would sooner or later acquire light, compact, home-built atomic explosives. *International Security* ran a pivotal article by a director of the Office of National Narcotics Intelligence, simply and starkly titled "Nuclear Terror." Research grants, working groups, faculty seminars got under way. But just about all inquiry fell by the wayside within three or four years, as attention shifted back to the excitements of big-picture strategic arms deals, spurred by the suddenly revealed "crisis" that America's Minuteman missiles had allegedly become vulnerable to Soviet ICBMs. "Nuclear terror" was not on deck at Aspen. No more articles were sought, or generated. "Sooner or later, a terrorist group or a psychotic working alone will build a nuclear device," Taylor told the *Washington Post* in 1983, but by then to no one's notice. Come 2010, for the first time, the Pentagon has made the aim of thwarting nuclear-armed terrorists a centerpiece of U.S. strategic planning; long-forgotten processes will need to be relearned.

Fourth among the reasons is "misplaced expertise." This gets us to the heart of the mystery of how smart, well-schooled men and women—even those deeply knowledgeable about one or another of the world's regions—can help bring down disaster, including on the very lands they know best. The problem is that too often their valid competence does not apply to the public policy controversies they choose to address. That is, they may be solidly grounded in the genuine realm of knowledge where they have spent exemplary careers, such as the study of Iran or of the Arab world, but they may be wrong about the up-to-the-minute, policy-relevant topics that have grabbed the excitements of political attention—such as the alleged might of monolithic militant Islam and determining how the United States should respond.

The imposing, white-haired, British-American thinker, Bernard Lewis is professor emeritus of Near Eastern studies at Princeton. The *Encyclopedia of Historians and Historical Writing* identifies him convincingly as "the most influential postwar historian of Islam and the Middle East." He is a recipient of the National Humanities Medal. Much of that influence was exercised as a singular authority in the run-up to Iraq before March 2003. In fact, he was "perhaps the most significant intellectual influence behind the invasion," according to Jacob Weisberg, editor in chief of *Slate*.[54] Lewis asserted that Iraq could be reconstituted easily from above as a Westernized polity, a bulwark of security for America and a model for the region. Surely one well-armed American jolt would "modernize the Middle East," argued this strong supporter of Israel, and a believer that Muslims "seem about to take over Europe." As a State Department official who sat in on some of Professor Lewis's advisory meetings with Vice President Cheney recalled, "His view was: 'Get on with it. Don't dither.'"[55]

Thereafter, while advising the White House on neighboring Iran, Lewis saw fit to predict that on August 22, 2006, President Mahmoud Ahmadinejad could attempt to obliterate the planet. The moment, he explained, was "the night when many Muslims commemorate the night flight of the Prophet Muhammed on the winged horse Buraq . . . [and] might well be deemed an appropriate date for the apocalyptic ending of Israel, if necessary of the world." This statement is absolutely, otherworldly, irrelevant, besides having stoked the fires of a White House already eager to fine-tune Iran through violence. Lewis surely understands the larger structure of Islam; but when it comes to the jeopardy of men's lives, only those of us who believe in miracles could accept a grand historical-literary observation like this one as helpful.

Fouad Ajami, director of the Middle East Studies Program at SAIS, praises Lewis as "a sage in Christendom" and "the oracle of this new age of the Americans in the lands of the Arab."[56] Ajami also was a fervent supporter of an Iraq War that would overcome the "centuries of defects" in the Middle East by U.S. invasion—the occupiers, he believed, to be greeted in Baghdad and Basra "with kites and boom boxes." To him the adventure was to be just one piece of a "Pax Americana," underwritten by "American primacy in the world."[57] But another point needs to be considered when Lewis, Ajami, and other authorities on Islam and the Middle East urge war: it is not just one's enemy, in the end, that one must know, but the enduring outlooks and strengths of one's own side. The power to gauge the depth of America's capacity even to stick with such a grand, blood-drenched experiment is utterly outside their grasp. On this, each wise man had no better understanding of what was at stake than did the emergency-man generalists of national security policy who were also calling for *action*.

An observer from another planet might expect the earth's only remaining superpower to deploy an intelligence service sharp enough to offset these misunderstandings. When rightly applied, intelligence by its nature leaves a lot of room for magic, because it depends on smoke and mirrors flashed or stirred with startling skill. But such artistry has seldom been part of the American experience. Contrary to myth, none of the CIA's failings spotlighted by 9/11 have anything to do with 1990s budget cuts or with new rules imposed following Congress's Watergate-era investigations, which blasted the Agency for "the fantasy that it lay within our power to control other countries through the covert manipulation of their affairs."[58]

Whether the competence of secret operations or of analysis is being weighed, the problem is less one of emergency-man appointees than of a hermetic bureaucracy.

Within a dozen years of its founding, the CIA was already beginning to acquire a reputation for omniscience at the same time that sophisticated veterans such as William F. Buckley were starting to mock it. An assassination attempt on Indonesian dictator Sukarno must have been designed by the CIA, Buckley wrote in a 1958 issue of *National Review*, because everyone was blown up—except Sukarno. Analytic deficiencies were equally pronounced. The Agency was nearly as wildly wrong about the fabled "missile gap" the following year as was the air force, projecting a further ramp-up of hundreds of Soviet ICBMs.[59] Estimates in the 1960s and '70s had their own grievous critical flaws, only swinging in the other direction.[60] And a full generation later the near-success of the plot to bomb a U.S. airliner on Christmas Day 2009 was just another sign of unfixed, systemic defects in the U.S. intelligence community, of which the Agency is the pivotal part.

All along, the CIA's primary calling—lest we forget amid the paramilitary excitements of our own day—is espionage: the stealing of secrets and their astute placement to create an instructive mosaic of understanding. Arguably, the most valuable intelligence product is the spotting, tracking, and interpreting of trends and patterns, the truly macro-indicators that should shape national policy. Intelligence does not show at its best in short-term specific prediction. Even estimates that concern particular events should rightly be treated as informed guesses. So, on one hand, Agency spokesmen have a point when they dismiss outside criticism as mere "hindsight bias." On the other, we encounter a track record that underscores the exasperated conclusion—not long before 9/11, in a report compelled by Congress—that CIA analysis suffers from "an 'everybody thinks like us' mindset." [61]

The CIA can do two things superbly. No other service is so adept at recruiting foreign agents, and this far less by blackmail or bribery than by pitching a belief that U.S. ideals and interests align better with the common good than those of other forces. It's a truly American skill akin to selling insurance, which the Clandestine Service regards as a useful prerequisite when selecting its trainees. [62] Furthermore, the technological achievements of U.S. intelligence have been breathtaking ever since the first flight of the U-2 high-altitude spy plane nearly a lifetime ago.

But nine years after September 11, it's the CIA's deficiencies that have expanded, not its attainments. Very similar mistakes obstinately recur decade after decade, and for substantially the same reasons.

"Think Dorothy and the Wizard of Oz," suggests Tyler Drumheller, until 2005 the chief of CIA clandestine operations in Europe, and probably the foremost recruiter of foreign agents in the Agency's storied history. Already in 2002 he had been reporting to Langley that Saddam had no active WMD programs, let alone fissile material. His analogy to Oz captures the ever-accreting layers of bureaucracy that arrive as more money is appropriated, more people assigned, all marshaled under the managerial conviction that a new organization chart brings a transformative quality. "The yellow brick road just seemed to get longer and longer" as station chiefs struggled to report to the top. And along the march to folly, the magical persuasions of a culture that refuses to admit error is "one explanation that sure makes sense to me." [63]

From an earlier generation we hear the same assessments. Tennent "Pete" Bagley is the former chief of counterintelligence for the Soviet Russia Division and author of *Spy Wars*. Bagley handled the apparent defection in 1964 of KGB officer Yuri Nosenko, who after rough interrogation about his veracity would prosper in

America under an assumed name as a valued adviser to U.S. intelligence on the workings of the KGB. Today, evidence prevails that he was a double agent, as Bagley had come to conclude long ago in Geneva while Nosenko set about "defecting." Yet to this day the Agency refuses to consider the possibility of Nosenko's being a KGB plant—and actually reached out *forty-five years later* to ensure that Bagley's appearance at a Washington, D.C., book talk was cancelled. "It's a culture that can't ever admit that it deceives itself by its dreams," Bagley says.[64] From the analytical side of the intelligence community, William T. Lee, in the judgment of key former Soviet officials the foremost interpreter of Soviet military affairs during the Cold War, grimly assessed the Agency on the afternoon of 9/11: "We've been left wide open by an organization impervious to change."[65]

Four examples of absentminded repetition speak of the daydreaming.

First, the workings of the international economy were long deemed irrelevant by U.S. national security decision makers. That changed with Reagan's arrival, when U.S.-imposed financial, technology, and trade constraints helped to cut the Politburo's oxygen. The CIA developed excellent agents within the world's banks and financial ministries. After the Soviet collapse, MIT chemistry professor and, briefly, Deputy Secretary of Defense John Deutch was appointed director of central intelligence by President Clinton. He would be out of the Agency within eighteen months, but while there had no interest in economic reporting. He wanted none of its sources, methods, and outcomes even discussed in his presence. This form of global monitoring just wasn't Langley's business. Moreover, the CIA by statute responds to the needs and requests of its "customers," as the top people at the White House and at Defense, State, and Treasury are called. And at Treasury sat Deputy Secretary Lawrence Summers, on leave from Harvard's economics department. This combination created an unfortunate twist.

Summers let it be known that he could simply pick up the phone to get whatever he wanted from, say, the president of Banco de México, directors at Barclays and their counterparts at Paribas, or from Basel or the Bundesbank—and, of course, from the world's finance ministries. So Langley was clearly wasting money and everyone's time by covertly inserting itself into these channels. This made sense to Deutch, and, therefore, to the CIA's obliging deputy director, George Tenet. Agents who had been painstakingly concealed in such institutions—many of them by now for fifteen years—and who had risked much, were terminated overnight by their U.S. handlers in 1996, whether in Japan, Brazil, or the Middle East. Of course, officers in the field warned about what was being lost.

Before long the Agency had to backpedal but the damage was done. It began to reactivate these sources in Asia though not in Europe during the 1997 Asian financial crisis. Trying to reposition human assets within banks worldwide had to await 9/11. It then occurred to Langley's seventh floor that resources of their kind might be useful to track terrorist financing, maybe even that of drug cartels. But such a web of secret talents had been swept away. Replacements had to be recruited from scratch—years of work crudely squeezed into months.[66] Only in 2009, with another change of administration, did a newly appointed CIA director announce that the Agency had launched a new secret daily bulletin, the Economic Intelligence Brief, for its prime consumer, the president. Summers is the president's principal economic adviser and will have due access. After folly is reached, embarrassments such as these get classified.

Second, each incoming CIA director invariably demands better language abilities among his analysts and clandestine officers, and insists that the number of deep undercover spies, known as NOCs (those under Non-Official Cover) be expanded. Linguistic competence has almost from the beginning been a problem.

After all, one of many reasons for disaster at the Bay of Pigs in

1961 when an invading force of 1,453 CIA-backed Cuban exiles was wiped out by Castro's forces, was that few Agency officers working with the brave insurgents spoke Spanish. Twenty years later, entrants into the career training program could be waved through as fluent in French after little more than spending half an hour of schoolboy patter with two elderly Parisiennes. Until the Cold War's end, most Soviet analysts had no competency in Russian, original documents having to be translated by contractors. None of the CIA officers working with the resistance movement in Iraqi Kurdistan during 1994 and 1995 spoke Kurdish; only one spoke Arabic. When the Senate Intelligence Committee in 2009 pronounced the intelligence community's foreign language capabilities "abysmal," and the CIA's director disclosed that just 40 percent of clandestine officers were proficient in one, Agency veterans were delighted to learn it had risen to so high a level.

A third recurring reason for the checkered nature of the intelligence product is dependence on high-tech wizardry. A truism of intelligence work is that what is expensive must be accounted valuable. Americans have pushed this to the max, nothing being more exorbitantly priced than information harvested by such "national technical means" as satellite collection. Symmetrical with this fallacy are the telling observations of Cofer Black, the Agency's former head of counterterrorism, and Robert Richer, associate deputy director for operations, who left to open a risk assessment business. They were astounded in 2006 to learn that much of the information they had considered utterly secret is publicly available: "In a classified area, there's an assumption that if it is open, it can't be as good as if you stole it." Adds Richer, "I'm seeing that at least 80 percent of what we stole was open."[67] Such parochialism should have been discarded, oh, around 1957. That's when stacks of Russian-language technical literature—everything from the popular magazine *Radio* to documents circulated at scientific conferences—had been piling up unread (because untranslated) at the Library of Congress. They contained descriptions of the imminent Soviet Sputnik satellite launch, which would come close to panicking the nation.[68]

Fourth is the problem of too much cash, from which the CIA has just about always suffered. "There basically wasn't a limit," one of its inspectors general quietly observed in the 1960s, complaining that most any scheme could be approved. And this problem manifested in spades after 9/11. But all this abundance was not for the sharp end of the spear. "We were bombarded with dollars and ended up creating a giant bureaucracy," concludes Drumheller.[69] So does "Ishmael Jones," the pseudonym of a twenty-five-year NOC officer fluent in Arabic and raised in the Middle East, who is recognized in this shadowy world as having been one of Langley's more valuable deeply concealed spies. He resigned in 2006 to write a searingly unique chronicle, *The Human Factor: Inside the CIA's Dysfunctional Intelligence Culture.*

With too much money comes a casual exposure to corruption, as Ronn Richard, now CEO of the Cleveland Foundation, has observed. Camp Peary is the CIA training facility, known as "the Farm," near Williamsburg, Virginia. In a career training class there in 1982—which he attended as a young Foreign Service Officer, in a bold one-off bureaucratic experiment at cross-pollination—Richard encountered senior case officers boasting in private of the opportunities for skimming the cash secretly disbursed to agents. In March 2001, and by then president of the Panasonic Corporation, Richard returned to public service at the request of his friend George Tenet to become chief operating officer of In-Q-Tel, the Agency's venture investment arm. "It was burdened by kickbacks and self-dealing," he explained, just a glimpse of this being documented in 2005 by the *New York Post*'s keen business reporter, Christopher Byron.[70] Upon making his case directly to Tenet, Richard was ousted in August 2002 by intermediaries from the seventh floor. Advised by senior intelligence committee staff on the Hill and by Patton Boggs attorneys that there was no possible benefit in going public, he returned to private life.

Here too is no isolated deficiency. Among other unpleasant revelations, indicators of low-grade yet insidious corruption can be found in records brought to light by German and Italian prosecutors of CIA abduction teams in their countries after September 11: credit card charges at the four-star Gran Melia Victoria hotel on the Spanish resort island of Palma de Mallorca, plus massages in the spa; long stays at $600-a-night Italian hotels, like Milan's gilt and crystal Principe di Savoia, and more than $150,000 racked up in general expenses, including $9,000 in room service charges accumulated by just two operatives; as well as partying at U.S. government expense in the Hotel Danieli, about the most expensive place in Venice. But such wrinkles too are quickly wished away.

Many proposals exist to help to break these sleepwalking deficiencies, and the final chapter will offer solutions. But whatever the way out, the CIA needs to be steered away from the practice of convincing itself, and then others, that failures in operations and in analyses are in reality successes, that all has gone right when so much has gone wrong. Tenet's argument that 9/11 wasn't a failure of U.S. intelligence speaks for itself. There are plenty of further examples of Langley's trying to turn the past from black to white, two at least being egregious: the campaign from the early 1990s right into summer 2001 to deny the extent that it had misassessed—despite ready evidence to the contrary—essentially all vital elements of Soviet strength as the empire was dying; and a bizarre effort during that same decade, when U.S. intelligence might have been better occupied, to reach even further back, into the 1970s, in order to rewrite the story of how the Agency had then failed as well to understand America's most dangerous opponent.[71]

History—vast, ambiguous, acted on by more influences than we can ever tell—is always easy to misuse. By and large, that abuse otherwise usually occurs unconsciously or from carelessness; it too is an enduring strand of magical thinking.

6.

MYTHS OF HISTORY

ON 9/11, NOTHING ELSE SHORT OF THERMONUCLEAR BOMBARD-
ment could have blasted into overnight orthodoxy the obsessive
doctrine that "a different world" had been born. In this spirit,
President Bush addressed Congress nine days later. The meta-
phors provided the soundtrack for the next seven and a half years
of geopolitical assumptions: the destruction of Saddam at the
price of being able to commit only a "token" U.S. force in Afghanistan, a suffocating unilateralism, secret prisons and the "plunge"
into torture, plus warrantless wiretaps at home. Even today, intellectually rigorous people like former Colorado senator Gary
Hart, chairman of the bipartisan American Security Project,
argue that we live in a "different world" from all previous time
or, according to Thomas Kean, co-chair of the 9/11 Commission,
that after the atrocity "we are not the same people."[1] But that
dreadful day did not revise the list of the world's great powers nor
redistribute oil fields or micro-engineering labs. Nor did it change
the optimistic, pragmatic American character. Future historians
will be perplexed at how the reaching out of a European-based
terrorist cell to hijack airliners—two phenomena very familiar
from the 1970s—could reduce the United States to such dazed
horror when the jets were used as deadly missiles.

If we want to establish a true watershed between one world
and the next, it would be August 6, 1945. On that date, the planet
indeed reeled on its axis as unprecedented destructive power

blasted from human hands on other human beings. It would be symbolized by the mushroom cloud, an image brought before the nation when Vice President Cheney declared, and here he spoke for all emergency men who believed the world had been upended, "Simply stated, there is no doubt that Saddam Hussein now has weapons of mass destruction." [2]

Why do Americans take so offhand an approach to history, which encourages context to be so easily lost? Why do the most far-fetched historical analogies time and again shape the gravest of decisions? How do such illusory "lessons of history" work against us? And why does the U.S. military—which devotes intense effort to studying precedent in shaping plans and doctrine—allow these same misperceptions to undercut its performance in war?

Emergency men periodically detect shifts in the universe that are said to be recasting human destiny. Prophecies of final catastrophe take shape, swell prodigiously, and so far, have blown away. In the 1950s, the global ambitions of the "Sino-Soviet Bloc" were going to lap over not just Cologne and Taipei but Mombasa and Tierra del Fuego. The bloc's unity was of course visibly in shambles by the early 1960s, but President Kennedy's alarm rang out against a wave of guerrilla insurgencies backed by the communist be-hemoths and threatening to engulf "the whole southern half of the globe." His geography was vague, since Laos, Cambodia, and Vietnam are not in the Southern Hemisphere. But China none-theless appeared as "the Golden Horde . . . on-the-march," James Thomson, aide to McGeorge Bundy, was astounded to observe, the Middle Kingdom displaying once more its endless numbers and ravenous appetites. [3]

"It is a darker world," said the intelligence chief of the Department of Homeland Security five years after 9/11, in a judgment shared by eminent academics and former policymakers working on Princeton University's Project on National Security.[4] But darker than when? Than the years since June 25, 1950, when 94,709 Americans were lost on the Pacific Rim—nearly as many as perished in the Asia-Pacific theater during World War II—or when Stalin and Mao, history's most prolific killers, acquired hydrogen bombs as well as the means to deliver them clandestinely into the United States? All the world's terrorists in all their lifetimes would not be able to do what the Soviet empire, with its gargantuan SS-18 ICBMs, its anthrax as well as its nuclear warheads, could have brought about on a single bad afternoon.

People who proclaim themselves the Paul Reveres of the latest extreme danger can acquire high office, turn slogans into policy, and then policy into deeds. The existential horror they identify compels the public to ask chilling questions: How can life as we know it continue with a nuclear-armed China? Or with a nuclear-armed Iran? An illusory clarity emerges about what should be done. Familiar mantras are heard: "force projection," "special operations," "preemption." America has been able to navigate far worse dangers, whether by skill or serendipity, than those encountered today. But throughout there have arisen similarly hazardous overreactions.

Not long ago the mere rustle of a badly translated copy of Lenin's *Materialism and Empirio-Criticism* in Ayacucho or in Jakarta could be drowned out by the thunder of planes hurling in ambassadors, AID teams, Green Berets, CIA operatives, and, of course, money against the impalpable, but therefore more terrifying, threat. And again today a sufficiently astute warlord in N'Djamena, who professes to detect a "terrorist" within his cousin's rival clan, just might be able to bring in a Ranger battalion courtesy of AFRICOM, the newest of the Defense Department's six unified regional commands around the world. Perspective is easy to lose.

Yet what generates world attention at any given passing moment is unlikely to be the torrential mainstream of history bearing down on us. George Orwell exposed this fallacy during World War II when he mocked a rising American intellectual, James Burnham. That former Trotskyite political theorist, who would join the OSS and go on to become a pillar of *National Review*, had the habit of offering contrasting dystopian visions of the future based just on each bloody shift on the Russian front. Orwell knew there were deeper influences at work. Americans, however, may particularly be prone to being enthralled by the excitements of the moment. They rapidly seize on riveting new events in other parts of life, such as the Next New Thing in venture-capital-backed IT breakthroughs. In foreign affairs, once they are convinced of an alien threat, they become consumed by it—at least for some incandescent time, as with communism and now terror.

Americans have a Janus-faced view of history. On one side of the mask, the Republic is relatively unburdened by the past. It is truly Emerson's "country of tomorrow" and "the land where hatreds die." There are fewer memories of blood feud than in much of the world, whether compared to France and Germany, the Balkans and Turkey, Korea and Japan, or Pakistan and India. American practicality combines with a general goodwill, leaving the dead past to bury its dead. The 1990s phrase "move on," as used in a political sense of let's head forward and forget the latest mess, is now part of common speech.

Such disregard of the past facilitates the day-to-day functioning of America's operative position in the world, its role as the integrator among nations—securing the seas, undertaking huge-scale disaster relief, championing free trade, or at least more so than any other power. To that extent, minimal interest in the past might be called "constructive oblivion." Outside a few panoramas like the Civil War, Americans just don't dwell on their own history, let alone on that of other peoples. Which might be okay, except that the country's foreign policy leadership shares these lacunae.

Adam Garfinkle is an accomplished historian, author of *Tell-tale Hearts: The Origins and Impact of the Vietnam Antiwar Movement*, and editor of the *American Interest*. He also served as speechwriter for Secretaries of State Colin Powell and Condoleezza Rice. "No one in a senior position in this administration seems to have the vaguest notion of modern Middle Eastern history," he observed at the time.[5] Foreign statesmen display enough knowledge gaps of their own to answer for. But such a degree of ignorance about a crucial region, let alone during a war, would not apply to a Chirac, or a Sarkozy, a Blair, or a Cameron, let alone their foreign ministers such as Bernard Kouchner or William Hague.

A readiness to dust away the past also makes Americans susceptible to the wizard's pretense that history has only begun right now. There are deliberate assertions that yesterday is irrelevant, as were loudly raised while Iraq spiraled downward in 2006. The challenge was to look ahead, said the architects of that war, not to dwell on how we got into the debacle. Little changes from administration to administration. Today's White House is similarly intent "to look forward, not back." It opposes a congressional inquiry to explore the origins, and the accountability, of how torture came to be practiced after 9/11 by people in the service of the United States. America is "looking ahead," insists President Obama.

On the other side of the mask is a culture of law, lawyers, and legalism, as found in no other country. Lawyers are the true aristocracy of America, Tocqueville observed nearly two hundred years ago. A people so heavily rooted in the law pay particular heed to the magic of precedent, if not to the specifics. Precedent is used to uphold arguments and to make points. Its influence compels those entrusted with protecting the national security of the United States to invoke lots of alleged historical likenesses; respect for precedent has much to do with why the public responds.

The use of analogies is a primitive mode of referencing history. But it is part of the American "national style" of foreign policy making, argues Stanley Hoffmann, longtime director of Harvard's

Center for European Studies.[6] It is why highly dubious analogies such as the "Munich" sellout are used so often. Since France and Britain botched the Czech question in 1938, Americans must remember in 2008 that "we are all Georgians"; since tyranny was to be overthrown in Iraq, American troops would be welcomed "just like [in] Normandy," or in Paris after D-Day. It becomes proportionately easier to make facile comparisons the less one knows about the places being discussed, and preferably the less one knows about the events being cited.

Emergency men eschew elementary qualifiers: B is just assumed to follow A by inevitable progression. The grim consequences of failing to respond forcefully to a Russian incursion into Georgia, they argue, can be gauged from what happened after Munich 1938; all Russia's neighbors will surely be cowed as the aggressor's appetite is whetted. Except that this assertion proved wrong.

A great power that pays minimal attention to the ironies of history is poorly equipped to resist converting its passions into military force. It's tempted by calls to action offered from well-credentialed enthusiasts who ignore the basics of the discipline: an attempt at objectivity, a sense of complexity, and being aware of how truly little can be known about the past. On the march to folly, those enthusiasts convince themselves that history is on their side as thoroughly as did any true believer in one or another of those collectivist "waves of the future" of the 1930s—Soviet communism, Italian fascism, German national socialism.

A disregard of the past also keeps every sort of plan from the sophomoric to the insane circulating—from President Kennedy's notion in 1962 of using "anonymous planes" against China's emerging nuclear weapons program to President George W. Bush advancing the possibility of painting a U.S. surveillance plane in the United Nations colors in hopes of drawing fire over Iraq, thereby provoking a confrontation with Saddam in 2002.[7]

The late Arthur Schlesinger, Jr.'s final essay, written in 2007, was called "Folly's Antidote." "For a superpower," he argued, "a sense of history is a moral imperative." The excitements of trying to interpret wars and crises, however, can put historians off-stride. Soon after the 2009 inauguration, the eminent presidential historian Richard Norton Smith addressed this phenomenon. Periodically his profession ranks the U.S. presidents. At the time, the departing one's popularity was dismal. "But if we have anything like a stable quasi-democratic Middle East 30 to 40 years from now," Smith observed matter-of-factly, "then I guarantee you that he'll rank very favorably." Smith might have added "deservedly or not," because he, at least, knows that this is not how history unfolds.[8] To use an analogy, it is like saying that the U.S. Marine Corps interventions up and down the Caribbean in the days of Wilson and Coolidge have brought about the relatively constitutional governments of present-day Central America. Technology and demographics, agronomy and the growth of a middle class, stamp more new worlds into existence over the decades than do the boots of long-forgotten battalions.

Emergency men flatten out time and space. Thomson placed such "abuse and distortion of history" at the core of his Vietnam autopsy. Thirty-five years after publishing *The Best and the Brightest*, Halberstam addressed the problem head-on for the Iraq War. He found a White House obsessed with making historical parallels, few of them based on fact. To him, the president, the vice president, and the entire inner circle were "the History Boys" as they groped to rationalize another failed war. When decision makers then as today pepper their speeches with "History teaches us . . . We know from history . . . History shows us," emergency men are likely to be at work. All involved in a decision have already convinced themselves that they possess historic mandates for action.

President Bush consumed history books by the yard, according to his political adviser, Karl Rove. He and Bush competed on the amount they gulped down, including "the number of pages and later the combined size of each book's pages," what they called the "Total Lateral Area" of their reading lists.[9] "The president is one of my best students," Dr. Kissinger let it be known. "He reads all the books I send him." [10]

Policymakers possess different levels of historical depth. Some, like George Marshall and, a lifetime later, General Brent Scowcroft, have a sense of history in their bones—Scowcroft attesting that one lesson is "don't change your objective simply because you are doing well," as occurred in Korea and, in the turn to nation-building after ousting the Taliban during 2001, in Afghanistan. Occasionally policymakers are themselves historians. As a professor in Harvard's government department, McGeorge Bundy had taught GOV 185: "The United States in World Politics." [11] It was a tour de force of contemporary history; there was standing room only during his annual lecture on the capitulation to Hitler at Munich. After leaving the Ford Foundation in 1979, he would spend ten years as a professor of history at New York University. It was said at Harvard and in the White House that no one was sharper at puncturing specious analogies than he. Arthur Schlesinger, Jr., had actually taught history at Harvard since 1946 and was the son of an eminent social historian who had taught there for three decades.

Bundy and Schlesinger came to Washington with a president whose confidence in his ability to change the world melded with his own penchant for the historic overview. His favorite book was Lord David Cecil's *Melbourne*, the definitive evocation of a skeptical, enlightened patriciate governing an empire. Jacqueline Kennedy spoke of being married to "an historian," a more dignified calling in her opinion than a politician's. "You are a writer and an historian," Schlesinger echoed. Bundy more coolly complimented the president on being an "ex historian." [12] It was not only the relatively applicable history of Barbara Tuchman's *Guns of August* to which Kennedy turned, but also less credible lessons such as "Munich" and the "loss" of China to communism in 1949.

The deep knowledge of history in the Kennedy White House,

however, didn't prevent that hyperalert cadre from performing any better or worse than the History Boys. In both cases, the country lurched into war; the national security teams of the Kennedy/Johnson and the George W. Bush administrations rival each other as the worst in modern American experience. Bundy could appear as much at sea about history as any twenty-first-century autodidact. He was blind to the implications of the so-recent agonies of French soldiers and legionnaires in Indochina. Surely a fight in Vietnam wouldn't require the full forceful commitment of U.S. power, as shown by his proposal that "Only Americans Who Want to Go [to Vietnam] Have to Go." His idea was no more or less thickheaded than many heard from the History Boys, such as, in 2003, "More people get killed in New York every night than get killed in Baghdad." Nor is it more despairing than to hear President Obama's ambassador to Kabul ponder "the wisdom of dropping 2,000-pound bombs on houses when it is unknown who is inside." [13] Not much mystery there.

President Bush, who majored in history at Yale, in fact raised a wise question during one of the seminars he conducted at the White House with visiting historians and public-policy savants. "What can I learn from history?" he asked Andrew Roberts after reading his *A History of the English-Speaking Peoples Since 1900*. It would have been timely had Dean Bundy, Professor Schlesinger, and the Pulitzer Prize–winning President Kennedy pondered the same question. Among the answers they might have heard: history does not prevent us from making mistakes; it teaches us how to make new kinds of mistakes, or old mistakes in new ways. That is because people are susceptible to overvaluing those shreds of the past that they have picked up, especially people who eagerly seek precedents; they are so intent not to repeat a mistake that they are more likely to commit the opposite error. Another answer the Kennedy/Johnson cohort might have heard would have been that the sound-bite "lessons" that resurface in U.S. foreign policy debates rarely hold up under detailed scrutiny.

Only one vice president in U.S. history other than Dick Cheney has served as secretary of defense or, as the nearest role to the office before 1947, as secretary of war: that formidable South Carolinian John C. Calhoun in the early nineteenth century. The temperament required for each office is profoundly different. This does much to explain why Cheney's voice of knowledgeable, rational restraint in the moment of 1991 Gulf War victory—that of a defense secretary who had backed George H. W. Bush against emergency men eager to go "on to Baghdad"—promised a dozen years later an overnight democratic remaking of the whole Middle East. Cheney's switch from hardheaded administrator in the Pentagon, and thereafter in business, to the White House sound-bite grand strategist after 9/11 offers a textbook map of the avenues through which magic can flow.

Puzzles remain about the former vice president. He is indeed the "student of history" who "cares about history" depicted by his wife, Lynn Cheney, a scholar of nineteenth-century English literature, among other interests. Together they've written an engaging, personality-filled history of nine legendary Speakers of the House.[14] Yet why did a man so attuned to his country's past and to its constitution champion the myth after 9/11 that danger follows an adherence to the rule of law? Why was he so evidently unconstrained by the founding ideals of the nation, as in implementing his belief that waterboarding terror suspects is a "no-brainer"? And what catapulted Cheney into the vice presidency in the first place when, unlike all but one or two of his twentieth-century predecessors, he disposed of no coherent political base of his own?

Dick Cheney's life story has the American West–going quality of legend: born on the Great Plains, a childhood in the Wyoming high country, a huge business success in Texas. In truth, the deals and intrigues of Washington lie at the center of his achievements. His five successive draft deferments, as the United States sank deeper and deeper into Vietnam, gave him opportunity to make his mark early. His unself-conscious 1989 response about them to the *Washington Post*—"I had other priorities"—reveals a lot of ego in his cosmos, even for someone who has climbed the greasy pole in the nation's capital.

Having been White House chief of staff at thirty-five, in 1978 he ran for Congress from his home state. Wyoming forms one congressional district. Whoever holds that office has particular, well-defined responsibilities and a singular voice. Cheney would be five times reelected. He considered running for the presidency. Instead House Republicans elected him their conference chairman in 1987 and minority whip in 1988. He seemed destined to become Speaker, should his party ever oust the Democrats, who had been in the majority since 1955. That change, back in the 1980s, seemed most unlikely. So he accepted from George H. W. Bush the post of secretary of defense in 1989. The Senate confirmed him unanimously. As directed, he dutifully cut the defense budget and downsized the post–Cold War military. He headed the Pentagon when both houses of Congress authorized President Bush in 1990 to drive Saddam from Kuwait.

Cheney's best hours came when he argued, along with the president, that easy triumphs in the desert, if pursued to the illusory limit, would entail colossal problems in Iraq's turbulent cities. "Going on to Baghdad" to topple Saddam, he'd explain after the Gulf War, would have been "a bad idea" leading to a "quagmire" of wider, incoherent violence.[15] And the responsibility of occupying Iraq, as he didn't elaborate, would have fallen primarily into his own lap at the Defense Department. In any event, he was certain enough that Saddam would be overthrown in a year or so as to place a friendly bet on it. During 1989–93, he succeeded at the Pentagon by shunning the merchants of grand ideas, by focusing on the mission, and by being loyal to the fighting men for whom he was accountable. Significantly, he was answering to a combat veteran steeped in foreign affairs.

Such victory did not enable the elder Bush to beat Bill Clinton. The secretary fell softly, bringing to the corporate sector a much-in-demand political record when he left the Pentagon in 1993. "All of a sudden," observed *Fortune* magazine, "Cheney had become Mr. Business." [16] He developed a sound reputation as a CEO at Halliburton—based largely on his ability to wangle government contracts on behalf of an oil and engineering services firm and to use his contacts "to get doors open." Meanwhile he challenged President Clinton's attempt to isolate oil-rich, radical Iran. Eventually his record at Halliburton made him appear to Washington as a proven, bottom-line leader of American enterprise. In a country that extols tough-minded businessmen and their achievements, he was now a doer from within Houston's Petroleum Club who also knew his way around the capital as an "insider." The "CEO President"-to-be, as George W. Bush was already being called due to his MBA, scooped Cheney up from the vice presidential search committee, and this was fine with the Republican Party.

When Cheney returned to Washington, he was expected to supply a shrewd understanding of the world to a president unfamiliar with both international affairs and corporate America. Cheney's experience "in business"—on the apparently harsh testing grounds of capitalism—took conspicuous precedence on his White House biographical Web page over his earlier political record. Post 9/11 it was pretty much an article of faith that his master repertoire as both a former defense secretary and a driving CEO embraced winning wars. All the world seemed new to him after 9/11. There was no precedent for what had occurred, he argued. Nonetheless, rhetoric and analogies borrowed from the past proved useful. Americans, he kept insisting, had discovered that ocean moats no longer protected the homeland. It was as if the country had never lived under the shadow of Soviet ICBMs, had not come within a whisker of war over the Cuban Missile Crisis, or as if Sputnik hadn't lofted forty-odd years earlier. Any cool calculus of armed geopolitics as in 1991 was displaced in Washington by a ferment of raw responses passing as ideas.

But the American vice presidency is a peculiar role. Being able to exercise cool, cold-eyed, essentially supportive leadership from that office is starkly different from performing as a congressman, a cabinet secretary, or a government contractor. There is no executive objective for which a vice president is responsible. He or she, hopefully, is a source of wisdom and experience, not tied to specific line successes or failures. Or at least that was the role until Dick Cheney redefined it.

In the fraught "new world" following 9/11, moreover, it was increasingly apparent that Cheney's achievement of ten years earlier stood compromised: Saddam remained in power and the regime of sanctions imposed by the United Nations had helped to starve, according to a cross section of authoritative sources, roughly a half-million Iraqi children to death. Saddam now posed a fabulously tempting target once the Taliban was apparently crushed in late 2001 and the Afghan war surely won.

Cheney may have believed there was no precedent for the threat to America, yet at the same time he looked to the past to justify what lay ahead: "It'll be like the American Army going through the streets of Paris," he assured the skeptical Republican House majority leader in September 2002. "The |Iraqi| people will be so happy with their freedoms that we'll probably back ourselves out of there within a month or two"—one of the worst assessments in modern American history. It was a Procrustean comparison, hardly to be rethought when *L'Express*, France's *Time* magazine, declaimed three weeks before the invasion that "the Near East is not the Europe of 1944." [17] Instead, the classic emergency-man mantra rang ever louder: "The dangers of inaction are greater than those of action."

Scores of notions, simplifications, and slogans—and even a few seriously propounded arguments—screamed for the vice president's attention as elder statesman. Cheney faced a trickier task than he had ten years before. This time, as second to an untested president, he was no longer surrounded by the sober leaders of the first Bush White House, such as General Scowcroft at the NSC and James Baker as secretary of state. Former JCS chairman Colin Powell and his appointees at Foggy Bottom—such as Deputy Secretary Richard Armitage, who had three combat tours in Vietnam, and policy planning director Richard Haass, all of whom counseled patience and a thorough lining-up of allies—were being outmaneuvered by Rumsfeld, Wolfowitz, and Perle. Those diplomats, says Feith in his memoirs, were prone to "fret about the risk" of war. The ground had shifted under Cheney. Conveniently, he was also no longer in the direct line of responsibility for the success of military intervention: should worse come to worst, it was now Rumsfeld who was in the notional line of fire.

Cheney swallowed the neocon gibber about transforming Iraq and the Middle East—all the enthusiasm about "moving history forward" to shake up "the complacency of the Sunni Arab" world. Immensely capable though he was, Cheney in his "new world" of 9/12 was not up to busting these fantasies, and readily yielded to the American penchant to affirm that the world today is utterly different from yesterday.

In the process, this often socially tolerant man convinced himself that delivering terror suspects to the cellars of friendly dictators, and torturing them ourselves beyond the reach of law, "was done in accordance with our constitutional practices and principles." [18] The pressures of defined, disciplined line responsibility that had kept him rational at the Pentagon and at Halliburton fell away. Ironically, he converted from the competently cautious senior establishment figure of a decade earlier into an emergency man, a supremely effective one, almost overnight. He combined a belief from the mid-1970s in the largest possible constructions of executive power with a demeanor of unequivocal certitude and bullish directness. It could play out fantastically as "we know that [Saddam] has a long-standing relationship with various terrorist groups, including the al-Qaeda organization." Then, in an argument over judicial nominees, he would deliver on the Senate floor a casual "fuck yourself" to the senior senator from Vermont. And he'd help to push through a doctrine of preemptive license to "act, and act quickly, against danger," with armed forces "ready to strike at a moment's notice in any dark corner of the world."[19]

FDR and Eisenhower had no one like this, nor did the elder George Bush—a quasi-independent force who could be counted on to raise the temperature and skillfully to turn the worst impulses of other emergency men into policy. Cheney's role came to be that of a heavily armed majority whip for the executive branch, with a bruising presence that hadn't been exerted so visibly since Vice President Spiro Agnew, "Nixon's Nixon"—though Agnew, who had commanded a 10th Armored Division tank company at the Battle of the Bulge, had earned a Bronze Star for steady conduct under fire.

Emergency men are far more often bored than frightened. Cheney had starred as a previously useful wielder of power, and then as a corporate go-between, for all of which he had been well rewarded. But emergency men tend to want something more. They believe that they have a greater, richer contribution to make beyond mere competence—vision, courage, fortitude. Where can that better be displayed than on the edge of a precipice? Cheney had previously passed all the tests of plain determination, skill, and intelligence. But as with so many other self-enclosed men, the world's drama came to be reduced dangerously and trivially to personal conflicts, refusals to compromise, an inexperienced belief in what can be accomplished by force, and finally to foolish analogies.

In 1948, the Cold War temperature plunged with the Berlin Airlift as America and Britain countered Stalin's attempt to cut off the former German capital; tellingly, around a million Americans were reading, or at least buying, Arnold Toynbee's *A Study of*

History. This tome abridges six of what would become twelve volumes describing the collapse of civilizations since Egyptian and Hellenic times under the stress of war and religious peril. Forty years later, as the Soviet Union was just about to go down in defeat, historian Paul Kennedy hit the nerves of another worried generation with *The Rise and Fall of the Great Powers: Economic Change and Military Conflict from 1550 to 2000*, a mega-seller that took Americans through a new cycle of empire. He maintained that now it was they, the Americans, who were imperially overextended. Today the political culture again searches for past wisdom, as well as for heroic inspiration. The reading lists of the History Boys show this quest, as does the abundance of books at Barnes & Noble on America's founding fathers and on the stalwart generation that got the country through World War II. Likewise, many authoritative-sounding references to ancient Greece, Rome, the British Empire, World War II, and the Cold War dot the op-ed pages and the articles of policy magazines. We seek signposts when the going gets tough and revert to the national passion for analogy-making.

Other nations of course deploy analogies to clarify war and peace. Some of these are sound, others preposterous. Even eminent historians voice ridiculous ones. In 1870, as the railroad enlarged its grip on warfare, Leopold von Ranke, so great a historian as to be called "forever the Head of the Profession," solemnly announced that Germany was "fighting Louis XIV!": the Sun King had been dead 155 years, yet Ranke was insisting that France had *always* been set on European supremacy, no matter that Bismarck had just provoked this modern, fast-moving war. But only America has elevated a yearning for inferences and similarities into a "national style."

The analogies that result serve more as prepackaged would-be solutions than as helpful instruction. They shape decisions through exemplary tales and moral fables. A doctrine of resemblance follows: events are cast in the light of their gross similarities, rather than their telling, dangerously particular differences.

Even when they appear apt, historical analogies carry psychological risks. They become mental aids or emotional crutches when the country faces disorienting events abroad. They provide false comfort by offering illusory guidance. They help to win arguments on issues such as whether to transform Iraq, or North Korea, but tend to reinforce ill-conceived beliefs, such as the need to proceed immediately or essentially alone. And none of these inferences can be tested, unlike the use of analogics in the natural sciences. In national security, elementary analysis gets smothered under dubious pasts.

Research into the psychology of analogical reasoning indicates that decision makers are more likely to misguide themselves when deploying analogies than when not. Vietnam, Iraq, and many other wayward grand-strategic decisions offer depressing proof. A "confirmation bias" tempts those in power to support their opinions with ready comparisons—of which, examined in that spirit, the history books offer an unlimited supply. The mind has a tendency to focus on historical evidence not just as a clarifier of how things stand at any one moment but as a guide to the future. That's why it's easy to assume, for instance, that the Marshall Plan, which catalyzed Western Europe's postwar rebirth, could be an equally successful model for reconstructing a conquered Iraq.

No matter how instructive an analogy may seem, a welter of forces have shaped any specific historical event. For example, U.S. success in helping to crush communist insurgents in Greece in 1947–49—the very real Marxism-spouting "terrorists" who energized the Truman Doctrine—might prove treacherous support for what could be achieved in different terrain, against different people, and embroiling different nations. The ferocious Viet Cong, heavily supplied by Moscow, were merciless disciplined veterans of a war of independence against the French Foreign Legion—not ragtag rebel bands armed by Bulgaria. But the analogy of that initial success in Greece seemed to offer a convenient handbook fifteen years later in Vietnam.

Occasionally, analogies work for restraint. The 1962 Cuban Missile Crisis fascinates the nation to this day because it remains a stark demonstration of U.S. vulnerability. At the height of those "thirteen days," President Kennedy rejected the Joint Chiefs' call for preemption. He used analogies of 1914's runaway "guns of August" to slow down the clock by imposing a blockade. He also feared the condemnation of history—if history survived—for committing a "Pearl Harbor in reverse." In Vietnam, fear of provoking a Chinese intervention, as in Korea, was among Lyndon Johnson's reasons for not invading the North or mining its harbors.[20] During the Reagan administration, the ghosts of Vietnam constrained any deeper U.S. military involvements against Soviet-backed insurgents in Central America. But by and large, Washington uses analogies as counsel for action, a sample of which were heard in summer 2008 during that five-day war between Georgia and Russia.

Consider four categories of analogy that keep shaping decisions.

One is the resort to ancient history. Toynbee, for example, described the great essential movements of humanity as inevitably climaxing in violence. His rich descriptions impart a mystical sense of these grinding cycles. He at least provided Americans with newfound perspective: To those reading of the dazed hordes of slaves led away from fire-ravaged Carthage or Thebes, post–World War II fears of Stalin's reaching into Western Europe could appear a bit less unprecedentedly paralyzing.

But that modest level of guidance is rare when classicists address today's national security problems. Daniel Mendelsohn, a student of Greek tragedy, has observed the penchant to find in Greek history an argument for "plain hawkishness, a distaste for compromise and negotiation when armed conflict is possible" among today's militant conservatives, several of whom are serious scholars of the ancient world. Mendelsohn detected this fondness nine months after Iraq was invaded, noting a considerable "finagling with Thucydides," as these hawks called on the greatest historian of political misfortune and therefore, ironically, the chronicler of imperial hubris.[21]

The finagling continues. For instance, Yale's Donald Kagan, the definitive historian of the Peloponnesian War, in which Thucydides was an admiral, has seen fit to denounce a U.S. Army lieutenant general for being skeptical of the troop surge into Iraq. General Douglas Lute's appointment as deputy national security adviser for Iraq and Afghanistan by President Bush, Kagan insisted, would lead to repeating the Athenians' disaster at the Battle of Mantinea in 418 B.C. because they had appointed a general tied to the political faction opposing decisive action against the Spartans. (A serious professional, General Lute now holds the same role for President Obama.) Victor Davis Hanson, a historian at the Hoover Institution and author of *The Western Way of War: Infantry Battle in Classical Greece*, among other important contributions, became known as Dick Cheney's "war guru." He regularly drew encouraging comparisons between the Peloponnesian War and the war in Iraq—and, in the twilight of that vice presidency, bemoaned America's weakening will to make "war on terror."

A couple of key problems emerge when comparing current events with ancient history. These fine scholars write stirringly of hoplites bearing swords and twelve-foot spears and facing each other across open country by daylight, steadily closing up their phalanxes as comrades to their left and right fall sliced and disemboweled. But the feature of classical warfare from which we can learn the most about today's events is essentially ignored. For example, the Greeks used small, stealthy strikes full of concealment and trickery, time and again toppling a city-state overnight. In this way the destiny of a region could be reset—and, given

Greece's significance in our civilization to the present day, perhaps the direction of history was truly altered. To neglect the most focused and imaginative tactics of the art of war leaves a significant gap in Western military history overall. But it's especially notable in studies of Greek warfare. Classical archeologist John R. Hale also draws attention to this puzzling inattention within the discipline. Nonetheless, war guru Hellenists turn to an era of muscle power, crude iron, and tightly held slaveocracies in which news traveled at horse pace as a guide to understanding our nuclear-powered, satellite-connected refractory planet of twenty-four-hours-a-day CNN and Al Jazeera.

It's unlikely that presidents, vice presidents, or anyone else would seek enlightenment on U.S. economic policy, or on matters of contemporary faith or on transportation from Athenian finance, Mallian religion, or Spartan technology. Yet in the area of national security, the Greek experience of war and peace keeps getting pressed into service. Robert Kaplan, the *Atlantic* correspondent now on the Obama administration's Defense Policy Board, touts as a model for the mobility of the U.S. Army the example of Xenophon's hideously bloody extraction of a failed force of Greek mercenaries playing at dynastic politics in fifth-century B.C. Persia. "What's that all about?" asks a bemused General William Hartzog about this fanciful connection, Hartzog actually having been responsible for U.S. Army mobility as head of its Training and Doctrine Command.

Kissinger, too, has weighed in with loopy formulations. In 1973—at a pivotal juncture of the Cold War, as America struck arms control deals, pulled its soldiers from South Vietnam, and as the Nixon presidency began to fall apart—he offered his view of the tides of time: the chief of naval operations, who promptly made notes of their conversation, reports him as saying America had "passed its high point like so many other civilizations." Since Americans refused to stay the course against the Russians, who played "Sparta to our Athens," Kissinger explained, he could only try "to persuade the Russians to give us the best deal we can get." [22]

Ancient Rome is brought onstage with similar unhelpfulness. In but one instance, Paul Kennedy suggests that U.S. politico-military practices are akin to the Roman Empire's "worldwide imperial ambitions" as he compares U.S. forces to Roman legions—though the difference is that the legions pretty much put down long-term roots of twenty to several hundred years wherever they were deployed. A "reset" button would be valuable, therefore, whenever anyone discussing U.S. national security is tempted to reach for Thucydides or Xenophon or Caesar.

A second category of misleading analogies can be grouped under the phrase "clash of civilizations," a collision presented as akin to the Goths entering Rome in 410 or Byzantium's fall to the Ottomans in 1453. Now "the fault lines between civilizations will be the battle lines of the future," Samuel Huntington instructed us in 1993, in an article that set the stage for his now best-selling *Clash of Civilizations*.[23] Twenty-first-century America, the emergency men then avow, is certain to collide with some sort of restored fifteenth-century caliphate—"a radical Islamic empire that spans from Spain to Indonesia." [24] Their alarmist apparitions roll over a map without borders. Dangers appear enormous, cohesive, and immediate. Perspective dissolves and real-world distinctions are the more thoroughly erased as Al Qaeda, Hezbollah, and the Muslim Brotherhood have conferred on them similar designs for global conquest. This band of geostrategists has been as emphatic about the green peril as were their predecessors about a clash with the Golden Horde. The heated theorizing may have cooled nearly a decade after September 11; but any major attack in America that includes shouts of "Allahu Akbar" will pull these notions back into the councils of power.

Today, antimodernist surges toward fundamentalism in several of the world's largest societies, including in the United States with its megachurches and in Israel with its Gush Emunim West Bank settlers, may form the most nearly simultaneous pan-planetary religious movement in history. Many religions are reasserting themselves on political issues. But this does not mean that the world will shatter into competing religious blocs. The sticky, grubby history of religion and ideology challenges this illusion. The Reformation, the Great Schism, the repeated flight of popes before Catholic princes, the wars between Sunni and Shia and all the spectacular internecine butcheries of Christianity itself already compromise such finger-painting of tomorrow's map of the world. As emergency men dramatize the impending showdown, a hard old saying is overlooked: "And God's alone the victory," sighs a Spanish emir, riding back from destroying another Muslim sovereign with Christian assistance. Here are the enduring ironies of history: popes might preach the holy war; they might also pocket stipends from a sultan to hold his brother in captivity.

An optimistic corollary exists for the religious twists of this "clash," as offered by the great Anglo-German historian Lord Acton. He wrote of the terrible, strong, and distinctly non-ideological forms that religion takes "from abiding with us": sloth and greed, fatigue and cynicism, and all-around selfishness and vindictiveness. Religion starts with setting aside self-interest while seeking peace, and then rapidly begins to burn heretics, or to desperately kill other Muslims as does Al Qaeda. Such diversions will save most of the world from any civilizational collision where sacrifice and brotherly love will not.

The third category of analogical folly is the grandiose description of America's world presence as "imperial." "We're an empire now, and when we act, we create our own reality," a senior White House adviser, widely believed to be Karl Rove, notoriously told the author Ron Suskind in 2002. "And while you're studying that reality—judiciously, as you will—we'll act again, creating other new realities." Just so spoke the Soviet ideologues. Moscow's true believers also convinced themselves that they were reconfiguring the world: Trofim Lysenko's sham doctrines of biology even insisted that Charles Darwin was wrong and that "socialist man" would evolve overnight; the "scientific realism" of Marxism/Leninism could meanwhile revamp the globe, "creating other new realities," too.

But America's emergency men usually prefer to invoke the British Empire rather than the Soviet one, adopting the master tones of stern viceroys. It can be fun to hear General Petraeus refer in a briefing to the "Great Game" that his soldiers are playing in Afghanistan—drawing a parallel with Britain's nineteenth-century wars and intrigues along the outer defenses of imperial rule in India. But it's unhelpful when Pentagon advisers and influential pundits draw on the *arcana imperii* of Victorian power for operational examples, a conceit to be found in the earliest of post–World War II emergency men, as in George Kennan's talks with skeptical Foreign Office mandarins about America's coming "frontier wars." Misguided U.S. operatives in forward positions of the emerging Cold War also spoke admiringly, to the disgust of upright men in Washington, of British political officers who were deftly able to "rub out" native troublemakers.

Robert Kaplan is now among the latest to extract lessons from those good old days of empire. "American hegemony post Iraq," he says, "will be as changed as Britain's was after the Indian Mutiny" in 1857/58.[23] He argues that America should move from an "an ad hoc imperium" to a "calmer, more pragmatic and soldiering empire built on trade, education, and technology." In his conception, the brutality of the eighty-nine years that followed the mutiny in that model empire, such as 1919's Jallianwala Bagh massacre, is airbrushed away. His book *Imperial Grunts: The American Military on the Ground* pays due tribute to the worldwide exploits of American warriors, but its subtext portrays the United States as no less an imperial power than Britain and Rome in their times, definitely news to the country's soldiers and marines. And from the Council on Foreign Relations, senior fellow Max Boot urges policymakers to "think imperially" of a "Pax Americana" as troubled lands like Afghanistan "truly cry out for the sort of en-lightened foreign administration once provided by self-confident Englishmen in jodhpurs and pith helmets." [26]

Fashion notes aside, all this analogizing is based on shaky his-tory: its fans impute to the British Empire a formidability it never possessed. The years of Palmerston, Gladstone, Disraeli, and Salis-bury get mashed into a much misunderstood Pax Britannica—an epoch of peace that happened to occur over the years when Britain's was the most pervasive presence in the world. But the empire's significant strength did not shape the world system or uphold the peace. Nevertheless, all could be so straightforward, suggest the emergency men, for a similarly imposing "Pax Ameri-cana" today if the country only had the backbone to embrace its destiny. This crowing about America's responsibility for "imperial policing" is a superb way for a liberal democracy to undercut it-self among allies, enemies, and its own electorate.

Empire is a multiplex word that stretches from before Athens's design to be supreme in Hellas to America's half-conscious ad-vance to its present powers of cultural assimilation and military preeminence. *Imperial* has the overarching quality of "we're here, we're the boss, you can't get rid of us." This ambition has rarely gripped Americans. Yet some historians argue that "there were no more self-confident imperialists than the founding fathers themselves." [27] It's a playful contention, but one that causes con-fusion and means little for today. To Washington, Jefferson, and Jay, *empire* meant sovereignty over the great empty lands of North America. In fact, contiguous authority was also the original meaning of *empire* when the English first used it in the late six-teenth century, to describe their hegemony over all the British Isles. [28]

Although America sometimes exhibits imperial behavior, the romanticizing of "American empire" is not even close to taking material, let alone constitutional, form outside academic phrase-making. And that's true whether one is imagining an empire bent on imposing ideas, material penetration, or plain strong-arm assertion. The country would have to produce an effective administrative class or an elite cadre to oversee such relationships, and Americans, God forbid, would have to want to be even more involved with the complicated politics of foreigners. The officers in U.S. military training missions in Niger and Chad, whose soldiers Kaplan, among other romantics, dubs "America's African Rifles," would have to speak the postcolonial unifying language, French. The chances of any of this occurring are remote.

The fourth category of analogy that is commonly used to underpin emergency-man action is World War II, with the Korean War quick to follow. "Munich" and "appeasement" tap the simplified moral capital of previous times. Concession brings catastrophe, most likely world war. MacArthur used the rhetoric as he tried to rally the country for a wider conflict with China in 1951, as did young McGeorge Bundy that year when criticizing Senate Republican leader Robert Taft for trying to restrict President Truman's power to send troops abroad without prior approval by Congress. The rhetoric reappeared in strength by 1965. "Can't we see the similarity to our own indolence at Munich?" argued the U.S. ambassador in Saigon, Henry Cabot Lodge. "It will be World War III if we don't go in." More than thirty years later, Secretary of State Madeleine Albright was fond of telling reporters "Munich is my mind-set," though she at least had reason, having fled Czechoslovakia as a child after Britain and France abandoned it to Hitler. But "Munich" is the mind-set of many other U.S. policymakers as well, spoken of in tandem with that history-laden term of discredit, "appeaser," stuck to those who question immediate, go-it-alone *action*.

Munich is an acute but scarcely universal justification of resolve. Emergency men resort to this analogy to argue about principle, which is fair enough, but the comparisons serve to obscure differences of places and peoples, leaving aside the moral trump card of stopping debate by referencing Nazis. The possibility of upholding the peaceful, constitutional, democratic Czechoslovak republic behind its Bohemian Bastion mountain ranges gets conflated with making a stand in Southeast Asian jungles to defend an autocrat or plunging into Mesopotamian deserts to preempt a tyrant. With the Soviet Union gone, it is "fascism" that finds its way into this muddled thinking, as in the increasingly embarassing term "Islamo-fascist." To have branded the latest menace with so retro an epithet as "communism"—a byword for archaism and failure—would not be as morally resonant.

Talk of Munich had filled the air in Washington when North Korea invaded the south on June 25, 1950, nearly ten years to the day after France capitulated to Nazi Germany. Munich would echo during Vietnam, saturate arguments to invade Iraq, and raise the heat over Russia's 2008 clash with Georgia.

"Think of it as an opportunity to confront Fascism in 1920," General John Abizaid, head of U.S. Central Command, which covers central Asia and most of the Middle East, said about America's invasion of Iraq during a speech at Harvard. "If only we'd had the guts to do it then." It would be difficult to find a British or a French officer of that rank who would be so historically obtuse: "fascism" in 1920 meant Mussolini, and he didn't seize power for another two years. Meanwhile, in Germany, the movement humbly claiming to be the little brethren of fascism had eleven members.[29]

Otherwise astute, historically minded journalists such as Christopher Hitchens and Michael Barone get equally confused when calling on those pre–World War II years to explain their support for having backed the invasion of Iraq. Because Hitler and Stalin struck a momentary alliance in 1939, they say, it was natural to expect Al Qaeda "Islamo-Fascists" to collaborate with the anti-Islamic-oriented Baath party of Saddam, an avowed admirer of Stalin. But, first, such an Al Qaeda/Baath party pairing up never occurred. And, second, the prospect of it ever happening in any way comparable to the ghastly Teufelsfreundschaft between Hitler and Stalin was remote. That "Devil's Friendship" would have been unlikely had Hitler and Stalin not previously liquidated the ideologues in their respective movements. For better or worse, Al Qaeda hadn't wiped out any of its own fanatics, a prerequisite to working with anti-Islamist Saddam.[30]

Grave operational illusions also arise from analogies based on World War II itself. As the Iraqi insurgency took root by late summer 2003, Rumsfeld, Rice, and Cheney each explained the violence by raising the specter of Werwolfkommandos—"SS officers," said, Rice, who "attacked coalition forces . . . much like today's Baathist and Fedayeen remnants." Pundits echoed the theme of "Nazi-like" killers in Iraq.[31] Except such tales of defiance in the heart of Europe at any time during the Allied occupation were entirely make-believe, as historians in the Pentagon had warned.[32] What there had been of Werewolf units had closed down like good obedient Germans with the Reich's surrender, never having gotten into gear. Yet the changes in strategy needed to meet a growing, full-blown Iraqi insurgency were delayed; administration publicists as well as such useful think-tank analysts as Brookings's Michael O'Hanlon imagined that America was merely facing Saddam's fanatic "dead-enders" rather than enraged popular movements.[33]

Paul Bremer of the Coalition Provisional Authority was similarly lost in another century. He and his staff spent a lot of effort during the first eighteen months of occupation matching week-by-week charts of apparent U.S. progress in Iraq with the week-by-week U.S. accomplishments in the 1945–46 occupation of Germany. He touted one hundred indicators of success in Iraq. It was a fantasy of time and place, as if American Expeditionary Force commander "Black Jack" Pershing's generals in the Rhineland in 1919 had set out to make sedulous comparisons with the U.S. Army's capable occupation of the Confederacy in 1865.

• • •

By late 2009, President Obama was audibly studying Kennedy's approach to Vietnam to guide his decision making on Afghanistan. A new foreign policy myth then emerged once he ordered in thirty thousand more troops: Kennedy, it was said among those who disagreed with this decision, had instead chosen *not* to escalate, indeed had steadfastly "held the line" against ratcheting up. Except that is not how journalists and the Republican National Committee saw it in 1962. Instead they exposed the fact that the growing U.S. presence was a lot more than "advisory." President Kennedy, clearly embarrassed, parsed his response: the soldiers were "not combat troops in the generally accepted sense of the word."[34] But of course they were, call Green Berets, SEALs, and other fighting men what one might. Decision making by analogy becomes all the trickier when history gets muddled.

As might be expected, the planners of the Vietnam War themselves drew on a rich mix of analogies. Munich would be heard of frequently, but mostly it was later in the tragedy, when America found itself in desperate combat and the stakes had to be ever more dramatized. "Kennedy and his counterinsurgency enthusiasts considered Malaya, the Philippines, and Greece to be the more pertinent analogues to Vietnam," explains Oxford political scientist Yuen Foong Khong in *Analogies at War*. "The administration of fine-tuners fine-tuned their analogies as well." Bundy and Secretary of State Dean Rusk particularly used the Greek regime's tenuous survival during 1947–50 as an example of successful American "police action." Kennedy himself examined the dollars spent, the U.S. military mission's training duties in Athens, and the relatively few advisers committed. Yet it was soon enough apparent how irrational was any comparison of that reassuring "police action" to the utterly different one metastasizing in Vietnam.

Once the initial attempts at counterinsurgency failed in Vietnam, the Korean War became the prevailing analogy for internal analysis as well as public justification. Elite opinion had shifted magically. The U.S. Army's drive to the Yalu was wished away, and the longest of American retreats went unmentioned. Images of victory in Korea shaped the decisions to escalate in 1964–65, helping to explain why America pursued a war of attrition. The impact of the Viet Cong guerrillas was discounted. International aggression from North Vietnam had to be met. As in Korea, the North could be thrust back by conventional U.S. divisions and airpower. References to Korea also rationalized America's early reverses as well as Saigon's dismal leadership. America, after all, had rebounded from the initial defeats in the summer of 1950 that had nearly thrown U.S. forces off the peninsula. It had eventually built up the Republic of Korea's army to formidable strength. South Korea had been held, *and so could South Vietnam.*

Bundy brought together two sets of analogies, remarking that policy derived significantly from "the lessons of the thirties and of Korea." [35] George Ball, the far-seeing number two at the State Department, marginalized himself in the councils of the Kennedy and Johnson administrations by opposing U.S. involvement, later reflecting that "Practically everybody thought that Vietnam was another Korea." His boss, Secretary of State Rusk, certainly did, and China again appeared to be the predator.

Dean Rusk was a dignified Georgian lawyer, a Rhodes scholar, then a professor at Mills College who served with distinction as a colonel in the China-Burma-India Theater during World War II. A fast-rising assistant secretary of state for Far Eastern affairs early in the Korean War, he was to be appointed president of the Rockefeller Foundation in 1952, and came to Washington with John Kennedy in 1961. No one was more open-minded toward different places and people: he had zero qualms about his daughter marrying an African-American when that was illegal in seventeen states of the Union. Though overshadowed during most of his years in office by National Security Adviser McGeorge Bundy, he had full opportunity to press his well-intentioned views of uplifting Asia. He is the longest serving post–World War II secretary of state, leaving Washington in 1969 with LBJ.

When Bundy had departed as national security adviser three years earlier, he was replaced by Walt Rostow, a professor of economic history at MIT before joining Kennedy's State Department. Rostow, the adviser who had counseled a "High Noon stance" in Vietnam, allied himself with Rusk. Operational carryovers ensued. The "same analytical methods," averred Rostow, would now be employed to select targets for U.S. bombardment of North Vietnam—an agricultural land with few industrial hostages—that he had used to select bombing targets in Germany when he was with the OSS.[36]

The Iraq War, like Vietnam, is unlikely to diminish this national style of analogizing. The habit endures in part because Americans know little about the overall exercise of their country's power since World War II. It is a vagueness about the recent past that reaches deep into the country's leadership as well as into intellectual discussion. That is why even Yale's John Lewis Gaddis, known as the dean of Cold War historians, can conclude that Americans "proved surprisingly adept at managing an empire." And year after year, significant inaccuracies on pivotal events—such as when and how the "missile gap" was finally debunked in 1961—get repeated despite readily available evidence.[37]

Ceaseless analogies between present times and the beginning of the Cold War demonstrated this imprecision toward the end of the last presidency: Secretary Rice spoke of the Bush administration having laid a policy groundwork in the Middle East for the next fifty years, as Acheson and Marshall had laid one in Europe. Finally, the History Boys drove the Korea analogy full circle: President Bush suggested that an ongoing large American presence in Iraq could be like what he called "the Korean model," in which sizable U.S. forces have remained in South Korea since the 1953 armistice. That is unlikely to be in the cards, either in Iraq or Afghanistan. The absence of a clear division between two sovereign countries, like the armistice line, is but one difference to consider. In Iraq and in Afghanistan, the "38th Parallel" would lurk around every corner, everywhere and nowhere.

America's political leadership could barely conceive what the country faced after 9/11. "It's impossible for someone to have grown up in the 50s and 60s," said the president, "to envision a conflict with people that just kill mercilessly, using techniques that are kind of foreign to you—to modern warfare—but it's real."[38] Real, that is, as if the Viet Cong had been using their punji sticks and plastique on Mars.

In Bush's lifetime, and those of other American leaders today, the country has repeatedly confronted unconventional warfare, insurgency, and transnational terror. Such an inability to contextualize the violence of 9/11, of Iraq, and of Afghanistan might be expected of politicians, and many national security experts. But our military commanders also lose context, though it is their duty to study the continuities of war.

America's record has been disturbing when we look at the country's three major wars since 1950. The reasons vary, but this ominous history cannot solely be laid at the feet of the civilian emergency men. In Iraq, concludes Thomas Ricks, "perhaps the worst war plan in American history" confused swift entry with victory. In Vietnam, there was a "dereliction of duty," in the words of Brigadier General H. R. McMaster, by the Joint Chiefs in their failure to insist that LBJ's attrition/graduated escalation strategy would likely fail. In North Korea, America endured its terrible retreat.

The blunders are united by a common illusion that too many commanders share with emergency men: an abiding belief that an enemy's lack of particular strengths is the same as absolute weakness. "They can't beat us on the battlefield," generals as well as politicians insist. "They just cannot defeat the United States military." [39] With minor variations, those judgments have been voiced in all three wars, and now in Afghanistan—and are equally beside the point. One reason they keep echoing is that the U.S. military, like the rest of America, convinces itself that the next war, like any great event involving the nation, will be entirely different this time—either unconnected with previously ugly lessons or distanced from past experience by hard-won but finally thorough learnings from past mistakes. It's a comforting belief that rests in part on faith in the Next New Thing, the latest technology that, as science fiction philosopher Arthur C. Clarke defined it, is likely "indistinguishable from magic."

Americans are uniquely receptive to the hottest magic—from the universal availability of the automobile to the opening of the electronic marketplace. Largely trained as engineers, the country's command cadre may be the most enthusiastic of all. There was a "cult of the new" at the Pentagon in the run-up to Iraq, conclude the distinguished co-authors of *Cobra II*, but we've seen overconfidence in technology many times before. The magic that MacArthur expected to hurl against the People's Liberation Army was strategic airpower. In Vietnam, it was to be helicopters providing radically mobile and dispersed airborne assault capacities, an advantage the French never had. And in Iraq the silver bullets were to include breakthroughs in information technologies sure to grant decisive, unprecedented "dominant knowledge" of the battlefield—enabling a relatively small force to blow away the fog of war and make lightning-fast decisions. Or so thought the largely civilian theorists of military transformation until reality did not match their doctrines. The result of this continuingly seductive yearning is that the soldiers, like the emergency men, will soon enough find themselves "winging it," in the words of Marine Corps Major General James Mattis. [40]

"Self-delusion about the character of future conflict weakened U.S. efforts in Afghanistan and Iraq," explains McMaster, previously commander of the 3rd Armored Cavalry Regiment in Iraq's Tal Afar and a trained historian who wrote *Dereliction of Duty: Lyndon Johnson, Robert McNamara, the Joint Chiefs of Staff, and the Lies That Led to Vietnam.*[41] Currently directing concept development for the army, he could have said the same thing about Korea and, again, about Vietnam. The self-deceiving faith in high-tech wizardry keeps being followed by amazement—whether after a few agonizing months, as in Korea, or painful years, as in Vietnam and Iraq—that "we are engaged with a thinking enemy" and that America is facing, as now in Afghanistan, "a far more sophisticated adversary than expected" with "Taliban leaders showing a surprising level of sophistication and organization." "They're not stupid," exclaims a marine after a firefight, "and they don't make the same mistake twice."[42]

So too in confronting Al Qaeda and its offshoots: the report that President Obama demanded after the Christmas Day airliner bomb plot concluded, in January 2010, that "the government's counterterrorism operations had been caught off guard by the sophistication of a Qaeda cell."[43] By May, Washington was startled that the Pakistan Taliban could reach into Times Square. Consistently, commanders, and their civilian superiors, cast the runes to make the enemy suit them—patronizing the opponent and then deceiving themselves that they are fighting the enemy they want to fight.

MacArthur's headquarters could not envision China's rugged peasant soldiers advancing without supply lines, in quilted white jackets. When U.S. reconnaissance aircraft passed overhead, these tough veterans simply lay down in the concealing snow and then attacked at night, during blizzards, or in morning fog to negate U.S. airpower. In combat, they were presumed to gain the upper hand by relentless, mindless "human wave attacks"—except often the tactics used to drive the GIs and Marines back down the peninsula could better be described as a high level of "infiltration assault" through small-unit encirclement at night. During the next war, the North Vietnamese Army felt no more compulsion than did the Viet Cong guerrillas to fight according to U.S. manuals, preferring their own style of jungle warfare as they moved in and out of the shadows. They kept adapting, from the intricate tunnels of Cu-Chi to the lone Viet Cong frogman who sank the USS *Card* with an explosive charge in 1964 to maintaining the Ho Chi Minh Trail's complex of roads under B-52 bombardment.

Napoleon said that the prime military sin was reliance on "making pictures" of the world one wants, not the world as it is deadly likely to be. Korea, Vietnam, Iraq, and now Afghanistan have filled a whole gallery of picture painting. For instance, "those people that just kill mercilessly" get dismissed routinely as "cowards" whether during the Vietnam War or in the current struggle. And opponents are branded alike as "terrorists" whether they plow a truck full of explosives into a playground in Pakistan or, in contrast, wipe out a CIA targeting team right within a U.S. forward operating base on the Pakistani border, as did a Jordanian-born Palestinian physician in December 2009.[44]

The enemy may indeed use terror, such as mass executions in Korea or pedicab bombs in Hue or truck bombs in Baghdad and Kabul, but that barely describes his talents. And throughout we're revolted by his embrace of suicide—whether it's China's "human waves" at the Chosin Reservoir, the one-way missions of half-naked Viet Cong sappers crawling with satchel charges into Green Beret firebases, or Dr. al-Balawi's attack. It's always a fresh revelation of the enemy's inhumanity, whether he's Oriental or Arab or Pashtun. Pathology, of course, is what the other side manifests: "heroic sacrifice" is what one's own side performs. As usual, the denigrating labels become standard wartime rationalizations of fear and anger that work only to a clever enemy's advantage.

Other refrains familiar from Iraq and Afghanistan echo through the decades: "population protection," "infrastructure development," "expansion" of the indigenous army, and arguments that there can be no "military victory" and that civilian deaths by napalm or 2000-pound bombs "contain the seeds of our own failure." Unfortunately, those are just a few of the verities once again to be relearned. The army not only forgot everything it had been bloodily taught about counterinsurgency in Vietnam, as is now well-known, but—in Vietnam—it had forgotten everything it had learned about counterinsurgency in Korea as well. In Korea, the armed services—consumed by turf battles, by a rivalry with the new CIA's ambitious operatives, and preoccupied by faith in air strikes—came belatedly to raiding, counterinsurgency, and conducting guerrilla warfare of their own.[45]

This movie has truly been seen before. "The war will be won by brains and on foot," the British officer who had served as a defense secretary during the Malayan insurgency of 1948–60 had told Kennedy in 1963 about Vietnam, warning that U.S. air supremacy would mean little.[46] Yet some forty years later, as violence worsened in Iraq, the U.S. Army had to catch up fast by offering a crash course in counterinsurgency, repackaging old knowledge as new.

By 2006, the *U.S. Army/Marine Corps Counterinsurgency Field Manual*, written under the direction of General Petraeus, with rarely acknowledged input from the Marines, had attained such popularity among policymakers and defense intellectuals as to be reprinted by the University of Chicago Press. *Foreign Affairs* described it as "a coffee-table staple in Washington."[47] To be sure, it provides a pragmatic interpretation of the topic for the battalion-level officers and NCOs at whom it is aimed. And its potted history might be instructive. Today's problems, however, differ markedly from guerrilla resistance to Bonaparte on the Iberian Peninsula, and so, too, from twentieth-century counterinsurgencies in such highly contrasting theaters as the Malay Peninsula, Kenya, Algeria, and Vietnam. History is here being used to provide reassuring reference points as well as some vague empirical support that might enable U.S. fighting men and women to make a bit more sense out of the corrupt disorder of invertebrate states.

But the wider excitement over the *Field Manual*'s oft-described "paradigm-shattering content" is hard to share.

Readers learn that the key to successful counterinsurgency is to protect civilians and that "sometimes, the more force is used, the less effective it is." That revelation is accompanied by calls to synchronize "military, paramilitary, political, economic, psychological, and civic actions." Yet this common knowledge was bitterly learned on the ground decades ago. To pick just one example, see Jeffrey Race's *War Comes to Long An: Revolutionary Conflict in a Vietnamese Province* (1973) in which a former lieutenant explains how ruthless communist insurgents used populist appeals to run a key southern province—and how the U.S. Army offered the worst response possible.

Thermonuclear war called for genuine reconceptualization; the ancient conflict of the more developed urban sections of the state with the resistant backlands has been all too well documented for millennia. Meanwhile, other modern classics sit on the shelf unread, such as Lawrence Durrell's *Bitter Lemons*, which describes how a few passionate malcontents in the Cypriot "Enosis" movement were able to manipulate an otherwise undefeatable British garrison to lash out at a previously affable population: before long, people responded with ambushes, abductions, and with the homemade bombs that, fifty years later, would be known to the U.S. military as improvised explosive devices, or IEDs.

Nonetheless the *Field Manual*, laced with history, is right now the *newest thing*, to its readers in uniform as well as to civilian decision makers around the Washington coffee tables, and it comes with a star-power imprimatur.

After eight years of war in Afghanistan, a new U.S. general arrived to reapply the wisdoms of counterinsurgency. He repeated the point that civilian casualties are counterproductive, that killing the enemy is not so important as winning over the population, from offering medical care to seriously engaging such men who end up as mayors and imams, and that efforts must be redoubled to ensure humane treatment of detainees. "It's all about people," insisted General Stanley McChrystal when he took command in summer 2009. Might not the Vietnam mantra of fighting for "hearts and minds" have also come earlier to light?[48] By then counterinsurgency had "become almost a religion," says Paul Pillar, a twenty-eight-year CIA veteran who now teaches at Georgetown. Other savvy observers call its disciples a "cult" and the entire current preoccupation a "fad, as it was in the 1960s."[49]

General McChrystal was being described in Washington as "a rising superstar" in the mold of Petraeus even before he took over in Afghanistan; "Stan McChrystal all but invented counterterrorism," gushed a prominent think-tanker with the faux familiarity and historical obtuseness of the academic carried away by knowing the top brass.[50] This remarkable officer was trained as a Green Beret and spent a year each during his rise to four stars as a fellow at the Kennedy School and then at the Council on Foreign Relations; when he insisted by autumn 2009 that "there is no *alternative*" to committing more troops, this was backed by reassuring policy-oriented credentials.[51]

But ultimately we encounter a profounder discontinuity than all this shattering of paradigms. U.S. commanders speak of our forces likely having to spend another three, four, five, or more years in Afghanistan—and they've already been there for nine. Yet generals who believe they have a decade or more to defeat insurgents are forgetting their Clausewitz, the preeminent practical philosopher of the Napoleonic War experience. War is an instrument of policy. And the policy world of a modern developed society is filled with a hundred substantial priorities—global warming, swine flu, bond ratings, steroids—while less advanced societies, or determined factions therein, can focus on one life-consuming cause. Thus insurgents can suffer for a decade or two, while their enemies get more quickly distracted. American impatience naturally sets in to bring dismal, protracted experiences to a close as we get on with something new.

To dramatically expand America's Special Operations Forces, as the Obama administration is doing, doesn't avoid these obstacles. Green Berets, SEALs, and other elite units project an illusion all their own that appeals to a politician. They seem to offer clandestine, relatively cheap, and "surgical" solutions, as in today's increasingly aggressive behind-the-scenes assaults against far-flung radical groups. It's an enchanting vision right out of the Kennedy years—and full of the same possibilities for secret wars soon to be followed by big messy commitments.

In one of the more memorable White House encounters of the Vietnam War, an aide confided to Bundy: "The thing that bothers me is that no matter what we do to them, they live there and we don't, and they know that someday we'll go away and thus they know they can outlast us." "That's a good point," replied the national security adviser.[52]

7.

WE'LL SHOW THEM THE LIGHT

"THE BALLAD OF THE GREEN BERETS," SUNG BY AN ACTUAL Special Forces soldier, Sergeant Barry Sadler, swept to first place on the pop charts and stayed there for five weeks in 1966. It served as a rearguard tribute to the idealism in action of President Kennedy's worldwide New Frontier: those "fearless men who jump and die . . . for those oppressed." Twenty-three years later Sadler would be shot to death in a domestic dispute outside a Guatemala City bar. In between, the Vietnam War had mustered the Special Forces front and center in the national imagination; by the 1980s, counterinsurgency missions in Central America usually appeared, at best, to be commitments to lesser evils. Sadler's parabola makes him a sadly representative man of U.S. involvements—from the hopes of bringing a bold all-American democratic leadership to Southeast Asia, to the bitter sequel of repeated entanglement in the squalid world of client states.

The ballad would play often in the months after 9/11. Well-coordinated twelve-man Special Forces "A Teams," some on horseback, helped to rout the Taliban from Kabul. In the years thereafter, as the country fought on two fronts, it would be stirring to hear the ballad sung by the 82nd Airborne Chorus, particularly at reunions of aging Special Forces veterans from Vietnam. The motto *De Oppresso Liber*—"To Free the Oppressed"—means as much to today's operators as it did when contesting the night against Viet Cong terror. "It is what we do," a young Special

Forces lieutenant colonel recently told a visitor to the Green Berets' tightly secured compound within a sprawling U.S. forward operating base in Iraq. "We defend freedom, whether here or in Afghanistan or around the Sulu Sea." His sergeant major joined the discussion as two captains, one near fluent in Arabic, the other in Farsi, joined in. The sergeant had twenty-eight years in Special Forces and had been among the first into Afghanistan, where he had been gravely wounded at Mazar-e-Sharif. "We uphold the rule of law," he said matter-of-factly.

The conversation at the firebase summed up the spirit of *De Oppressor Liber*, and of core American beliefs: humanity is one; all peoples prefer the freedoms that the United States offers; and to such ends, we can find in ourselves the skill, strength, and determination to bring this about when needed, decently and without arrogance. It is how we like to see ourselves, and how we often are. Only later will suspicion arise that the price of justice in the painful regions outside the advanced democracies comes so high as to make order preferable on most any terms.

Why are Americans convinced that we can transform other people about whom we know little, that just about everyone truly wants to be like us, and that we can easily help them become so? Why would Americans want to? Why does an Illinois industrialist, say, who would never think of placing one of his factories in Hue or Samara, nonetheless switch off his bunkum detector when the supposedly informed leaders of his country assert the urgency to democratize South Vietnam, Iraq, or now Afghanistan? And then what happens when he discovers that much of the sacrifice is in vain, and that even what has been presented as a pressing moral as well as strategic problem just can't be solved?

• • •

Faith in the ability to transform others comes strongest to those who have successfully transformed themselves. Belief in transformation, redemption, and recurring makeovers is due to more than being a country of immigrants. It stems from deep ethical traditions and material experiences.

National surveys show that about 50 percent of the American people claim to be "born again." For longer than its life as a nation, the Republic has had, as G. K. Chesterton observed, "the soul of a Church." Not that this compels religion per se. Rather it is a spirit of generous convergence that arises from being the only nation in the world founded on a creed, as laid out with the face of reason in the Declaration of Independence. To this end, Americans find it logical that other people can be equally enlightened, even converted. When we reach out, we expect other countries to be pervaded by our visions with similar alacrity. Are not the redemptions of Germany and Japan after World War II supreme examples?

This intoxicating good news has taken many shapes and has had numerous motivations over the generations—secular and religious, private philanthropies and government concerns. A combination of moral certainty, excitement, and confidence permeated the lyceum movement's drive to send missions to Latin America in the days of Van Buren. It infused America's presence at the first general diplomatic gathering that the country ever attended—the 1880 Conference of Madrid concerning the standing of Morocco; the United States showed up in order to speak for Morocco's brutalized Jews. We see that creed appearing too in the far-from-selfish rebuilding of Europe after World War II; and it is also apparent in the efforts after 1991 to uplift the struggling pieces of the Soviet wreck. "Would we ever have done that for a collapsing United States?" asked Genrikh Trofimenko, renowned professor at Moscow's Diplomatic Academy. "No, to put it mildly." [1]

The doctrine of the moment can almost automatically mobilize moral energy and assent, whether it seeks to conciliate the Politburo through a spurious "détente" or to substitute some halfway temperate polity for the dark passions of Afghanistan.

"We are responsible for the maintenance of freedom all over the globe," John F. Kennedy emphasized, as would President George W. Bush, who insisted "we have a duty to free people." Such conviction could not have been stated better by the Special Forces colonel in Iraq and, to believe the account of former White House press secretary Scott McClellan, this determination "to free people" may have been the preeminent reason for war in 2003.[2] *De Oppresso Liber* still imparts a driving impulse to involvement in the hills beyond Kabul, even though a new administration insists that the United States is no longer committed to Afghan "nation-building." Besides the great-power anxiety about upholding U.S. stature in the eyes of friends and opponents, few Americans are so weary as to see Afghans left to the tender governance of the Taliban. Yet.

Americans of both parties want to frame their country's role in the world in moral terms. Britain's Foreign Office is unlikely to experience a spasm of excitement over "transformational diplomacy," as recently did the State Department, whose top functionaries were instructed as a matter of the latest cause to set about building democracies worldwide; and as democracy slips in Francophone Africa, the Quai d'Orsay doesn't think twice about siding with despots.[3] If relatively uninterested in foreign policy, Americans are intense on principles, as was characteristically apparent in the lead-up to Iraq. The bill of particulars for invasion made no mention of the hard, real U.S. interest in oil. It was as if Saddam's despotism had been located on the Central European plain. For millennia, great powers have used transcendent principles to justify their wars and interventions. But Americans take such justifications seriously enough to act on them, repeatedly.

To be sure, one shouldn't push the moral element in American energy too far as an explanation of why we believe that other people—friend or foe—just can't wait to become like our intensely pragmatic, good-hearted selves. A nation that destroyed the tribes through the Indian Removal Act, and whose leaders aligned with the likes of Trujillo, the Shah, Somoza, and, for over a decade, Saddam Hussein, is unlikely to be single-mindedly principled. But when it is, take great care. Highly moralistic peoples can be dangerous indeed as they set out to spread the word. They mean very well. Their intentions are noble. So the compromises that result along the way, when they notice them—civilians killed by U.S. munitions, dictators befriended for the sake of "stability"—are purely secondary costs of the larger undertaking.

Moreover, Americans believe that their good news of practicality and high ideals can be spread rather easily. Here's where crass material experience comes into play. Our faith is reinforced by observing the global response to American popular culture. Such shared tastes encourage us to hear the "dreamtrain of wishing for democracy," as James Mann, former *Los Angeles Times* bureau chief in Beijing (home of sixty-eight Starbucks) calls the American equation of economic with political liberalization.[4] If Madonna, *Rambo II*, Coke, Ford, rock, Apple, and McDonald's are received so enthusiastically in Caracas and Novosibirsk, surely we can believe that the principles of 1776 will go down just as easily. But even though Starbucks's green logo also shines in Mecca—as in other modern, cosmopolitan, and ethnically diverse cities worldwide— this promises nothing about transforming the divine politics of the holiest venue of Islam. The roilings of material culture can be matched with just about any form of political and religious order.

We keep assuming that people who imitate us are more or less inclined to believe with us. The "dreamtrain" keeps chugging on, drawn by the perennial hope that even consumerist, capitalist, but far from democratic China must click over into a constitutional mode with the same zeal with which it has embraced the stock market. It is an illusion of resemblance that might have been disproved rather spectacularly by Saddam Hussein's campaign theme song during the Iraqi election of October 2002: Whitney Houston's "I Will Always Love You" played incessantly over loudspeakers as he gathered 100 percent of the vote.

Throughout this faith in the power of resemblance runs the conviction that the world wants to be reasonable on American terms. Vast and various peoples are eager "to fully join the progress of our time," as a U.S. secretary of state has defined it.[5] Whole peoples are expected to forget immemorial bloody pasts and yesterday's bombing of a Jerusalem pizza parlor or of UN schools in Gaza. This goes beyond faith in management. We get our hopes up that other people can see our light: Israelis and Palestinians, Sunni and Shia, Burman and Karen.

Spreading American ideals worldwide also requires placing a lot of faith in nominally democratic processes in a lot of fraught places where the U.S. approach can best be described as "winging it." The fraudulent 2009 Afghan presidential election is just one exemplary disappointment, the greater for being so publicized. In Vietnam, U.S. determination to stay the course was reinforced by what the White House hailed as "the 83 percent turnout" in Saigon's 1967 presidential contest. It was the "keystone," said the *New York Times*, "in President Johnson's policy of encouraging the growth of constitutional processes."[6] The balloting had indeed been relatively honest. But by then lots of people in South Vietnam, as well as an increasingly cynical U.S. press, couldn't believe it and, in any event, the victors' opponents were thrown in jail right after. Elections become magic rites of their own. People stand in line for hours and choose a paper slip or get their thumb dunked in purple ink—simple deeds, but often true acts of courage. Meanwhile, Americans assure themselves that ancient worlds are changing as they watch, though the locals are unaware.

R. James Woolsey, who formulated the objective of "Athen-izing" the world, was a Washington lawyer who moved in and out of government as an arms negotiator and top Pentagon appointee for the Carter, Reagan, and George H. W. Bush administrations. His achievements at Stanford and Yale and as a Rhodes Scholar combined with a calmly authoritative demeanor to encourage his friends to liken him to Mac Bundy. He became Bill Clinton's first director of central intelligence but was unable to establish a rela-tionship with a president minimally focused on the mechanics of foreign policy. He left within two years, soon to join Booz Allen as a management consultant. By 2003, a decade after he went to Langley, few people in the capital were more eager to invade Iraq than he. After all, he had appeared on CNN within twenty-four hours of 9/11 to suggest Iraq's complicity. The following year, as Congress debated whether to authorize President Bush to use force against that country, Woolsey insisted that Saddam Hussein had also been connected to the 1996 Oklahoma City atrocity.

At the start of the Iraq venture, he rationalized pressing de-mocracy on the rubble of Baghdad in one overarching phrase: "It's not Americanizing the world. It's Athen-izing it. And it is doable."[7] North Korea was to follow. And this purpose could be applied to Afghanistan, Woolsey claimed, and potentially to Syria, Iran, and Saudi Arabia as well. He didn't identify the Afghan Socrates or Plato; such revelations would come about through U.S.-sponsored elections and the rule of law—though, first, "I think we ought to execute some airstrikes against Syria" (when Israel was at war with Hezbollah in 2006).[8] Here, "Athen-izing" would be accomplished through airpower. Today his public com-ments are more tempered; having stepped back from "the case for bombing Iran," he speaks only of "economic pressure" to compel a halt to its nuclear weapons program.[9] But listening to such a smart, erudite, and deeply experienced man talk about "democracy" and America's use of force is unlikely to help our Illinois industrialist to know which source of foreign policy wisdom to believe.

Democracy, after all, is what Stephen Potter, author of mocking self-help books like *Gamesmanship, One-Upmanship*, and *Supermanship*, labels an "OK word," one of those terms invoked to fill needs rather than to clarify issues. They buy time and blur objectives. They are a valuable part of the mantras of officialdom—with *democracy* being foremost in Washington. One of America's old clients, however, had a more refined interpretation of the sacred word. Knowing something about moral compromises, and not bothering to care, General Rafael Trujillo, the sadistic U.S.-backed "Benefactor" of the Dominican people until his assassination in 1961, memorably described his governing philosophy as "neo-democracy." For America, however, he provided "stability," then as now a prime "OK word" as well. So did the Shah of Iran, whose police state is still fondly remembered today by some observers in Washington, such as *Post* columnist David Ignatius, as a "nascent democracy." [10] And so does Mubarak in Egypt and the House of Saud. Here the United States routinely displays extensive flexibility and patience.

"We always raise democracy and human rights," said Secretary of State Hillary Clinton to Egyptian democracy activists. "It is a core pillar of American foreign policy." [11] Just so, but will anything "rise" forth when summoned? And we don't have to venture to the Middle East for evidence. We have only to cross to the western side of Hispaniola, the island split between the Dominican Republic and Haiti, to encounter a prime example of noisily promoting democracy and undercutting it. Seven hundred miles from Miami, Haiti grabs periodic U.S. attention when it labors under ghastly tyrants or, as in 2010, horrific temblors that drew in 22,000 American military service members to provide humanitarian relief. But the previous well-intentioned U.S. involvement—1994's

"Operation Uphold Democracy" intervention—simply replaced crude thugs in uniform with courteous crooks in suits, while deluding ourselves that the United States had "liberated Haiti from decades of dictatorship." [12] At least ecumenical America upheld one of the five freedoms enshrined in the Bill of Rights: voodoo symbols could not be used in leaflets calling on Haitians to remain calm during the U.S. intervention, the White House instructed the landing force, because that would show support for one religion over another.

Other great powers have cultivated myths about their ability to transfer, if not to impose, their ideals. They too have believed that less fortunate peoples may readily be made to undergo, at last, a benevolent reworking. But the British Empire's white man's burden and France's *mission civilisatrice*, for instance, were different. No one in Whitehall or at the Quai d'Orsay presumed that such ends could be accomplished overnight, or simply by appearing on the spot with good intentions, great examples, and lots of money (and guns). No one expected to charge into India or Algeria, demonstrate generosity and perhaps bestow tutorials about the "rights of man," and then turn the place back to the locals in, say, five years. Yet even when the U.S. took the Philippines from Spain in 1898, trying its hand at a brief episode of imperialism, it disembarrassed itself within a short lifetime—July 4, 1946, the Philippines' long-scheduled independence day. Nothing like a good example.

Americans take it for granted not only that other nations will sooner or later assimilate themselves to our exemplary ways, but also that an outright enemy will likely be converted, smacking his forehead and exclaiming, "How could I have been so wrong?" as American ideals finally sink in. This is part of the myth that surrounds the end of the Cold War. It would seem that Gorbachev, for reasons unknown, suddenly changed his mind about the tyrannical system that it had long been his profitable career to enforce, tearing open his society in 1987 and letting in the light.

We bring our hopes for conversion right into the war zones. Lieutenant General Douglas Stone, who commanded all U.S. detention facilities in Iraq through 2008, calls this process of conversion "the battlefield of the mind." Here again a particular type of expert must play. It's a battle to be won with American "psychiatrists, psychologists, counselors and interrogators [who] help distinguish the extremists from others" among prisoners trapped in a detention morass that offered no means of establishing who was likely guilty of anything in the first place. General Stone approached his charges through a process of expert counseling that "replaces their destructive ideology" with more fruitful ideas. Thereafter, under his successors also, prisoners demonstrate the sincerity of their conversion before being returned to the street, which is always the last resort of politicized penology. They are subjected to a polygraph—the weird-science partner of the softer aspects of magic—to prove that they have been "unbrainwashed" and "de-radicalized," as former homeland security secretary Michael Chertoff described the longed-for results.[13]

But how much does "brainwashing" have to do with the dangers that truly confront America? To what extent does this tangle of Oprah self-help, biofeedback electronics, and pop deprogramming therapies lead anywhere remotely reliable? All we know for sure is that General Stone would review "an overhaul" in 2009 of the troubled American-run prison at Bagram Air Base outside Kabul, as well as the jails of our Afghan allies. The chairman of the JCS has ordered all field commanders to "redouble" their efforts to treat detainees properly, though in 2010, a federal district judge ruled that Bagram's screening process was even "less sophisticated and more error-prone" than that applied at Guantánamo—which the Supreme Court had found inadequate. Nearly a decade into the Afghan war, concern arose that arbitrary and brutal imprisonment just might prove a splendid recruiting ground for the Taliban.[14]

Leave aside evidence that America's opponents are besting us at changing hearts and minds; Americans not only keep believing that entire cultures can be made over, but that this can, of course, occur fast. Our tempo of change, greater than that of any other country, fosters the illusion that if given half the chance other people will adapt at the same speed; they'll throw off their old ways while joining us for a sprint into the future. Sooner or later, this all-American faith will prove again to be a source of bitter letdown. Expecting more than "neo-democracy" out of post-Soviet Russia is an example.

"You are going to the most changeable country in the world," young British diplomats are still instructed at the Foreign Office before heading west. America has few qualms about radically repudiating great slices of its past. American life has conditioned us to know that no moment, however proud, can endure, and that sooner or later the established order will be brushed aside. Even our literature reflects this awareness: *The Last of the Mohicans, The Last Puritan, The Last Tycoon, The Last Hurrah, The Last Picture Show.* No other nation has such a sense of dramatic transience in its writings, not Russia, France, Britain, Germany, or Japan. In the process, Americans consistently jettison illusions on the home front, most powerfully those of race and gender. Almost at the same time, tens of millions of Americans fruitfully, it would seem, change their minds overnight. Surely people in other countries can do so, too, disenthralling themselves from their old, brainwashed ways as pawns of "extremism."

Frustration follows American hopes for the malleability of other cultures, and we act on that, too. In 1966, after spending several weeks in Vietnam, radical investigator-journalist I. F. Stone captured this toxic, demoralizing, morning-after taste: "The young Ivy Leaguers arriving briskly at the Embassy of a morning. . . . Under the supposed benevolence of our policy one soon detects a deep animosity to the Vietnamese and a vast arrogance. We assume the right to remold them, whether they chose to be remolded or not." [15]

Similar enthusiasts—even if not "Ivy Leaguers," who are now more drawn to Wall Street, management consulting, and to law than to foreign policy—can be seen today dashing in and out of embassies in Baghdad, Kabul, Sana'a, and the usual roster of places barely registered by America until the next "crisis" bursts out. What ill feelings result come less from animosity toward an Iraqi or Afghan than from impatience. "Get on with it!" demand those supervising the remolding. Local soldiers don't show up for joint patrols at dawn with a 1st Cavalry Brigade Combat Team; their politicians funnel aid dollars to Credit Suisse Private Banking. Soon arises—not once but again and again—from the Green Zone or a Kabul compound the cry "Why can't these people get their act together?" It can be heard alike from embassy officials who should know better and from grunts in the dining facilities of the supersized U.S. bases.

In his autopsy of America in Vietnam, Thomson wrote of "the subliminal belief that we are smarter, cleverer, just better" than those whom we presume to set about uplifting. He even raised what he called the "unprovable factor" of racism to try to explain America's conduct as it shoulders a providentially bestowed task to bring a brighter future to others: "Would we have pursued quite such policies—and quite such military tactics—if the Vietnamese were white?" A similar question is asked today in the Middle East. "They all look alike" can be the unifying factor as Americans conflate peoples as different as Egyptians and Palestinians, with stereotypes abounding, as in debating "whether or not, you know, Muslims can self-govern," and concluding that "Arabs' fear of dogs" is helpful for interrogation. [16]

Resentments accumulate, which is why Iraqi prime minister Nouri Maliki proclaimed "a great victory" when the 2009 bilateral security agreement required U.S. troops to pull out of cities and towns. The nearby archipelago emirate of Bahrain offers another wearying example of dislike. Tehran's officials menacingly describe Bahrain as "part of Iran"; the United States maintains a navy base at Manama, the capital. But in Manama itself, seat of our ally the Emir, people fly black flags in front of neighborhood shops and houses to signify *Americans not welcome here*, particularly U.S. fighting men, including special operators on their way to Afghanistan.

America backs with its unparalleled wealth what, today, is Washington's sincere hope, more often than not, for democracy. And it's a degree of wealth that itself separates us from other countries. Wealth shapes our international behavior, and our image. It brings with it the freedom to make wide-ranging choices well beyond common sense. We simply are not bound by the practical constraints that more or less immediately drag upon most, if not all, other nations. As in Vietnam, the United States can double down in Iraq and in Afghanistan on its hopes of not just breaking the spirit of terror but, one way or another, of fostering America's vision of a world set free.

A more significant aspect of the disorientation that comes with wealth has actually gone unnoticed. Expansive ambition arises from the giddy sense of omnipotence that can accompany the windfall of *sudden* fortune. And America is, not for the first time, *newly* rich. The country has accumulated by far the greatest part of its resources in this lifetime. To have the new-rich knowledge that more money is easily come by lays us further open to a sense of possibility unmarried to risk. We can embark on such truly quixotic ventures as trying to turn Iraq into "a normal democratic country," replete with a thriving tourism industry "in a year or so," according to AEI's Frederick Kagan in 2008, who advised the U.S. Army on what *New York Times* columnist Frank Rich calls "the supposedly magical powers of the 'surge.' "[17]

Sudden wealth blinds us to the many things that still can't be bought, such as reconciling the millennial antipathies of Sunni and Shia beyond finessing a decent interval for U.S. withdrawal from Iraq. Meanwhile the $25 million bounty for bin Laden goes unpaid, as did the billions in development aid pledged to Hanoi by Johnson and then by Nixon, if only North Vietnam would give up its ambition to reunite a nation several times older than the Republic. America is like a Silicon Valley billionaire who believes that, sooner or later, everything has a price. He is only momentarily surprised to lose a slice of his capital when a new, apparently extraordinary investment falls flat. With entrepreneurial optimism, he takes his knocks, forgets the last failure, and plunges on to the next venture. Sometimes his journey is rewarded. But it is still a magical progression, because the illusion is one of fundamental invulnerability and endlessly renewable success.

"Each and every time we have to relearn how to do this," says James Dobbins, a Foreign Service pro, former special envoy to Afghanistan, and author of the mischievously titled *Beginner's Guide to Nation-Building*.[18] He draws on insights from experience in Somalia, Bosnia, Kosovo, and Haiti—weighing best practices and assessing the different elements involved, such as the administration of justice and humanitarian aid. Afghanistan, however, is the "place where every mistake ever made in an underdeveloped economy is being repeated," and in which U.S. participants found reconstruction funds being pulled from under them as early as 2002, when Washington's attention shifted to Iraq.[19] The U.S. inspector general who monitors this largess in Afghanistan argues that the difficult lessons of accountability from the U.S. reconstruction effort in Iraq—which saw $53 billion go to economic and governance assistance that Iraq's planning minister says has had no discernible impact—have yet to be applied. But that's partly because his office wasn't created until 2008.

Half a century ago, President Eisenhower also swooped into Kabul. "Faces were weather-beaten, often hidden by full beards and turbans, more than faintly similar to biblical pictures of the time of Abraham," he'd write in his memoir, *Waging Peace*. "Few, if any, women were present."[20] His visit presaged the arrival of the American engineers who would soon after start to build an asphalt artery between the Afghan capital and Kandahar. That "Eisenhower Highway" epitomized how Americans threw money at places of which few of them had heard. But it did not take long for the usual Afghan wars to turn the gift into a ribbon of rubble. Prosaically renamed "Highway 1," it required four years of reconstruction after the U.S. Army descended in pursuit of bin Laden; and only five more years after that for U.S. soldiers to call this three-hundred-mile road the "Highway of Death."

Secretary Clinton calls the record of aid to Afghanistan "heartbreaking" as vast amounts of waste turn out merely to be short-term fixes to complex, long-term problems, insoluble with more cash and concrete. Others call it a "nightmare."[21] Meanwhile, our Illinois industrialist grows skeptical about what a lot of this frantic activity has to do with keeping his grandchildren off gas lines and out of wars. It does not take the chairman of the Senate Foreign Relations Committee to recognize, as when the country was escalating in Vietnam, that had Americans been offered any sort of referendum on foreign aid, they would have soundly rejected just about all of it.

Whatever Afghanistan's future, retrospect is likely to show 2009 as a pivotal year. It went barely noticed outside the bureaucracy that the Agency for International Development, the federal government's key organization to provide economic and humanitarian assistance, had no director in its headquarters in the Ronald Reagan Building. That high political appointment went unfilled amid competing claims from the Office of Presidential Personnel and from Capitol Hill. Without an administrator in place, according to Charles Allen, who has been working on DABS, the new national electric utility corporation in Kabul, "a lot [was] on hold because this means that the assistant directors, the office directors, even some consultants, all know that we're essentially on temporary duty." It was like trying to run a business without a CEO until an impressive new administrator—Ragiv Shah, M.D., a political appointee from the Gates Foundation but welcomed at the State Department as "a superstar waiting to be discovered"— briskly took office in January 2010.[22]

Of course, there are many inspiring examples of benevolent American outreach. The U.S.-funded programs against tuberculosis in Pakistan are unambiguously successful, boosting detection rates in a country where seventy thousand die annually of this curable airborne disease. Girls' schools are being opened in Afghanistan, and in Iraq's Diyala Province dollars go to providing wheelchairs to children without legs or feet (unsettling though it is to look more closely at how they lost those limbs). Yet all around the troubled world, Americans face an ugly reality learned the hard way in Vietnam: money cannot elicit enduring loyalty when the price for accepting assistance in the villages is murder in the dark, and when it is too dangerous for aid workers to travel outside the capital.

The incisive *New York Times* columnist David Brooks offers a capsule wisdom about effectively altering hearts and minds. "If you're going to do nation-building," said this early advocate of the Iraq War, "you have to understand the values of the people you're going to build a nation with."[23] His point, old news in Vietnam by 1967, reveals more about notionally well-informed American elites than about Iraq or Afghanistan. It illustrates the ignorant goodwill of the clever initiator who sweeps forward magnificently—from new uncomplicated beginnings to messy disillusioning endings; an intellectual's version of Sergeant Barry Sadler's journey.

America has indeed helped to transform devastated nations. Barack Obama, for instance, has promised a "Marshall Plan for the 21st Century" with development assistance as a vital step toward global security: "That was true with the Marshall Plan, and that must be true today." And President George W. Bush vowed to lead an international effort to rebuild Afghanistan on the model of the Marshall Plan. Pakistan has demanded "some kind of Marshall Plan" for Afghanistan.[24] But comparisons to the Marshall Plan, which heaped today's equivalent of $100 billion on Western Europe after World War II, just don't fit, and attempts to replicate generosity on anything approaching that scale disappoint. After all, it was applied to highly developed, capably administered nations. And there were startlingly few violent enemies on the ground, however many strikes the communists fomented.

The original Marshall Plan succeeded because American objectives fit hand-in-glove with the structures and dispositions of the societies concerned. American strengths of drive, material resources, and optimism were playing to the similar if battered strengths of Europeans stricken by war but still richly endowed with wealth and talent. The plan was more pump-priming than a new reservoir. Yet ever since, just about any problem that exhibits a conspicuous gap between wealth and poverty—and that appears to overlap U.S. security concerns—has brought forth earnest calls for another "Marshall Plan": Vietnam, the Balkans, the Middle East, recently Haiti, though that cry has faded fast.

It is profoundly magical thinking to believe that one or another great success can be replicated in entirely different conditions. The Marshall Plan was indispensable to reviving postwar Europe. But committing billions of dollars and all-American levels of intense effort to South Vietnam, or Iraq, or Afghanistan will not similarly lift those places to peaceful, let alone democratic, prosperity. Still we try, and even attempt to adhere to what seem like the timelines that had worked long ago.

Meanwhile, we try to communicate better—and all the more intensely so since 9/11. "The most powerful woman in advertising," Charlotte Beers, a former CEO of Ogilvy & Mather and account manager for Frito-Lay, was therefore recruited into the high ranks of the State Department soon after the terrorist attacks. Her assignment was to launch a mammoth Madison Avenue campaign—ranging from forests of booklets to years of broadcast time—to refurbish America's image in the Arab world. There was no need to know anything at all of the Middle East or of Islam; advertising is advertising, and the worlds of *Mad Men* PR and of the souk meet through a U.S. government Arab-language TV station called Alhurra, which Arabs refuse to watch, and a radio network called Sawa. By the time she quit on the eve of the Iraq invasion, the office and the ad campaign were in chaos.

She'd be followed as undersecretary of state for public diplomacy by White House political adviser Karen Hughes, though Hughes as well had never seen a minaret before she embarked on helping her country "do a better job of engaging the Muslim world." Now President Obama's appointee in this role, a former CEO of Discovery Communications (parent company of the Discovery Channel) and former general counsel of MTV, tries to build bridges, one stated purpose being to "to try to understand the source of much of the anti-Americanism in Pakistan," a land where 59 percent of the population—after decades of U.S. fine-tuning—tells an Al Jazeera poll that the United States is the biggest threat to their country.[25]

Having more experience in the world than these new arrivals in government, the chairman of the Joint Chiefs puts their efforts at "strategic communication" in rather obvious perspective, and concludes that this is a war that the United States has been losing. "We need to worry a lot less about how to communicate our actions and much more about what our actions communicate," says Admiral Mike Mullen. "Each time we fail to live up to our values or don't follow up on a promise, we look more like the arrogant Americans the enemy claims we are." It's a reason, he might have added, why, in 2010, Al Qaeda is still better at communicating its message on the Internet than America is.[26] Mullen then takes the truly outsized American next step of urging that we must therefore battle Afghanistan's "culture of poverty" and proposes initiatives no less audacious than fixing the whole Afghan polity and society. But wealth is far more easily transferred than the attitudes that created it.

The world-remaking rituals got rebooted when a new administration arrived in Washington. President Obama ordered seventeen thousand additional troops to Afghanistan in March 2009 and "AfPak" Special Envoy Richard Holbrooke urged an overhaul of public diplomacy programs. Think-tankers who double as advisers to the military—including Frederick Kagan and his spouse, Kimberly Kagan, who runs a new organization, "the Institute for the Study of War"—wrote an op-ed that month stating, "There is no doubt that we can succeed against these much weaker foes," comparing the Afghan insurgents dismissively to those in Iraq. By August, however, a new vision was on offer once these foes were discovered to be not so weak after all. Mrs. Kagan joined Brookings expert Michael O'Hanlon and participants from CSIS, Brookings, and AEI to urge "significant escalation" as they unanimously insisted "there is no alternative to victory." They were also channeling General MacArthur's testimony to Congress in 1951 after disaster near the Yalu. Catastrophe was the alternative, they argued, in an urgent opinion that had nothing to do with Democrat or Republican, liberal or conservative.[27]

Counterinsurgency has been called "armed social science." Yet as we proceed in Afghanistan, even the most well considered of PowerPoint policy recommendations read like parodies of the social-scientist-in-uniform pitches that cloyed in the Vietnam jungles. One of the most comprehensive from CSIS starts with "Ensure valid goals for going to war" and includes "There is no governance without security," "Development goals must be realistic," and "Strategic communications . . . will be an illusion unless the host country government wins popular support," binding all this together with the insight: "The national culture or cultures . . . will decisively reassert themselves over time."[28]

The last conclusion at least bears repeating: it's being encountered in the U.S. attempt to build up indigenous forces, and fast, if not for nation-building than at least for "stability" with the hope of an early American exit. But a nation's way of violence can be as distinctive as any other part of its culture, a fact that American timelines also overlook.

Afghans, for example, have anciently excelled as private-enterprise killers in a world of minute but intense feuds, running competent special operations in their own neighborhoods, though these excitements have for the moment been sedated by a U.S.-government-furnished "education program on ethical practices" and lessons in proper interrogation.[29] Iraqis can be characterized as individually brave but anarchic, which is a kind description of its army's current, unremedied logistical problems. Plus third-world security forces can be burdened by their own forms of magic. For the Iraqis right into 2010, that has been in the form of a small, handheld, bomb-detecting wand. U.S. advisers knew it to be as useful as a Ouija board. Yet Iraq's security forces spent around $85 million over two years on these charlatan devices with reassuring swiveling telescopic antennas. They've been brandished at hundreds of checkpoints as a substitute for the physical inspection of vehicles, and were a major factor in the security blunders that enabled the urban truck bombings of 2009–2010. But it has been a herculean task to disenthrall the Iraqi police from their faith in this sorcery. The general who heads the Ministry of the Interior's Directorate for Combating Explosives has insisted that he doesn't care "whether it's magic or scientific."[30]

Neither the Afghan nor the Iraqi forces, alas, have yet displayed the raw material and what turned out to be the hard-won professionalism of the reconstituted 1.2 million man Army of the

Republic of South Vietnam, which was going into action by 1972. Despite a mixed quality of leadership toward the top, the ARVN, contrary to myth, turned out to be excellent. But even this was not enough for the United States to succeed by that late date. Kenneth Moorefield fought alongside the ARVN as an infantry captain. Today he is the Defense Department's assistant inspector general for special plans and operations, responsible for assessing the progress of Iraqi and Afghan security forces. "Pound for pound, the ARVN's fighting men were about the best in the world—except for the North Vietnamese Army."[31] He wishes that he could again be serving with something like it.

Rory Stewart of Harvard's Kennedy School is the author of *The Prince of the Marshes*, as well as several other particularly instructive books, and was formerly a British soldier and intelligence officer. Competent in some four languages, he has directed a work-development foundation in Kabul. He comes closest among current observers of the Afghan struggle to offering the insight that James Thomson contributed during the Vietnam War. Stewart's piece "The Irresistible Illusion," in the *London Review of Books*, sums up all the familiar perspectives that certain temperaments bring to bear on the world, including the nightmares of "failed states" and "global extremism"—which, of course, can be stilled by counterinsurgency, Western-sponsored elections, and multibillion-dollar development projects.[32] Stewart dismisses the "final dream of 'legitimate, accountable governance'" in Afghanistan. It's an illusion, he explains, that "makes our policy seem a moral obligation, makes failure unacceptable, and . . . does this so well that a more moderate minimalist approach becomes almost impossible to articulate." And he underscores that a central deadly defect in this current struggle is the fact that Americans are particularly unwilling to believe any problem insoluble. So cut deals with the Taliban? Consider the likelihood that a lesser U.S. armed presence may be greater, that the more the Predator drone campaign works, the more it fails? Put up with the Taliban returning to power, if its chieftains and warlords take sides against Al Qaeda, or at least don't harbor their former guests? Such alternatives run smack into the moral exaltations that influence U.S. policy. Or at least they do so for a while.

Determined resistance to evil takes two forms. One is exemplified by the emergency men already introduced: urgent action, confrontation, conscious decisiveness, and a resolve to forcefully hold the line against forever-erupting "crises." The other mode of resistance draws on a different moral script: the enemy can be won over by our idealism and sincerity. It's an approach that distills the revivalist conviction that the world—friends and enemies alike—will come forward to be saved by the better qualities of human nature as dramatized by the citizen do-gooder in work-boots and jeans. This is the man or woman who builds habitats for humanity, and who believes that, if we can just get alongside those who wish us harm, the sheer force of our goodwill and moral experience will convert the misguided. If Jimmy Carter is not in the pantheon of emergency men discussed so far, he has no less of their certainties, good intentions, and authentic horror at the world's dangers.

The representative emergency men above—President Kennedy, Defense Secretaries McNamara and Rumsfeld, McGeorge Bundy, Dr. Kissinger, and Vice President Cheney—are each in their different ways establishment figures. They were as familiar with Washington as they were with the Council on Foreign Relations. But Carter cast himself as a professional outsider, a product of the South: a commodity grower, a governor who slept on people's couches to save money, a Christian who played up being "born again" to a degree that would have embarrassed any other presidential candidate before George W. Bush. In demanding "a government as good as its people," he ran noisily against the established elites. Indeed, he denounced the last cadre of emergency men, Democrat and Republican, who had brought disaster: war in Vietnam, rates of unemployment and inflation unprecedented since the start of World War II, the stain of Watergate.

A truly presidential-sized ego, however, lay behind the energetically asserted humility and mechanical smile. That is once more apparent from the title of his recent book *Palestine: Peace Not Apartheid*, which presents itself as a call to reconciliation for Israelis and Palestinians but invokes that supercharged term *apartheid* to describe Israeli practices in the West Bank and Gaza. It is a word he was willing to claim as his own rather than hiding behind the robes of his fellow Nobel laureate, South Africa's Archbishop Desmond Tutu, who had first so described the Israeli occupation.

Jimmy Carter believed himself both an embodiment of popular virtue and a manifold expert in many disciplines. He called himself a "nuclear scientist" during the 1976 presidential campaign; hyperbole going on falsehood that only matched the absurd claims by the Republican Party for the stellar diplomacy of the Nixon/Ford years. In reality Carter was a competent nuclear engineer and the only president so far from the high-tech U.S. Naval Academy. He served in the navy's rigorous fledgling nuclear submarine program before resigning his commission in 1953 to keep the family business going. No matter what one calls a student of nuclear power plant operations, he was nonetheless the most technologically qualified president ever.

He brought a sharp intelligence to Washington when he arrived in January 1977, knowing more than enough to be justly shaken by the nuclear demon thrust into his hands. The rest of what he needed to know could surely be bridged by moral certainty, and he didn't conceal his disgust with his predecessors' foreign policy, particularly deploring Kissinger's enthusiasm for "kissing China's ass."[33] But he was committed to furthering the Nixon/Ford "détente" overtures to the Soviet Union, including yet more arms control deals. He believed devoutly that the fitting response to the Politburo's brutal ambition was to get it to understand truly and exactly America's sincere longing for peace.

Even more than most presidents, Carter thought he was changing the world. Speaking out with moral clarity is a kind of laying on of hands. He intended to remake things existentially—not by Green Beret advisory teams, as Kennedy had tried, or by "linkage" of a grab bag of foreign policy issues, as had Nixon and Kissinger. Instead he would do so by championing human rights and by changing the hearts (and then the minds) of suddenly illuminated friendly dictators and even outright opponents, as in Moscow.

The remaining fifty thousand U.S. troops in South Korea were to be withdrawn, he insisted in 1977, until this proved an idealism too far—North Korea five years later getting around to dynamiting to death half of Seoul's cabinet. But there were some good instincts. At a time when experts spoke of "the decline of the United States as an economic and industrial system," as some do again today, Carter had the plain businesslike foresight, however ineptly acted on, to call not just for energy conservation but also for freeing America from dependence on foreign oil. And he began to champion a Palestinian homeland, already comparing the Palestinians' plight under occupation to that of American blacks under Jim Crow—while, at Camp David, he rammed through a peace agreement between the Egyptian president and the Israeli prime minister, leaders who had each tried to escape that particular summit. And not a shot has been fired in anger between Egypt and Israel for more than thirty years.

Carter's relations with foreign leaders were highly personalized, as might be expected from a man who believes that his own sincerity can be grafted onto all vast troubled humanity. For instance, he unctuously welcomed the Shah of Iran to the White House in 1978—and then refused to communicate with him fourteen months later as that tyrant tottered to his fall, though a dialogue might have been useful when it was important to keep this suddenly fleeing client out of the United States. With a catastrophic evenhandedness, Carter also refused to communicate with the triumphant rebel, Ayatollah Khomeini, and forbade U.S. diplomats to do so either.

Carter got the old emergency religion soon enough, once the Soviet Union invaded Afghanistan in December 1979. Party secretary Brezhnev had "lied to me!"—a fairly standard piece of Russian imperialism taken personally, given Brezhnev's earlier platitudes. Carter called for spending $1 trillion on defense over the next five years, an average real increase of 5 percent annually. He declared that America would go to war against any "outside power" (there was only one) that might try to control the Persian Gulf, only a stone's throw, it sounded, from the Afghan mountains. And, as has been forgotten, he also modified the U.S. nuclear doctrine of "mutual destruction" by approving a concept—shaped by defense intellectuals appointed to the Pentagon, and drawing on the guidance of Samuel Huntington, to be known for *The Clash of Civilizations*—of a "countervailing strategy."[34] Henceforth the United States intended to destroy select Soviet military targets first, getting Moscow to give up before an all-out exchange that would bring down civilizations everywhere. Disillusion an idealist and you get *real* trouble.

Only one other president has insisted that he saw into the souls of men, even the brutish interior of Vladimir Putin. And only one other president has so personalized the search for peace in the Holy Land. Speaking of the Islamist movement that had swept the Palestinian legislative elections (and that Washington brands as "terrorist"), Carter emphasized that "Hamas has committed to me" its readiness for compromise. In turn, George W. Bush discerned "a man of peace" in Israeli prime minister Ariel Sharon, better described by scholar Avi Shlaim as "the practitioner of the most savage brutality towards Arab civilians."[35] Each president invokes his "Heavenly Father" not only to pray to for guidance in the gravest decisions, but to assert afterward that God has discernibly offered it.

Other emergency men have been convinced that they'll solve intractable problems like the Arab-Israeli antagonism (or Vietnam, or Russian truculence, or Afghanistan) through their own stellar capacities. In contrast, Carter, like Bush, has been at home with miracles, his authority while in office resting on a divine presumption to which neither Lincoln nor Washington dreamed of laying claim.

Today the Middle East is the primary realm of American fantasy. It's a very real place that we turn into a fantasmagoria of mystery and morality plays—akin to the contradictory ways in which we once regarded the Orient in the days of opium dens, nobly suffering peasants, crazed rebellions, and merciless potentates. "We might think of Arabs as being not too different from us," says Jonathan Brown, a professor at Georgetown University's Alwaleed bin Talal Center for Muslim Christian Understanding, "but many also think of them as uncivilized relics from the Arabian Nights."[36] Americans may care little about foreign affairs, and the Illinois industrialist will cheerfully acknowledge being vague about African or Latin American excitements. But everyone believes they know the Middle East, the lands where all three great monotheisms began, the sphere of permanent emergency, year in, year out. Chances are that the "3 A.M. phone call" to the White House is going to relate to a crackup in the Middle East.

The Israeli/Palestinian antagonism is the most dependable emergency of all, and one inseparable from U.S. national security, no matter how constructed. It defies reality to believe that U.S. entanglements in the conflict don't undercut America in the Muslim world. Al Qaeda has long asserted Israel's dispossession of the Palestinians as one of its reasons for being at war with America, bracketed by the U.S. military remaining in Saudi Arabia after the Gulf War and by the loss of life in Iraq caused by the sanctions that followed. "It's illusory to think that Israeli policy doesn't spur a wider radicalization," adds Brown, "let alone when those policies are enforced by US-supplied F-16s and cluster bombs." General Colin Powell has long argued that the biggest step America could take to counter ideological support for extremism is to help resolve that antagonism—and it's a core security interest addressed starkly by General Petraeus before Congress in 2010: "The conflict foments anti-American sentiment due to a perception of U.S. favoritism toward Israel."

However one interprets the Muslim extremists' maelstrom of aims, it's stirred by the "Green Zone-ism" surrounding the U.S. presence. Richard Cohen, the columnist who coined the term, applies it to the basing of Middle East policy on imaginary worlds. Fantasies include the "raising" of democracy through pro-American oligarchs as in Egypt and Saudi Arabia; seeing U.S. opponents as no more politically driven than zombies as they rejoice in their slaughters; and the growing fantasy, only intensifying by 2010 as Israeli settlements expand into cities, that negotiations can achieve a viable Palestinian state.

Presidents Carter and George W. Bush sought a *solution* that would establish two enduring authentic sovereignties—the ritual invocation of "two states living side by side." It is a reasonable-sounding ideal. To both men it is not only a humane vision but also an attempt at common technical progress: this piece of land will be given up for that piece, changes of heart will follow, a legitimate order will ensue. But to treat the Israel/Palestine dilemma as a fundamentally manageable issue—even a soluable problem—requires a whole set of illusions and self-deceptions. This all raises the question of what pragmatic, problem-solving, and ethical conclusion Americans might come to when they realize that—after enormous expense of money and hope—a problem simply has no solution, indeed after "solution" has become a mocking "OK word."

Well, we play out the illusions into grim indefiniteness, believing that we're working in our own enlightened self-interest. We apply our national style of analogy-making to the dilemma. In this case, not only can the Israeli/Palestinian antagonism be solved, but precedents abound in which deep-rooted conflicts of nation, culture, religion, frontiers, *have been* solved. Ireland is an example, and George Mitchell—former Senate majority leader and later special envoy for Northern Ireland—has been President Obama's Special Envoy to the Middle East. Just as the wounds of Ireland began to close when the intensity of American goodwill was brought down on both sides, so should bitter memories of mass killings in Gaza, or of a bus bombed in Jerusalem.[37]

But behind the tone of disinterested American friendship, the Israeli-Palestinian dilemma presents an array of big, zero-sum differences. "We found it absurd that sovereignty was being discussed between two parties, when one of those parties kept constructing towns and highways in the territory of what was being examined as a sovereign state-to-be," says Michael Durkee, a veteran Foreign Service officer who until 2009 was the deputy special envoy for Middle East regional security (viz. Israel and Palestine). "They [the Israeli government] tried to game us throughout, as they did the Bush White House," he adds, "getting [then national security adviser Stephen] Hadley to focus on the minutiae of which border crossing they'd agree to open at nine A.M. or eleven A.M." And here the "us" being referenced includes the special envoy at that time, General James Jones, currently President Obama's national security adviser.[38]

White House rebukes of Prime Minister Benjamin Netanyahu in Spring 2010 didn't just result from a dispute over the latest housing project, U.S. anger stemmed from this Israeli tactic of focusing only on procedural issues as settlement construction continues. Yet the Israeli settler constituency and its destinarian supporters are an inherent, and explosive, element of the Israeli state—which makes a one-state solution, as Carter now sees it, "more likely than the present debacle."

Meanwhile fantasies accumulate. We keep trying to convince ourselves that America is an evenhanded mediator and that it is "raising democracy and human rights." But this is hard to reconcile with the unequalled amount of foreign aid extended to Israel, including U.S. tax breaks to pro-settler organizations that underwrite self-described "gated communities," over the same four decades that Israel has defied repeated U.S. censure of its expansion into occupied territory.[39] To try to maintain an ostensibly evenhanded posture, we also convince ourselves that the side we know the less of is inevitably intransigent, though the dehumanizing language that Israelis and Palestinians throw at each other is equally chilling, and both sides have killed and maimed Americans of goodwill.

Desperate to find one side primarily culpable for unleashing terror, we often blame the Palestinians for shedding more innocent blood. It's a simplification that is hard to reconcile with the Israeli record, whether the thousands of civilians killed during the 1982 Operation Peace for Galilee invasion of Lebanon—with the "indiscriminate" bombing and shelling of West Beirut that President Reagan denounced as "a holocaust" to Israel's prime minister—or the 2009 judgments of the report of a UN fact-finding mission led by the respected jurist Richard Goldstone, which accused Israel of deliberate attacks against civilians during December 2008–January 2008.[40] Palestinians and Israelis offer similar rationalizations. Hamas ludicrously calls Israeli civilian deaths a "mistake"; Israel, in turn, has its own excuses for the nine dead on the *Mavi Marmara*; for more than a thousand in Lebanon during 2006, including U.N. observers; and for 106 refugees at Qana in 1996, too, with Israel dismissing that international investigation—by the United Nations and the Dutch military—as well.[41] Terror by definition makes us lose perspective as we witness appalling acts against noncombatants, meant specifically to horrify. Whether terror is the flailing recourse of the weak or the formal, uniformed kind offered up by the state, the outcomes are the same. To this end, it is increasingly difficult to see Israel as unquestionably an American moral interest.

Despite all of the country's dreams, ideals, and optimism toward the world, Americans, who under pressure show themselves to be in their deepest involvements intensely practical people, ultimately return to conduct that suits themselves. Here's a test case for how firmly America, this time—after inconceivable disappointments, miscalculations, and reversals in Iraq and in Afghanistan—holds to its overseas illusions.

To that end, a U.S. reassessment of the Israeli relationship is likely to arrive as Israel finds itself unable to integrate a Palestinian majority population within the single state that its current policies are bringing about. As the terrible context of Israel's founding recedes, the trade-offs to U.S. interests will be assessed as a whole. And here the record also consists of nuclear proliferation, which includes Israel having been "absolutely vital" to apartheid South Africa's nuclear weapons program that resulted in six Hiroshima-size bombs; inflicting on Washington "one of the most devastating cases of espionage in U.S. history" in 1985; and, nearly twenty years later, "deceptive" sales of U.S. military technologies to China. By 2010, more than settlements lay behind Vice President Biden's statement in Israel that "What you're doing here undermines the security of our troops."[42]

Ultimately, an ever more diverse America is likely to feel ever less impulse to uphold an arrangement by which an already expelled population is kept under armed foreign sovereignty. America failed in its principles of refuge when the Jewish people were in stark danger seventy years ago. But as often occurs when disgrace in one land and time is being made up for in a very different context, the price is incoherence, dishonesty, and a host of new angers.

It is a cliché in Washington that the United States is committed to Israel on any terms—but clichés wear out, and we don't know what "any terms" may be. But we do know that American opinion has a way of reversing itself at lightning speed. And we know the degree of bitterness that follows not just from overseas politico-military failure but from being unable to win peoples who we believe should be grateful for America's protection, aid, and goodwill. Moreover, we have also seen America distance itself from real kindred spirits before, such as the vibrant high-tech democracy of Taiwan, while still committing seriously to security guarantees, as could be extended to a single democratic binational state embracing Israel, Gaza, and the West Bank.

Roughly every American generation for at least 150 years has committed itself to a grand venture of democratic conversion of another culture, not too different from the recent one of having attempted to transform the "people and politics of the Middle East and the Moslem world."

Forty years before invading Iraq, America was gearing up for Vietnam. Forty-five years before that, America had pledged itself not just to war, but very quickly to the certainties of the "War to End All Wars," as many Americans rode the high tide of Woodrow Wilson's inflexible idealism. Commitment to the anticipated "democratic revolution the world over" and an international order that that would guarantee went deep—but the sobering result was "a peace to end all peace." Forty years back from this disillusion, the United States found itself at the end of Reconstruction (1865–77) attempting to bring the victims of the just-defeated slave power into the American nation, and to do so fast. But the idealism that had asserted "equal protection of the laws" also fell victim to fatigue and politics. (*A Fool's Errand* was an enormously popular book of the time.) Once it proved more difficult than expected to remake a culture so different from that of the North, hopes for Reconstruction collapsed: a campaign of organized terrorism and the reluctance to deploy federal troops any further ensured that America returned to its business of doing business.

Each time, there comes about a "shift in policy," whose practical outcome is a wearily accepted minimalism, a pursuit of "stability" as the highest object of statesmanship, and, perhaps, a diminished concern with justice. Magic, of course, lies in the belief that purposes so good as *De Oppresso Liber* must be impossible to thwart: "My strength is the strength of ten, because my heart is pure," sings Sir Galahad—and, for a while, we join in the chorus. But then we awaken.

CONCLUSION:
FINDING OUR BETTER ANGELS

Confirm thy soul in self-control . . .
Oh, Beautiful, for patriot dream
That sees beyond the years . . .

—"AMERICA THE BEAUTIFUL," BY KATHERINE LEE BATES

WE CAN SAFELY CONCLUDE THAT THE AMERICAN FOREIGN POLICY establishment is not up to the task of world leadership as posed by the country's far-flung political and military involvements, which it has done much to create. In particular, what's not up to the task is the "national security establishment," meaning the think-tankers and professors, appointees and former officials, lawyers, lobbyists, and businesspeople who concern themselves with the nation's security—in fact, most of those authorities at the Council on Foreign Relations, at the Aspen or the American Enterprise institutes or at the Kennedy or Wilson schools. There's a lot of talent among all these high-powered men and women, but also a lot of inherent unreality. This is no special deficiency of left or right, Democrat or Republican, and neither does it matter whether the players rally under the banners of Wilsonian idealism or Nixonian realism, whether they are nostalgic for the Kennedy excitements or the quiet triumphs of Reagan. Whatever the specifics of their compelling doctrine, most of these foreign policy enthusiasts hold to the half-dozen unifying illusions explored above.

The second conclusion derives from the first one: America will benefit from reducing its well-meant but readily militarized and poorly conducted ground commitments around the world. Time and again, American energy propelled by the valor of ignorance plays into the hands of our opponents, whether marching to China's border on the Yalu, throwing a half million men into Vietnam, or, today, playing all too dynamically into Al Qaeda's hands by setting out to remake Iraq, Afghanistan, the Middle East, while appearing to equate every Muslim resistance or independence movement with terrorism. Already a sober half of all Americans conclude that the United States should "mind its own business." It's silly to regard this as some outburst of "isolationist sentiment," rather than a levelheaded response to a lifetime of emergencies and to realizing that those responsible, no matter how exalted, are mostly winging it.[1]

A minimalist approach to the nation's security in no way seeks to restrain advancing America's advantages of industrial, financial, commercial, and cultural engagement with the world. In practice, this means continuously expanding trade, promoting our political values as convenient, and using force only when the nation's interests are directly threatened—as by the peril to European order that drew us into the Balkans a dozen years ago, the security of oil and international borders for which the Gulf War was fought, and the need to retaliate swiftly upon the murderers' lair in Afghanistan after 9/11. Dangers like these press so strongly on general world stability that they bring in major democratic allies, and even temporarily but genuinely useful troublemakers like Iran and Syria.[2] Such an approach entails deploying the full gamut of U.S. power: military strength need not be the first, or the second, mode of response. For example, cutting tariffs on manufactured imports from Pakistan may well be America's best step against extremism in that country by boosting its stability and prosperity.

A lower, less habitual politico-military profile would mean reevaluating the more than seven hundred military bases and stations around the world that compose an interlocking system of six enormous regional commands. It would also compel a higher level of justification—before Congress, before the country—when force may have to be used. So too when getting acutely into other people's business, such as treating every sign of China's mounting power as endangering America rather than as a natural advance from preeminence to an unsurprising hegemony in Asia.

It's also safe to assume that a lot of what Washington has been up to in Iraq, Afghanistan, and elsewhere since 9/11 wouldn't be occurring if the country's attention were focused by a draft. Let decisions be made as if there were indeed conscription. This degree of self-control requires an ongoing sense of proportion, a resistance to slogans, and realizing that no single seemingly crucial place of the moment—Afghanistan, Iraq, Vietnam, Georgia, Israel, or Taiwan, which was a key source of 3 A.M. phone calls to our parents' generation, and for which America was ready to go to nuclear war—is vital to our future.

America can no longer afford the expensive, dangerous learning curves that accompany each feckless foreign policy venture. Every time the geostrategic bubble bursts the more forthright of the would-be global architects admit all that they have just discovered about the world: "I didn't think it would be *this* tough"; the "society was more complex than I anticipated"; that failure, it's now realized, was "predictable in advance."[3] Much of the other half of national opinion will be inclined to agree about the United States minding "its own business" after two separate aimless trillion-dollar wars. The Iraq and Afghanistan nation building ventures have piled on debt unprecedented since World War II while America itself lags way behind other advanced countries, to pick just one indicator, in amenable mortality—that is, deaths preventable with timely and effective health care.

Can America accept a nuclear-armed Iran, and could it live at peace with, say, the Islamic fundamentalists who'd likely sweep any free election against our aging client orders in Egypt or Saudi Arabia? Perhaps. In any event, such crude endurable outcomes are preferable to the mayhem that would result from "surgical strikes," attempts at coups and countercoups, at destabilizing and propping up the many familiar parts of politico-military fine-tuning that ride on the notion of "fighting for the Middle East of the 2020s and 2030s," as *New York Times* columnist Tom Friedman justifies Washington's motivations.[4] After all, depending on how emergency men surge forward to interpret China's ambitions, we may in a couple of years be fighting once again, as we did in South Vietnam and North Korea, for "the future of Asia."

Skepticism contributes usefully to examining the persuasions of magic. To take a skeptical stance does more than raise questions or offer the clarity of hindsight. It can help to deliver answers about problems of ability or of the latest ringing doctrine. "The purpose of recriminating about the past," as Churchill reminds us, "is to enforce action in the future." So let us proceed sequentially through each of these six self-deceptions and work out how best to elude them all.

First, the emergency men. These will always be with us to some degree. Emergency men and women are part of the country's freewheeling enthusiasms, no more likely to be kept out of Washington than Wall Street. A big step toward restraining them and their urgencies, however, would be to limit the number of political appointees in the national security slots of the executive branch. There have been periodic attempts to reduce such appointments throughout the federal government for the sake of effective performance. What is proposed here is less ambitious but likely more significant, given the stakes and the track record. Although it can be difficult to catalog these national security positions, the roles that would generally be closed to political appointment would include the slew of undersecretaries, associate undersecretaries, assistant secretaries, deputy assistant secretaries, and directors at State and Defense, to which we may add those NSC staffers who are neither civil servants, Foreign Service officers, nor military. Equally their counterparts in the vice president's office should be limited. A lot fewer decision-making responsibilities would be left to the vagaries of political appointment. When it comes to national security, the arguments for business as usual, like those raised in the first chapter from long-time public servant Peter Rodman, have shown themselves too dangerous.

A strengthened Foreign Service as well as civil service would start to substitute. That there are currently more members of U.S. military bands than Foreign Service officers, and that Pentagon spending is some fourteen times greater than the State Department's budget, are Washington clichés, but nonetheless true. Let this be changed, as is already being endorsed by Secretary of Defense Gates as well as by Secretary of State Clinton.

Along the way, ever more talent would be drawn into the Senior Executive Service once it was less likely that a seasoned career professional would be elbowed aside by the likes of, say, Elizabeth Cheney, a thirty-six-year-old lawyer appointed deputy assistant secretary of state for Near Eastern affairs in 2002, to serve off and on between political campaigns until 2007—the civil equivalent of four-star rank. Men and women of such modest experience, whether in the Bush or Obama administrations, don't glide into public service as, say, vice chief of staff in the U.S. Army or a full general of the U.S. Marine Corps. Perhaps they would perform superbly, but we don't know. Meanwhile, we would have to deal with erratic conduct and the unneeded risks that stem from illusions about what could be accomplished and how—as has long existed among inadequately prepared civilian appointees entrusted with the nation's defense.

Emergency men will still abound among politicians, journalists, academics, and lobbyists in the national security arena. Defense intellectuals could still contribute as policy consultants to State and to the Pentagon, where there are hundreds of them already. And plenty of military-related advisory work remains to go around, as for our top brass in Central Command—though why U.S. generals seek policy and strategic guidance from national security academics is unclear, beyond the need to co-opt civilian opinion leaders. Of course, critically valuable outsiders should be invited into national security roles as needed, as in the case of the Obama administration's head of cybersecurity—a former chief information security officer at Microsoft who now reports to the National Security Council's principals. And, to be sure, the Foreign Service, like the civil service, also has its own emergency men and corner-cutters, even ambassadors profoundly weak in history. But despite exceptions all around, reducing the hands-on presence of political appointees would provide a ballast of somewhat boring, slightly weary professionalism against the ideological crosscurrents of each administration. That there should be fewer illusions of urgency and of certainty, and fewer emergency men with their hands on the levers, will have a ripple effect on the five other key modes of self-deception.

Second comes the mystique of management. A simple start to breaking away from it is to acknowledge what is intrinsically unmanageable. Four years ago, for instance, Princeton University's Project on National Security published the findings of an immense three-year undertaking funded by Ford, by other foundations, and by industry, chaired by two former secretaries of state and led by a professor who was to become President Obama's director of policy planning at the State Department. Leave aside that most of the conclusions could have been offered at any time over the last half century ("We need to reassure other nations about our global role and win their support to tackle common problems"), the title of the final ninety-two-page report reads like a parody of an American civics class: *Forging a World of Liberty Under Law*.[5] However noble a sentiment, these are "OK words" that perpetuate loose thinking rather than impose precision. Little is about to be "forged" by Americans in, say, Nakhodka or Jeddah, let alone structures of liberty and law as envisioned at Princeton.

Citizens should be alert to the absurdities of national security experts unable to recognize the things that lie beyond their rational control. Americans must be "competent occupiers" of Afghanistan, says the Brookings Institution's Michael O'Hanlon, who notes his advisory duties to General Petraeus, while his Brookings colleague Bruce Riedel, a former CIA officer and Obama White House consultant, insists that "we've got to fix Afghanistan's election fiasco."[6] Ultimately it becomes front-page news in the *Washington Post* when the capital's global architects decide *not* to attempt something as elaborate as trying to influence the internal theological struggles of 240 million Indonesian Muslims.[7]

Such grandiosity would be funny if lives weren't being spent. It's also a sign that sufficient due diligence—to invoke a necessary process for vetting management teams in business—hasn't been conducted before many of these well-credentialed men and women reach the influential positions where they can put their opinions into action. "How do you know that?" and "Why do you think that's realistic?" are necessary queries, but asked too rarely. These are questions that would be unremarkable in a boardroom; when lives are at stake, it becomes imperative to enforce similar reflection on energetic goodwill, and to compel the smart people around the table to justify the general principles that are otherwise so easy to sign off on.

• • •

Third is star power, much of whose enchantments in public life would be diminished once a higher proportion of long-term functionaries, rather than political appointees, is routinely assigned to key offices. Such people are less likely to be singled out as world-altering wizards or to delude themselves that they even have deep-going impact on the workings of this planet. Furthermore, they themselves will be more skeptical of all the self-identified "experts" that clutter the subject. And having seen America's overseas client heroes come and go over the years, their antennae will be up against the pretensions of the latest Ahmed Chalabi and his Washington supporters.

Much of the hype about national security wizards, magicians, and dream teams comes from the Washington press corps. Rather than naïveté, this uncritical enthusiasm shows that many journalists are far too close to the political elites with whom they interact socially and professionally as peers. Their own healthy skepticism erodes. They themselves can be emergency men and women, their sparkling, highly visible careers boosted by dramatic accounts of the nation's latest peril. The heated, usually wildly unrealistic reporting and commentary that Peter Braestrup, a correspondent for the *Washington Post* and the *New York Times* in the Vietnam War, called "crisis-journalism" has been going on for years, from "Matter of Fact" columnist and John F. Kennedy pal Joseph Alsop in the 1950s, to the "excitement that war was coming" that editor Evan Thomas felt in newsrooms in 2003, through to today's excitable commentators like Charles Krauthammer whose "existential" dangers leap regularly from television and the opinion pages.[8]

Readers, or viewers, keep in mind that even the best journalists get starstruck, and that particular enticements arise during wartime. Consider so superb a correspondent as the *New York Times*' Dexter Filkins. "Who owns the land here?" he quoted General McChrystal asking while visiting a dusty outpost along the Helmand River. "Is it owned by the farmers or landlords?" Filkins explains that "it was the sort of question a sociologist, or an economist, would ask."[9] Actually, it is a question that any good officer would ask, since the cry "Land to those who till it!" has made warriors out of peasants in countless rural despotisms. Moreover, generals who're turned into stars develop their own political constituencies in the capital, as did Westmoreland; it becomes difficult for a commander in chief to set them aside even when they no longer appear indispensible.

As for the truly dubious experts who intrude into the national security arena, it won't be easy to pry them off. Illusions of masterly ability continue even after incompetency has been exposed. Consider the most noxious example of magical expertise—the CIA "professionals" whose knowledge of interrogation wouldn't stand up in traffic court. To this day, we hear torture rationalized as so-called enhanced procedures that were "continuously monitored" by other supposedly star professionals; the walls against which detainees were slammed were "flexible," and waterboarding at such expert hands is an acceptable means of questioning. Despite all, such "experts" are even said to have produced results.[10]

A bluntly effective way to document how powerful is the spell of "expertise" in defense matters—as here exemplified in the dark side of counterterrorism—would be to establish a truth commission with bipartisan investigative clout. The purpose should be to place the story on the public record, since the Justice Department, in 2010, has forgone prosecution by concluding that Bush administration legal officials' merely showed "poor judgment" in endorsing torture. Let such a commission be akin to the already up-and-running Financial Crisis Inquiry signed into law by the president in 2009 and due to report at the end of 2010. If the shaky expertise and inadequate oversight of bond analysts and bankers can be placed under a cold light, so might the claims to proficiency of the assorted overnight authorities, such as the ones of interrogation, whom the nation ingenuously accommodates during "crisis."

Fourth comes the illusion of expecting wondrous results despite committing nominal intellectual effort to understanding a problem. A much-needed seriousness of purpose can be introduced by leading universities as well as by changes in the CIA.

For starters, universities can curb the habit of bestowing plum teaching positions for a year or two, sometimes more, on outgoing high national security appointees seeking a safe harbor. The custom is utterly bipartisan, the latest arrivals on campus having been from the Bush administration, but ones from the Obama years inevitably to follow.[11] This habit is why George Tenet, previously director of the CIA, became "Distinguished Professor in the Practice of Diplomacy" at Georgetown University, further using his time to write memoirs that expressed "shock" at the lack of thought behind the Iraq War, and why former Pentagon undersecretary Douglas Feith was "Professor and Distinguished Practitioner in National Security Policy," with a parallel appointment as "adjunct scholar" at Harvard's Kennedy School, while using his office atop Georgetown's Intercultural Center to explain that he had been guardian of the Geneva Conventions, his misguided colleagues being responsible for dispatching Muslims to CIA waterboarding.

There's no need to close the door on such positions. Some "formers," as Georgetown undergraduates call them, prove superb in the classroom. But the quality of instruction is going to be as arbitrary as the earlier capriciousness that distributed talent and the absence thereof among the national security slots at State, Defense, on the NSC staff. Such grace-and-favor faculty roles are unknown in physics departments or at medical schools. In national security studies, they are one more marker of how a huge, prestige-buttressed edifice fails to offer the dispassionate understanding that it might give.

Another way the universities can contribute to better thought is to assess how "national security," let alone the new calling of "homeland security," is being studied in the first place. As much an academic field as a field of practice, "national security" is troublingly unanchored. "Might you want to consider anthropology or computer science or Arabic to then someday *apply* it to national security?" I ask students at Georgetown, where I've taught for fifteen years. Usually not; they're eager to jump right into the mix and "make policy," playing for the highest of stakes before they have proved themselves at the humbler but harder-edged crafts upon which the structure rests. For the sake of seriousness, political science departments as well as public policy schools might just drop degree specializations in "security studies." They can instead demand more rigorous concentrations, such as in international economics, with perhaps "national security" being offered as a minor. It's also time for university presidents and provosts to examine the extent to which members of their own faculty get seduced by the excitements of "security studies"—including all the consulting, conferencing, and punditry—at the price of lasting scholarship.

At the CIA—whose knowledge gaps compromise the nation's security as a whole—intellectual shortcomings do not stem from hypnotizing star power, political patronage, or emergency-man excitements, but from the other extreme of organizational dysfunction. Few authentic talents from the outside enter this guild. The Agency has never been a place "full of people who had problems with authority," as outsiders, in this case the author and New America Foundation president Steve Coll, imagine it to be.[12] Rather than a hotbed of Jack Ryans or Jason Bournes, or indeed of maverick analysts such as William T. Lee, it has long embodied the insular, turf-obsessed office culture of a savings bank in Buffalo. Even more so than the rest of the national security establishment, the CIA has excelled at keeping all accountability at arm's length, which virtually guarantees poor thinking. Not even twenty-five-year veterans can recall a single case of someone being fired for failing to perform.[13] (The 2009 felony conviction of the Agency's number three, its recent executive director, Kyle "Dusty" Foggo, was simply due to outright and unconcealable fraud.) Nor has any senior officer been held accountable for the 2003 Keystone Kops abduction of an annoying Muslim cleric from Milan, which, for the first time ever, got twenty-three Americans convicted in absentia in November 2009. While Italian justice made its creaky way, Jeffrey Castelli, the station chief in Rome at the time, was twice promoted; the only reason he did not advance to the coveted post of chief of station in New York City—that appointment finally being denied him in 2008—was that several mandarins in the Clandestine Service actually went to the mat to argue that this would set an appalling example to the several thousand young officers who had been brought on board after 9/11.

Of course, world-class intelligence officers are to be found in this mass of bureaucracy, and Al Qaeda has been degraded as much by spies recruited within its network as by targeted air strikes. But the CIA is the key example of an organization that can only work its way out of failure by concentrating on the basics. Here, less is assuredly more. How to change the culture and allow the country's premier intelligence arm to attain its full potential as an elite espionage service? Make it smaller, leaner, and more focused. A modicum of competition can also be introduced. For example, last year the director of national intelligence, one of four in that office since reforms were imposed in 2004, made a bold proposal. He urged that some chiefs of station—responsible for running clandestine operations and interacting with foreign spy agency bosses—might, for the first time, come from outside the Agency. It could make sense, argued the since-ousted Admiral Dennis Blair, for, say, a Drug Enforcement Administration official to take up the post of COS in Bogota. Langley defeated this challenge. It should be revived.

Other recommendations include hiving off the CIA's covert

paramilitary functions to the military's Special Operations Command; assimilating its geopolitical appurtenances, such as a redundant $100 million a year language school in Reston, Virginia, to State or Defense, which already dispose of such capacities; and moving the bulk of its analytical functions—akin to a university's graduate departments, except working with classified material— to State also, with money and additional Foreign Service talent headed to those functions. Additionally, Congress's main investigative arm, the Government Accountability Office, can contribute to better overall performance. Give it authority to audit the books of the CIA and other covert agencies, a power as fiercely resisted by Langley as by Congress's turf-conscious oversight committees, but one whose enormous scope can't be handled adequately by Congressional committee staffs. "I found in my job that when somebody says something is sensitive," explains David Walker, president of the Peter G. Peterson Foundation, who had addressed this matter of CIA accountability while serving as U.S. comptroller general from 1998 to 2008, "it normally means it's probably embarrassing."[14]

Finally, let me offer a recommendation that might improve judgment among up-and-coming CIA officers. Sure as clockwork, the blunders that can't be concealed get spun by operatives who are at least no strangers to disinformation. The latest embarrassments concerning torture have been handled just like the scandals of domestic espionage, poison plots, etc., exposed by Congress in the mid-1970s. The Agency turns to impressionable journalists, in this instance the *Washington Post*'s David Ignatius, to write that any public discussion of the subject will demoralize its younger officers, and that "foreign intelligence services that share secrets with the United States" will now hesitate to cooperate.[15] That is not to be believed. The latter spin never proves out and those emotionally vulnerable officers who are referenced can instead benefit from being compelled to think twice about obeying what any grad student in public policy would recognize as illegal orders.

Fifth is history, and how to accept its vast ambiguities. One recommendation is to notice the difference between how 9/11 has been interpreted by nearly all American politicians and by a cross section of more reflective people. It has become a ritual with the political class to declare that 9/11 recast the way they view the world and that they came to think anew about national security overnight. To see the world as every so often born again is a lamentable perspective that guarantees decision making to be full of illusions.

In contrast, look at the sixtieth-anniversary issue of *American Heritage*, in winter 2010. Thirty-five of the nation's finest scholars were asked each to select and explain a decisive event that has helped define our country. September 11, 2001, was not among a roster of moments that included Gettysburg, Midway, and D-Day and that also addressed FDR's closing of the nation's banks to fight the Depression, the first American deaths in Vietnam, the moon landing, and the inauguration of an African-American president. "It's an appropriate selection," remarks executive editor John Ross, "since 9/11 has become one of those magical episodes in American life that unites terrible drama with complete amnesia about all that occurred before." [16] And by this *American Heritage* has made a quiet, unstated contribution to calmer perspective.

Another recommendation: When men and women positioned as national security experts consult "the past," they are more likely to be trolling for outcomes to match their present certainties. And when historians themselves weigh in on national security affairs and apply their own lessons from the past, as in "finagling with Thucydides," then they're more likely to be doing so to score debating points than to elevate discussion. In both instances, the national security expert and the historian are each marshaling obscure dates and place-names to create seemingly authoritative analogies.[17] To flush out this pop history from the op-ed pages, policy-oriented magazines, and overall public discussion, let the many excellent historians who have no interest in the literary swordplay surrounding national security offer a public service: have them devote some time to policing this excited discourse, offering gentle corrections in their area of expertise to cool the froth. National security experts, members of their own profession, as well as "history boys" and the "best and brightest" alike at the White House, can be held to account.

The sixth figure of the magical pattern is the illusion that other peoples are primed and eager to adopt our ways, as in Nebraska senator Kenneth Wherry's pledge not so long ago that America would "lift Shanghai up, ever up, until it is just like Kansas City." [18] The latest manifestation of this idea is in the so-called new doctrine of counterinsurgency, which by definition presumes a lot of nation-building, call it what we will.[19] Here the recommendation is to beware of the seductive promises that counterinsurgency holds for Americans. Its precepts are tailored to American dispositions: the small band of individuals against enormous odds; the startling effects of meticulous organization; and most of all the surefire conviction that freedom-seeking people always side with us, eager for an extreme makeover of their customs, livelihoods, and ministries, even if they have to endure "the growing pains of democracy." This alluring vision can still draw the country into swamps that we have neither time, patience, nor energy to drain.

Effective counterinsurgency, as practiced by a democracy, by definition presumes a deep and respectful understanding of the folkways, faiths, and political systems among which one must fight—along with an extraordinary power of identifying the enemy within a sea of strangers. "All of these concepts are very important," explains General Petraeus, "and they have to be implemented with a really nuanced understanding of Afghani-

271

stan."[20] To be sure; but would he expect, say, an Afghan officer to acquire a "really nuanced understanding" of Chicago's aldermen and of its South Side, let alone of all of America, after two or three years on the ground in the United States? The comparison is no odder, and the conceit that U.S. soldiers, CIA operatives, and AID officials can do so from scratch is very American as well.

"Counterinsurgency is about the people," tolls the mantra from the Joint Chiefs, as if war itself had not been cast as an extension of politics long before Clausewitz crystallized the insight.[21] But when deconstructing the amazing litany of requirements, counterinsurgency proves to be a protean task that demands endless nuanced abilities: victory in the field; professionalizing Afghanistan's army and police; backing the private armies of warlords yet trying to put spirit and honesty into the country's judiciary; assuring free elections; expanding (and Westernizing) its school system; securing Highway 1. No other nation would contemplate so godlike a venture, whatever the tactics are called or however the strategy gets circumscribed ("restated") as reality takes a bite.

In Afghanistan, journalists write of U.S. Marines who have "embraced counterinsurgency methods to befriend and protect the local population." In spring 2010, such friendships were to be struck up in an area along the Helmand River called Marja, where U.S. engineers in the late 1950s had built a network of irrigation canals and urged Pashtun nomads to grow wheat, a crop since replaced by fields of opium poppies. The marines "buy sodas and food in the local markets," and some of these fighting men may be equally inclined to believe that their activities indeed offer a path to friendship. Now Yemen is the latest place to be eyed for American recasting: Special Forces teams train the country's police and troops while U.S. visionaries urge an American-made educational system to counter religious fundamentalism. Soldiers are reported to be "cementing friendships" with such gestures as handing out foot-long bowie knives to tribesmen. All this faith in the bonhomie of male bonding can only lead to disappointment. Washington ends up interpreting as solid ongoing and reassuring political fact what in reality are mere cultural courtesies. We "didn't realize how hard it was to do," said the U.S. commander in southern Afghanistan by summer 2010, when efforts at democracy in Marja proved disappointing.[22] Huge policy decisions get shaped by anecdotes out of Kipling.

These six strands of magical thinking do not, unfortunately, loop around all of our nation's intellectual whimsies. Other characteristics of American life affect the ways we encounter the world, though not so pervasively as those just examined—for example, the penchant for dreaming up conspiracies. Dreadful confusions about what is real and what is not insinuate themselves into fevered minds. This peculiarity is now further magnified by a generation of ever-increasing partisan antagonism, by blogs, economic calamity, ongoing war, and by the steadily mounting overall mistrust of government since the late 1960s. It's a refusal to believe facts that just don't fit with one's preconceptions, as with the "birthers" who insist that Barack Hussein Obama—intent on destroying what remains of the Constitution—is an illegitimate president for having truly been born in Kenya or Indonesia or somewhere other than in the Republic.

"The paranoid style in American politics," as it is nourished by the sense of an alien world outside, surfaces when all our hard work, bounty, and honorable ambition seem not to be enough to make things go right on a planet where every upstanding person of course shares our values and yearns to act on them. We turn on one another, laying blame on particular people or groups—upon them, not on our own inadequacies. "We were betrayed," conclude minds inflamed by disappointment—whether by "oil companies," "liberals," a "vast right-wing conspiracy," or perhaps by Skull and Bones.

This general paranoia can be found abundantly in France and Italy, though less so in Britain, Japan, or postwar Germany, and not at all in the Nordic countries. America has been particularly vulnerable to these obsessions since the Korean War because of the recurring magnitude of its overseas disappointments. "Concerting to deliver us to disaster" was Joseph McCarthy's line, and so much of the nation bought into it.[23] As Eisenhower understood, this fever burned straight out of the necroses of waste and disappointment in Korea. Who knows what the next frustrations will bring, or the extent to which we will once more turn on ourselves—as occurred too in the encroachments on civil liberties during Vietnam and after 9/11—in event of a future terrorist attack? The more expansively "national security" keeps getting defined, the more opportunity for embittered alarms to pollute the landscape.

The most dangerous consequence of all, when any great nation submits itself to magical thinking, may be for it to behave trivially, to feel small, and to shrink inward even from humanitarian responsibilities. After all, magical thinking not only overstresses the promises of action, underestimates the grimly repetitive sacrifices that all too likely must follow, and sees these quests as manageable. No, once the promises fail, a nation, still thinking magically, marches just as facilely into irrational despair. For America, that demeanor can show itself as an unrealistic gloom that tempts us to succumb to so circumscribed a foreign policy that we're not capable of even minding our *own* business. Real core interests, like, say, ongoing access to Saudi oil, get dangerously confused with the discarded excitements of the last disillusioning adventure in a chilling loss of perspective. It has happened before, as after Vietnam.

Victory, in contrast, has been called the ability to face greater problems without fear. The steadiness that makes that possible can be seen in the case-hardened, enduring qualities that the U.S. Navy brings to refueling its ships in a storm: "Not easy, just routine." These are strengths of focus, of deadly seriousness about the country's inescapable needs, and of seasoned professionals who seek to work with the fewest illusions. Such strengths abound in this most practical of nations. America has long been able to build on its customary union of competence and decency to keep overcoming ever greater problems without fear. It does so by being a magnet to the world's true best and brightest, by resourceful growth, and by opening its society to trade and to talent beyond what any previous generation thought possible. This is altogether the clear-eyed spirit that alone will carry us into a twenty-first century whose opportunities can hardly be imagined.

ACKNOWLEDGMENTS

I AM ESPECIALLY GRATEFUL TO ALICE MAYHEW OF SIMON & Schuster for her vision in acquiring this work, and also to her and Senior Editor Roger Labrie for their incisive guidance as the manuscript evolved. My literary agent and valued friend, Deborah Grosvenor, made a perfect match. Like so many writers—whether an author is addressing politics, history, biography, the arts, science, or global business—I've benefited from Timothy Dickinson's extraordinary counsel. Incisive editorial assistance was provided by Catherine Adams, with research insights offered by Karli Johnston, currently an analyst at NATO.

My mother, Jeanne Leebaert, and my sister Melissa are always indescribably supportive. Sergeant Onno Leebaert, USMC, is an inspiration when examining the hard issues of war and peace, as indeed is the memory of my father, Onno Leebaert, at one time of the Royal Netherlands Army. The wisdom of family and friends doesn't only make us think better; it gives us ground to hope for better decision making on these terrible matters that will not go away.

Georgetown University—its president, John J. DeGioia, the university's research librarians, and particularly its range of fascinating students—have for many years offered a rich intellectual home. Partners at MAP AG and in related ventures have patiently accepted the occasional diversions that come with having a co-worker who is also a writer. Particularly tolerant and encouraging have been Knut Revling, Anne Bohman, John May, and more recent colleagues Steve King and Pat Alagia, M.D. At the U.S. Army

Historical Foundation, I've benefited from the guidance that can only be offered by soldiers who've borne the heaviest responsibilities: General William Hartzog USA, ret.; Brigadier General Creighton Abrams, Jr., USA, ret.; and Lieutenant Colonel Lewis Sorley USA, ret.; as well as by historian Matt Seelinger.

To meet the demands of so tricky a topic as the magical deformations of foreign affairs requires a breadth of input from those who have been there. And no one could have benefited more than I from deep conversations with Bob Coulam and Stacey Wagner, who critiqued early drafts; literary entrepreneur John Henry; those distinguished authors Ann Crittenden, Liaquat Ahamed, Jim Strock, and John Ross; management wiz Donna Farmer of the Association for Competitive Technology; David Braunschvig; Arthur Houghton; Mark Felton; Susan Grimes; Bob Sevigny; LTC Dean Franks, USA; David Webster; Leon Aron, one of our country's foremost observers of Russia, and Michael Pillsbury, for a generation a pioneer in Chinese studies; Frank Samuel; William H. Taft IV; Buster Houchins; Schuyler White; Major Karen Douglas, USAFR; Professor Ni Shixiong of Fudan University, who honored me by having *The Fifty-Year Wound* translated into Chinese; and Terry Bradley, bibliophile, friend, and brownie baker. Chaplain (Captain) Brad Borders, USA, and the Reverends David Johnson Lowe and Alida Ward have brought inspiration from a kingdom not of this world.

NOTES

INTRODUCTION

1. Andrew J. Bacevich, the *Washington Post*, October 5, 2008, "Going for Broke." This acute analyst of U.S. foreign policy is quoting a May 2004 memo from Pentagon official Douglas Feith.
2. James Traub, "A Statesman Without Borders," *New York Times Magazine*, February 3, 2008.

1. SOURCES OF MAGIC

1. For example, defense spending increased sixfold from 1941 to 1944; aircraft production tripled and then tripled again; field artillery leaped fivefold. Figures come from the U.S. Army World War II "Green Books" and from the *Library of Congress World War II Companion*, as offered to me by Matthew Seelinger, historian of the U.S. Army Historical Foundation.
2. Lloyd C. Gardner, *Pay Any Price: Lyndon Johnson and the Wars of Vietnam* (Chicago: Ivan Dee, 1995), p. 32.
3. National Security Archive, Foreign Police Training file, HQ 62-107929, 1962–63, Hoover to Robert Kennedy, July 23, 1963.
4. Rumsfeld's "six days" reference is from BBC News World Edition, February 7, 2003; General Harkins's "six months" prediction in 1963 comes from David Halberstam, *The Best and the Brightest* (New York: Random House, 1972), p. 213; Harkins would offer it again the following year; for Friedman's numerous references to "six months," see the collected references in Christopher Cerf and Victor Navasky, *Mission Accomplished, Or How We Won the War in Iraq* (New York: Simon & Schuster, 2008), pp. 155–58.
5. Robert McNamara, *In Retrospect: The Tragedy and Lessons of Vietnam* (New York: Random House, 1995), p. 108.
6. Kai Bird, *The Color of Truth: McGeorge Bundy and William Bundy, Broth-*

ers in Arms (New York: Simon & Schuster, 1998), p. 327. Note the discussion between Bundy and Walter Lippmann about South Vietnam.

7. Secretary Rice offered this insight about 9/11 and Afghanistan to the trustees of the Brookings Institution who visited with her at the State Department on May 8, 2007. She spoke and took questions. The source attended this gathering but prefers to remain anonymous.

8. Fred Kaplan, "Rumsfeld's Pentagon Papers," *Slate*, October 23, 2003.

9. Cerf and Navasky, *Mission Accomplished*, p. 25, quoting Dick Cheney, March 16, 2003.

10. George Bush Inaugural Speech, January 20, 2005, re "ending tyranny."

11. "Deputy Secretary Wolfowitz Interview with Nolan Finely of the *Detroit News*," Department of Defense news transcript, March 5, 2003, re "exaggerated"; "dead-enders" is from the Brookings Institution's Michael O'Hanlon, with Stephen J. Solarz, in the *Washington Times*, February 17, 2004; "thugs" is from Secretary Rumsfeld, *CNN Late Edition*, March 14, 2004.

12. "Make a million" is Richard Haass, interviewed on *Imus in the Morning* radio show, May 13, 2009.

13. Peter Rodman, *Presidential Command: Power, Leadership, and the Making of Foreign Policy from Richard Nixon to George W. Bush* (New York: Knopf, 2009). Rodman cites Arthur Schlesinger, Jr., on lack of "energy" at State, p. 31; "diplomacy not working" is Rodman's judgment, p. 76.

14. In 1999–2001, I interviewed many of the principals in these activities, such as Gus Weiss, who had been at the NSC and then DOD, the CIA's Helene Boatner, and William Crowell, who became NSA deputy director. The inspiring story of the "American Trade Craft Society," as this cadre called themselves, remains largely secret.

15. Thomas Schweich, "Generation No," op-ed, *New York Times*, December 11, 2008.

16. Other countries can be "diverted," too, such as the Soviet Union. The United States explicitly intended to exact vengeance for Vietnam by supplying the mujahideen against the Red Army in the

1980s, but this one-time riposte that claimed 14,453 Soviet lives doesn't come close to the number of American dead in the two costly diversions of North Korea and Vietnam.

17. Richard A. Clarke, *Against All Enemies: Inside America's War on Terror* (New York: Simon & Schuster, 2004), p. 241; "token" is a quote from the NSC's Rand Beers in 2002; "If you're in Iraq and you need something," recalled commander General David McKiernan, "you ask for it. If you're in Afghanistan and you need it, you figure out how to do without it." See Rajiv Chandrasekaran, "Pentagon Worries Led to Command Change," *Washington Post*, August 17, 2009.

18. The official was Alvey A. Adee. He was second assistant secretary at the U.S. State Department for thirty-eight years until his death in 1924, without ever leaving the country.

19. Columbia University professor William T. R. Fox coined the term *super power* in 1944, primarily to describe the British Empire and Commonwealth; a common myth is that the United States assumed "the leadership of the world," "replacing" the British Empire in 1947 by aiding Greece. U.S. and British documents indicate otherwise, as referenced in Derek Leebaert, *To Set the World Right: The Final Decade of the British Empire and What It Means for America*, forthcoming.

20. See chapter 2, "Back to the Future," in Derek Leebaert, *The Fifty-Year Wound: How America's Cold War Victory Shapes Our World* (New York: Little, Brown, 2002).

21. *Time*, December 1, 1948, on Lewis Douglas; "The *Fortune* Survey," *Fortune*, June 1948, p. 12.

22. Marshall used the phrase "play with fire" several times during spring 1948, as recounted to me by his biographer Forrest Pogue, with whom I worked as a Smithsonian Fellow, 1983–84. "Twelve tanks in Europe capable of fighting" is from Lewis Sorley, *Thunderbolt: General Creighton Abrams and the Army of His Times* (New York: Simon & Schuster, 1992), p. 109.

23. Rumsfeld in a "town hall meeting" in the Kuwaiti desert, answering a soldier angered by inadequate armor on Humvees, December 8, 2004.

24. Matthew Ridgway, *Soldier: The Memoirs of Matthew B. Ridgway* (New York: Harper Brothers, 1956), p. 5.

25. Conventional wisdom among U.S. historians is that Moscow knew of the pending North Korean attack and approved it, but that encouragement was late and halfhearted. This is wrong. Soviet backing was extensive and long-planned. See my argument in *The Fifty-Year Wound*, pp. 90–91, including the seminal role of Stalin's ambassador Colonel General T. F. Shtykov, profiled in *Sovetskaya Voennaya Entsiklopediya*, vol. 8, p. 544.

26. As cited by Stephen Sestanovich, "The Right Strategy Isn't Enough," op-ed, *Washington Post*, January 24, 2007.

27. Mistaken "conventional wisdom" on this matter is to be found in David Halberstam, *The Coldest Winter: America and the Korean War* (New York: Hyperion, 2007), pp. 334–84. See my review, " 'Limited War' on the Edge of the World," *Army*, March 2008.

28. "Liberate" and liberalize" were the commonly defined U.S. objectives, as in *Testimony of General Douglas MacArthur before the Armed Services and Foreign Relations Committees of the United States Senate*, 82nd Congress, May 3–5, 1951, pp. 19, 246. So too "complete victory" and "liberate the entire peninsula," which percolate through the hearings.

29. See Bela K. Király, "The Aborted Soviet Military Plans Against Tito's Yugoslavia," *War and Society in East Central Europe*, vol. 10, ed. Wayne S. Vucinich (New York: Columbia University Press, 1982), pp. 273–88. Also see the CIA analysis NIE-29, "Probability of an Invasion of Yugoslavia in 1951," March 20, 1951, pp. 1, 4.

30. Elite opinion and "prevailed" are documented in Yuen Foong Khong, *Analogies at War: Korea, Munich, Dien Bien Phu, and the Vietnam Decisions of 1965* (Princeton, N.J.: Princeton University Press, 1992), pp. 110–11; Gordon M. Goldstein, *Lessons in Disaster: McGeorge Bundy and the Path to War in Vietnam* (New York: Times Books, 2008) quoting Bundy re the right decision, pp. 137–38. This last book needs to be used with caution. Bundy offered recorded interviews during 1995–96. But after his death his family refused Goldstein authorization to publish. As has not previously been disclosed, Bundy suffered from Alzheimer's disease. It is unlikely that his agonizing self-inquest would otherwise have occurred. That said, Goldstein's archival work is helpful.

31. Author's interview with General Mohammed al-Shawani, director, INIS, January 12, 2009, McLean, Virginia.

32. Secretary Robert Gates's speech at the National Defense University, cited in *Washington Post*, December 4, 2008.

33. General Wesley Clark, USA, ret., interviewed by Ryan D'Agostino in *Esquire*, January 2009, p. 99.

34. The phrase "national security establishment" is frequently used by the *New York Times* without elaboration, as in the August 17, 2009, editorial "Climate and National Security."

2. EMERGENCY MEN

1. "McCain to Georgian President," Robert Barnes, *Washington Post*, August 12, 2008.

2. Charles Krauthammer referred to "Old Europe" as he insisted that "the goal of this war is to . . . dominate Eastern Europe," column, *Washington Post*, August 22, 2008. Holbrooke comparing Russia's assault to Hitler in Czechoslovakia is cited in "Coming to Grips with the Kremlin's New Nerve," *New York Times*, September 7, 2008. Sean Hannity, on his syndicated *Sean Hannity Show* radio program, August 15, 2008, ludicrously proposed sending Stinger missiles to Georgia.

3. The term *emergency men* was coined by Jacob Burckhardt, nineteenth century Swiss historian, and author of *The Civilization of the Renaissance in Italy* (1860), among other classics. "Emergency men," he explained in his *Reflections on History*, are people whom the opportunities offered by the modern state tempt into an eternal trifling with danger and extremity.

4. John le Carré, "Tinpots, Saviors, Lawyers, Spies," *Baltimore Sun*, May 5, 1993; Al Gore on environment and "fascism" to Carnegie-Mellon graduates as reported by Fox News, May 19, 2008; Warren Buffett on "economic Pearl Harbor" from Bloomberg News, September 24, 2008.

5. Samantha Power, "Bystanders to Genocide: Why the United States Let the Rwanda Tragedy Happen," *Atlantic*, September 2001, p. 107. It was Secretary of State Warren Christopher who reached for the atlas.

6. "Implacable" is from the 1954 Doolittle Report for Eisenhower, as cited in "The Survivor," *National Journal*, June 6, 2009, Shane Harris, who also makes the comparison.

7. Douglas Schoen and Michael Rowan, *The Threat Closer to Home: Hugo Chávez and the War Against America* (New York: Free Press, 2009), as they said on C-SPAN, *Morning Edition*, June 7, 2009.

8. See *The Fifty-Year Wound*, pp. 32–40; additionally the observations of Britain's Foreign Office on Kennan are instructive, as with "frontier wars." See Public Record Office PRO, FO 371/100836, Gascoigne to Paul Mason, June 20, 1952, and Gascoigne to Strange, May 20, 1952.

9. For Kennan on "human blood" see *Foreign Relations of the United States* (hereinafter FRUS) 1950/2, "Memorandum" by the Counselor of the Department to the Secretary of State, pp. 601, 607; on Kennan's views of Japan, SEA, and "empire" see Lloyd Gardner, *A Covenant with Power* (New York: Oxford University Press, 1984), p. 112.

10. See my discussion of General MacArthur in *On Point* 13, no. 3 (Winter 2007–2008), which corrects the inept impression of MacArthur in Stanley Weintraub, *15 Stars: Eisenhower, MacArthur, Marshall: Three Generals Who Saved the American Century* (New York: Free Press, 2007).

11. UN General Assembly, 294 Plenary Meeting, October 7, 1950, Harry S. Truman Library; "complete victory" is in William Stueck, *Rethinking the Korean War: A New Diplomatic and Strategic History* (Princeton, N.J.: Princeton University Press, 2002), quoting MacArthur, p. 113.

12. Stueck, *Rethinking the Korean War*, p. 101.

13. One of MacArthur's countless references to the "Oriental mind" and "the Oriental psychology" is to be found in Richard H. Rovere and Arthur Schlesinger, Jr., *General MacArthur and President Truman: The Struggle for Control of American Foreign Policy* (reprint, New Brunswick, N.J.: Transaction, 1992), p. 141.

14. Halberstam, *Coldest Winter*, p. 382.

15. Author interview with Lieutenant General Edward Rowney, USA, ret., March 15, 2010, Washington, D.C.

16. "Inhibitions" is from Rovere and Schlesinger, *General MacArthur*, p. 154. General MacArthur used "appeasement" throughout the hearing, as on the first day. See *Testimony of General Douglas MacArthur*, p. 39.

17. "Alone if necessary" is from *Testimony*, p. 42; "Communist Jehad" was a term used by one of General MacArthur's chief aides,

Major General Courtney Whitney, who accompanied him to the Senate hearings.

18. Quoted in Rovere and Schlesinger, *General MacArthur*, p. 165.

19. This formulation is used in ibid., p. 227.

20. "Gobbledygook" is acknowledged in ibid., p. 235.

21. *Testimony of General Douglas MacArthur*, p. 104.

22. The Pentagon used the misleading number of 54,246 service member Korean War deaths until the end of the century. By the war's fiftieth anniversary, it had corrected the record to 36,516, no longer lumping together all the noncombatant fatalities that the military had suffered outside the Korean theater, including car wrecks and sickness from Germany to California.

23. Andrew Krepinevich and Barry Watts, "Lost at the NSC," *National Interest*, January 2009.

24. The abrasive secretary of state Alexander Haig was the self-styled "vicar" of foreign policy under Ronald Reagan from 1981 to 1982, and fostered an extreme form of internal bickering. Yet see the glowing cover story in *Time*, March 16, 1981: "Alexander Haig: The Vicar Takes Charge."

25. Stephen Ambrose, *Eisenhower: Soldier and President* (New York: Touchstone, 1990), p. 460.

26. FRUS 1952–54, vol. 13, Indochina, 194th NSC mtg., April 29, 1954, p. 1,440.

27. John B. Roberts and Elizabeth A. Roberts, *Freeing Tibet: 50 Years of Struggle, Resilience, and Hope* (New York: AMACOM, 2009), p. 18.

28. John Prados, "Laos, the Road to Vietnam," *Military History Quarterly*, Summer 2009, p. 26.

29. John Lewis Gaddis, *Strategies of Containment: A Critical Appraisal of Postwar American National Security Policy* (New York: Oxford University Press, 1982), p. 166.

30. *Public Papers*, Eisenhower, Item 421, "Farewell Radio and Television Address to the American People," January 17, 1961, pp. 1039, 1038.

31. Arthur M. Schlesinger, Jr., "On Heroic Leadership and the Dilemma of Strong Men and Weak Peoples," *Encounter*, December 1960, pp. 3–11.

32. "The tide began to run out" is JFK, August 24, 1960, at a Democratic rally in Alexandria, Virginia. "Bear any burden" and "hour of maximum danger" are from his Inaugural Address; Eisenhow-

er's "Cross of Iron Speech" was delivered on April 16, 1953, to the American Society of Newspaper Editors.

33. Kennedy spoke of the hit-and-run exile raids against Cuba as "probably exciting and rather pleasant for those who engage in them." See my discussion of the assassination and special operations attempts against Castro and Cuba in *The Fifty-Year Wound*, pp. 297–304, as well as in *To Dare and to Conquer: Special Operations and the Destiny of Nations*, Derek Leebaert (New York: Little Brown, 2006), chapter 18, "Invasion From the Future."

34. "Seething" is the description of JFK's "incensed" reaction to Prime Minister Ben-Gurion's efforts, as described to me December 1, 2009, by author Patrick Tyler.

35. "Edge of danger" is also from JFK's heated campaign. See Speech of Senator John F. Kennedy, Citizens for Kennedy Party, Waldorf-Astoria, September 14, 1960.

36. Quoted in James W. Hilty, *Robert Kennedy: Brother Protector* (Philadelphia: Temple University Press, 1997), p. 258.

37. Arthur M. Schlesinger, Jr., *A Thousand Days: John F. Kennedy in the White House* (Boston: Houghton Mifflin, 1965), p. 197.

38. Quoted in Geoffrey Warner, "Review Article: President Kennedy and Indochina," *International Affairs*, 70, no. 4 (1994).

39. JFK to James Reston, as cited in Stanley Karnow, *Vietnam: A History* (New York: Penguin, 1997), p. 267.

40. On "DOE," see Theodore White, *The Making of the President, 1960* (New York: Atheneum, 1961), p. 406.

41. See Leebaert, *The Fifty-Year Wound*, p. 302, and chapter 6, note 119.

42. On Bundy and assassination, see Seymour M. Hersh, *The Dark Side of Camelot* (Boston: Little, Brown, 1997), p. 190, documenting a 1961 conversation between Bundy and Richard Bissell. The best analysis of preempting China is William Burr and Jeffrey Richelson, "Whether to Strangle the Baby in the Cradle: The United States and the Chinese Nuclear Program, 1960–1964," *International Security*, Winter 2000/2001.

43. Richard Reeves, *President Kennedy: Profile of Power* (New York: Simon & Schuster, 1993), p. 201.

44. Goldstein, *Lessons in Disaster*, p. 137.

45. FRUS 1964–1968, vol. 3, Vietnam, July–December 1965, Document 104, Meeting with General Eisenhower, August 3, 1965.

46. Richard Nixon, "First Annual Report to the Congress on United States Foreign Policy for the 1970's," February 18, 1970.

47. Diane Kunz, *Butter and Guns: America's Cold War Economic Diplomacy* (New York: Free Press, 1997), p. 214.

48. H. R. Haldeman, *The Haldeman Diaries: Inside the Nixon White House* (New York: Putnam, 1994), p. 424.

49. An entertaining overview of Nixon's practice is James Carroll, "Nixon's Madman Strategy," *Boston Globe*, June 14, 2005. Also see Allen J. Matusow, "Nixon as Madman," *Reviews in American History* 27, no. 4 (1999), pp. 623–29.

50. Michael Schaller, *Altered States: The United States and Japan Since the Occupation* (New York: Oxford University Press, 1997), p. 221.

51. Ibid., citing NSC staffer Roger Morris, p. 212.

52. Quoted in Seymour Hersh, *The Price of Power: Kissinger in the Nixon White House* (New York: Summit, 1983), p. 126.

53. U.S. Department of State, FRUS 1969–1976, vol. 6, Vietnam, January 1969–July 1970 (Washington, D.C.: U.S. Government Printing Office, 2006), pp. 370–74.

54. Walter Isaacson, *Kissinger: A Biography* (New York: Simon & Schuster, 1992), p. 681.

55. Andrew Cockburn, *Rumsfeld: The Rise, Fall, and Catastrophic Legacy* (New York: Scribner, 2007), p. 27.

56. As quoted in Gabriel Schoenfeld, "Missing the Boat," *Commentary*, January 1995.

57. Statement of Secretary of Defense Harold Brown Before the Senate Foreign Relations Committee, July 9, 1979, Hearings on the SALT Treaty, 96th Congress, 1st Session, Part 1, p. 111.

58. This perspective on the Soviet Union was apparent in the hesitant response by those Kennedy School faculty concerned with national security to the June 1978 commencement address of Nobel laureate Aleksandr Solzhenitsyn, which I attended. Soviet "legitimacy," and even the "convergence" of the U.S. and Soviet political-economic systems over time, were staples of discussion during the years that I ran faculty/fellow study groups at Harvard's Center for Science and International Affairs, 1978–81.

59. See Leebaert, *The Fifty-Year Wound.* Chapters 10 (1981–85) and 11 (1985–89) concern the Soviet collapse. Jack Matlock, a former U.S. ambassador to the U.S.S.R., has returned to the argument

that neither side won the Cold War and that U.S. pressure was of no consequence. It can be found in *Superpower Illusions: How Myths and False Ideologies Led America Astray—and How to Return to Reality* (2010). See my review for the Claremont Institute, "Shaking Loose," June 2005, of Matlock's previous book, in which he makes the same unpersuasive arguments (*Autopsy on an Empire*, 1995).

60. Henry Fairlie, *The Kennedy Promise: The Politics of Expectation* (Garden City, N.Y.: Doubleday, 1973), p. 180.

61. The pivotal document is NSDD 75, "U.S. Relations with the USSR," January 17, 1983. It was preceded by NSDD 32, "U.S. National Security Strategy," May 20, 1982, with p. 6 being germane. An alternative view of what was under way can be seen in my Moscow discussions with George Kennan, in 1981. See *The Fifty-Year Wound*, pp. 498–99.

62. That this embargo was anything but highly effective is one of many Cold War myths. See evidence in Leebaert, *The Fifty-Year Wound*, pp. 520–24, and note the pivotal delays caused in pipeline construction and in oil and gas sales.

63. Robert McFarlane, who had been a national security adviser before his disgrace in the Iran-Contra scandal, argued in 2008 that withdrawing U.S. troops from Lebanon twenty-five years earlier after the deaths of 241 American servicemen "led to the rise of Islamic terror." See "From Beirut to 9/11" op-ed, *New York Times*, October 22, 2008. It's a simplistic matching of cause and effect, as if Israel's 1982 invasion, the ensuing civilian deaths, and the massacres thereafter at Sabra and Shatila have had nothing to do with the ensuing spiral of violence.

64. The most authoritative source is William T. Lee, *CIA Estimates of Former Soviet Union Military Expenditures: Errors and Waste* (Washington, D.C.: American Enterprise Institute, 1995).

65. This is attested to by the deputy director of the Soviet bioweapon program. See Ken Alibek, *Biohazard: The Chilling True Story of the Largest Covert Biological Weapons Program in the World* (New York: Random House, 1999), p. x.

66. Patrick Tyler, *A World of Trouble: The White House and the Middle East—From the Cold War to the War on Terror* (New York: FSG, 2008), pp. 303–304.

67. "Not 'Up-Tight' on Ortega, Bush Says," *Los Angeles Times*, October 27, 1989. "When we were contemplating action against Iraq, I

looked into other cases since World War II where we had undertaken military action and what lessons they might provide us. One of those cases, of course, was Korea." Brent Scowcroft email to author, March 4, 2010.

68. An ambitious discussion of technology in warfare, by a think-tank commentator on the "Revolution in Military Affairs," is Max Boot, *War Made New: Technology, Warfare, and the Course of History, 1500 to Today* (New York: Gotham, 2006). See my review, "Shooting Ahead: Revolutions in Military Affairs from the Rise of Gunpowder to the Iraq War," *Washington Post Book World*, November 19, 2006.

69. Irving Janis, *Groupthink: Psychological Studies of Policy Decisions and Fiascos* (New York: Houghton Mifflin, 1982). See his chapter, "Escalation of the Vietnam War," pp. 97–121.

70. Fred Kaplan, *Daydream Believers: How a Few Grand Ideas Wrecked American Power* (New York: Wiley, 2008), p. 191.

71. Josef Joffe poses the question in his review of *The Silence of the Rational Center*, "The Big Idea: Did America's View of Itself as Unique Lead to the Iraq War?" *Washington Post Book World*, April 8, 2007.

72. Hella Junz, the former resident executive director for Europe of the IMF, had already explained this matter of "dynasties" within the EU bureaucracy to me and to Timothy Dickinson in May 1994.

73. Richard Haass emphasizes this point in his *War of Necessity, War of Choice: A Memoir of Two Iraq Wars* (New York: Simon & Schuster, 2009), pp. 63, 152.

74. I was discussing the new administration with Richard Perle, and his own role specifically, during a visit to his house in Chevy Chase, Maryland, in May 2001.

3. THE MYSTIQUE OF AMERICAN MANAGEMENT

1. Jon B. Alterman, "Middle East Notes and Comment: Managing Iraq," Center for Strategic and International Studies, February 5, 2007.

2. Robert McNamara, *In Retrospect: The Tragedy and Lessons of Vietnam* (New York: Vintage, 1996), p. 207.

3. Jeff Stein, "Can You Tell a Sunni from a Shia?" op-ed, *New York Times*, October 17, 2006. Stein adds that such ignorance on foreign

policy priorities is "pretty standard"; discussion with author, September 23, 2008, Washington, D.C.

4. Robert D. Kaplan's "Ten Rules for Managing the World" are laid out in "Supremacy by Stealth," *Atlantic*, July/August 2003, David Rothkopf "Inside the Committee That Runs the World," *Foreign Policy*, March/April 2005; Ben Schwarz, "Managing China's Rise," *Atlantic*, June 2005. Norah O'Donnell, "Hardball with Chris Mathews," MSNBC, July 6, 2006; *The Opportunity: America's Moment to Alter History's Course*, Richard Haass (New York: Public Affairs, 2005), p. 163.

5. Nina Easton, "Paulson: Hot on India, Cool on China," Fortune Global Forum, October 26, 2007. And weeks later, right after the U.S. election, the new administration got slammed from the right for having "lost the appetite to coax China to democracy," as by Bill Gertz, author of *The Failure Factory*, interviewed on *Rush Limbaugh Show*, November 12, 2008.

6. NATO *Handbook*, chapter 7, "Policy and Decision-Making, Crisis Management," NATO Publications, October 16, 2001.

7. William Kaufmann, *The McNamara Strategy* (New York: Harper & Row, 1964), p. 43.

8. Bruce Kuklick, *Blind Oracles: Intellectuals at War from Kennan to Kissinger* (Princeton, N.J.: Princeton University Press, 2006), p. 101.

9. McNamara cited "every quantitative measurement," in 1962. It was featured in many of his obituaries, as in the *Economist*, July 6, 2009. Rumsfeld's overemphasis on "metrics" to indicate success was apparent on NPR's *Morning Edition*, March 30, 2005.

10. The assessment of Endy D. Zemenides, a Chicago attorney, who early in his career had been on the Touche Ross & Company audit team for G. D. Searle during Rumsfeld's years as CEO. Discussion with Zemenides, May 2006, Chicago.

11. "Army Chief: Force to Occupy Iraq Massive," *USA Today*, February 25, 2003. General Shinseki added that the force needed to be big enough to maintain safety in a country with "ethnic tensions that could lead to other problems." Wolfowitz was minimizing those ethnic tensions while, on the same day as Shinseki's testimony, Rumsfeld again insisted that Saddam Hussein had biological weapons.

12. Mark Danner, "Weapons of Mass Destruction and Other Imaginative Acts," *New York Times*, August 27, 2008.

13. Ron Suskind, "Without A Doubt," *New York Times Magazine*, October 17, 2004.

14. "His deputy" is Douglas Feith, and the "blizzard" quotations are from Feith's memoirs, *War and Decision: Inside the Pentagon at the Dawn of the War on Terrorism* (New York: Harper, 2008), p. 58. See my review essay, "Fog of War," *Army*, July 2008, which includes discussion of incapable war planning with a compliant General Tommy Franks.

15. Charles Duelfer, interview with Lisa Mullins, PRI's *The World*, March 10, 2009.

16. On the final memorandum, see George Will, "A Report Overtaken by Reality," *Washington Post*, December 7, 2007; on "Six Years of Accomplishment" see Al Kamen, "In the Loop," *Washington Post*, November 17, 2006. The Pentagon thereafter corrected its math: the revised praise for Rumsfeld and "six years of accomplishment" can still be found at www.defense.gov/home/features/2006/sixyears/.

17. See Larry Bossidy and Ram Charan, *Execution: The Discipline of Getting Things Done* (New York: Crown, 2002).

18. Secretary of State Rice spoke of the "promising new strategic realignment of the Middle East" at a press conference at the Department of Defense, January 11, 2007, among other references to "realignment" of this part of the world.

19. See Michael Wolff, "The Ultimate Bubble," *Vanity Fair*, February 2009, p. 82.

20. Thomas Ricks, *Fiasco: The American Military Adventure in Iraq* (New York: Penguin, 2006), p. 76.

21. The real number at the time was 726 dead, not "approximately 500," as Wolfowitz winged it to the House subcommittee on April 29, 2004.

22. "In Iraq, the Job Opportunity of a Lifetime," *Washington Post*, May 23, 2004.

23. Ben Arnoldy, "Why the Taliban Won't Take over Pakistan," *Christian Science Monitor*, June 7, 2009; the Qureshi admonition is described in "Pakistan Aid Places U.S. in the Midst of a Divide," Jane Perlez, *New York Times*, October 12, 2009.

24. Richard Clarke, *Against All Enemies: Inside America's War on Terror* (New York: Free Press, 2004), p. xix.

25. Milt Bearden, NPR interview, March 8, 2009.

26. See Michael Fullilove's review of this unconvincing book, "Forget Freedom," *Washington Post*, March 8, 2009.

27. Robert D. Kaplan, "Supremacy By Stealth," embodies this view, as in concluding: "And so for the time being, the highest morality must be the preservation—and wherever prudent, the accretion—of American power."

28. Bob Woodward, "The War Within," excerpt, *Washington Post*, September 9, 2008; "Army Historians Document Early Missteps," James Dao, *New York Times*, December 31, 2009.

29. Andrew F. Krepinevich and Barry D. Watts, "Lost at the NSC," *National Interest*, January 2009.

30. Mohammed Heikal, *The Sphinx and the Commissar: The Rise and Fall of Soviet Influence in the Middle East* (New York: Harper & Row, 1978), p. 164. Heikal reports Kosygin relaying this to Nasser.

31. I interviewed Ambassador Wall in Washington, D.C., early in his new position and, as follow-up, a year later: August 2008 and October 2009.

32. Rufus Phillips, *Why Vietnam Matters: An Eyewitness Account of Lessons Not Learned* (Annapolis, Md.: Naval Institute Press, 2008), p. 307.

33. Elizabeth Williamson, "How Much Embassy Is Too Much?" *Washington Post*, March 2, 2008.

34. Jason Zweig, "The Intelligent Investor: Why Many Investors Keep Fooling Themselves," *Wall Street Journal*, January 16, 2010, p. B1.

35. Lloyd Gardner and Marilyn Young, eds., *Iraq and the Lessons of Vietnam: Or, How Not to Learn From the Past* (New York: New Press, 2007), p. 65.

36. The question of the major allies' commitment to U.S. visions is unceasing, whether at NATO's thirtieth or sixtieth anniversary. See my opening chapter, Derek Leebaert (co-author), in *European Security: Prospects for the 1980s* (Lexington, Mass.: D. C. Heath, 1979), pp. 3–27.

37. *New York Times*, April 11, 1951, p. A1; *New York Times*, April 8, 1964, p. 12; and "America to Press Europe," *International Herald Tribune*, February 9, 2008.

38. "Perles of Wisdom," interview with Richard Perle by Amir Taheri, National Review Online, March 7, 2003.

39. Richard Haass, "The World That Awaits," *Newsweek*, November 3, 2008.

40. The application of the Mars and Venus pop psychology cliché ap-

peared at the time by Robert Kagan in *Of Paradise and Power: America and Europe in the New World Order* (New York: Knopf, 2003).

41. Secretary Acheson's message is described by Foreign Secretary Anthony Eden's private secretary in Evelyn Shuckburgh, *Descent to Suez: Diaries, 1951–56* (New York: Norton, 1987), p. 57.

42. The post–Korean War "never again" school was a near-consensus view that henceforth America would use massive force to protect its interests from Soviet-directed attack.

43. Kunz, *Butter and Guns*, pp. 157–58.

44. Interview with Major Ian Palmer, USA, who was an aide to Major General John Batiste, commander of the 1st Infantry Division, during their fruitless presence in Ankara to create a forward HQ, August 12, 2009, Kirkuk, Iraq, FOB Warrior.

45. Paul Wolfowitz, "Remembering the Future," *National Interest*, Spring 2000, p. 41; NBC *Meet the Press*, March 14, 2010, Karl Rove interviewed by Tom Brokaw.

46. The chronicle of CIA penetration of Turkey's General Staff during 2002, and the report of an agent in place about Wolfowitz's visit, is from CIA sources.

47. White House press release, March 27, 2003.

48. Ricks, *Fiasco*, p. 316.

49. In Paris two weeks after 9/11, en route to Senegal—U.S. speakers then being sent by the State Department to a range of Muslim nations—I received condolences in ministries and bakeries alike, with pledges of French support to retaliate in Afghanistan.

50. On strategy, see Robert Gates, *Washington Post*, October 9, 2008, p. A9; on European aspirations at the start of 2010, see Carl Bildt and Anders Rasmussen, "The U.S. Is Not Alone," op-ed, *Washington Post*, January 8, 2010.

51. Gardner and Young, eds., *Iraq and the Lessons of Vietnam*, p. 67.

52. "Nixon's Balancing Act," *Washington Post Book World*, February 25, 2007, review by Orville Schell of Margaret MacMillan, *Nixon and Mao: The Week That Changed the World* (New York: Random House, 2007).

53. My dialogues with PRC embassy staff in 1970 were shared at the time with Vernon Walters, U.S. military attaché at the American Embassy, Paris, later CIA deputy director. During September 1970, I recounted this experience with the PRC embassy to

Howard Boorman, editor of the *Biographical Dictionary of Republican China*, and his modern Chinese history seminar, Vanderbilt University. My observations in winter 1970–71 in Khabarovsk and the surrounding region were shared in early 1971 with U.S. intelligence.

54. Chou En-lai's response is in Schell, "Nixon's Balancing Act." This is an exceptionally misinformed review, Schell believing that at issue was the prospect of war between the United States and China and that Nixon's Beijing appearance "goaded the Soviet Union to yielding on SALT I."

55. Christopher Hitchens, "The Case Against Henry Kissinger Part Two," *Harper's*, March 2001, p. 60. The remarks are those of Winston Lord, as told to the staff of the Carnegie Endowment for International Peace.

56. Secretary McNamara blurted this out in fall 1966 in a meeting that included William T. Lee, as well as John Foster (head of Pentagon R&D), Deputy Secretary Cyrus Vance, and Julian Davidson, army chief scientist for Nike-X. I had discussed this meeting with Foster, and then later specifically with Lee on January 17, 2003.

57. I often spoke with Michael Howard, a thesis adviser at Oxford, about U.S. managerial conceptions of foreign policy. In this reference to "management," he is here praising Kissinger's presumed "management" of the Soviets. See Michael Howard, "Nuclear Danger and Nuclear History," *International Security*, Summer 1989, p. 182.

58. "Management" is from Gerard C. Smith, *Disarming Diplomat: The Memoirs of Gerard C. Smith, Arms Control Negotiator* (New York: Madison, 1996), pp. 170, 174.

59. Lee, *CIA Estimates*, p. 157. Former Soviet defense minister General Yazov unburdened himself of a similar belief after the Soviet Union's demise: "I was convinced we could fight a nuclear war and prevail," as he says in Eric Schmertz, ed., *President Reagan and the World* (Westport, Conn.: Greenwood, 1997), p. 122. In contrast, the United States never combined its offensive and defensive capabilities (let alone its armored divisions) to the extent that can be considered "war-winning." For starters, it would have included civil defense on at least a fraction of the Soviet scale, as

well as Soviet-scale antisubmarine warfare, anti-ballistic missiles and radars, and warhead stockpiling initiatives.

60. In his book, *Power Rules: How Common Sense Can Rescue American Foreign Policy* (New York: Harper, 2009), former journalist and State Department appointee Leslie Gelb recalls a discussion during 1978 arms control negotiations in Helsinki: his Soviet counterpart explained to him that "all you Americans really don't know much about the inner workings of Soviet politics, and we're not going to tell you. It's our real advantage over you" (p. 139). This should not have been news to any savvy U.S. negotiator; and, in fact, those "inner workings" were pretty transparent to those who looked.

61. "Engineered" is in Alistair Horne, "The Case for Henry Kissinger," *Independent*, August 18, 2009; "genius" is Gelb, *Power Rules*, p. 55; "statecraft" is in Paul Starobin, "When Love Is Not Enough," *National Journal*, July 25, 2009, p. 18.

62. Ibid., p. 21.

63. Analysis of the context of this "peril" is in Leebaert, *The Fifty-Year Wound*, pp. 508–10, and see the conclusion of the former Soviet commander of ballistic missile and space defense troops in D. Takhanov, interview with General Colonel Y. Votintsev, "My zashchishchali SSSR ot iadernogo udara" *Vecherniy Almaty*, June 1, 2, and 3, 1993.

64. President Kennedy's famous quip during the Cuban missile crisis, given his fear that a U-2 overflight of Cuba could, at that juncture, set off a cataclysm.

65. Richard Perle, "Too Heavy a Hand," *New York Times*, March 16, 2008.

66. *Journals 1952–2000, Arthur M. Schlesinger Jr.*, July 13, 1971, edited by Andrew and Stephen Schlesinger (New York: Penguin, 2007), p. 339.

67. Stefan Halper, senior fellow at Cambridge University's Center of International Studies, shared this insight during a June 2008 visit to his residence in Great Falls, Virginia, of McNamara's recurring use of "they" during the former secretary's final visit to Cambridge University during 2004.

68. Elliot A. Cohen, "A Hawk Questions Himself," op-ed, *Washington Post*, July 10, 2005. Cohen nonetheless praises the U.S. intention

to "change the pattern of Middle East politics," which, five years after he questioned himself, has hardly occurred, going by today's politics in Egypt, Saudi Arabia, and Israel, among others.

69. Richard Perle, "Time to Cut the Cord," *New York Times*, May 4, 2008.

70. Dana Milbank, "Prince of Darkness Denies Own Existence," *Washington Post*, February 20, 2009, p. A3.

71. The "loss" of the maps was described to me by Gus Weiss, interviewed in December 2001, and checked at the time. Weiss, the first non-CIA officer to receive the Intelligence Medal of Merit, had returned to CIA headquarters right after 9/11 as a consultant. The maps had been "found" by December. I reported the incident four months later in *The Fifty-Year Wound*. "This occasionally happens," says Tyler Drumheller, former head of CIA operations in Europe, "especially when the maps are rare." Drumheller telephone conversation, January 22, 2010.

4. STAR POWER

1. Jim Collins, "Misguided Mix-up of Celebrity and Leadership," *Conference Board Annual Report*, September/October 2001.

2. One of many references to Kissinger as "miracle worker" is in "Hard Work for a Miracle Worker," *Time*, June 3, 1974; Kissinger as a "magician" is from Isaacson, *Kissinger*, p. 581. On "dream team," President Bush insisted that "I've got one of the finest foreign policy teams ever assembled." Former Speaker of the House Newt Gingrich was one of many Washington pundits who agreed that it was a "dream team," and he went on to predict how well Vice President Cheney would work with Democrats. See "The Bush Team's Prospects," *Washington Quarterly*, April 2001.

3. Obituary of McGeorge Bundy, *New York Times*, September 17, 1996, quoting Max Frankel's profile.

4. "The Radical at the Pentagon," John Keegan, *Vanity Fair*, February 2003.

5. Fareed Zakaria, interviewed on *The Kojo Nnamdi Show*, NPR, May 15, 2008.

6. Ted Draper said "belong to the history of publicity" several times

to Timothy Dickinson, then an editor of *Harper's* magazine and currently at *American Heritage*, during 1979–80 conversations in Princeton and New York. Author interview with Dickinson, January 10, 2010, Washington, D.C. Draper expands on that remark in his *Present History* (New York: Random House, 1983). How did Kissinger position himself and gain this outsized reputation? "His greatest feat was to beat the President's media machine at its own machinations. . . . Kissinger's power over the American media may explain more about how he did it than his power over anything else" (pp. 245–46).

7. Henry Kissinger, *Nuclear Weapons and Foreign Policy* (New York: Harper, 1957) p. 152.

8. Ibid., p. 191.

9. Paul Nitze, "Limited Wars or Massive Retaliation?" *Reporter*, September 5, 1957, pp. 40–42.

10. "Wooing" is from Alistair Horne, "The Case for Henry Kissinger," *Independent*, August 18, 2009. Many of us who worked these U.S.-Soviet issues in the mid-1970s found the indulging of Ambassador Dobrynin to be naïve and outrageous. The result of such diplomacy, Ted Draper concludes, was "tragicomic confusion" (*Present History*, p. 222). Within days of entering office, President Reagan cut off this ongoing "wooing."

11. Charles Krauthammer, "Milestone in Baghdad," *Washington Post*, December 5, 2008.

12. Tyler, *A World of Trouble*, p. 160. Tyler adds "even to the detriment of U.S. national interest" (p. 175).

13. Henry Kissinger, *Years of Renewal* (New York: Simon & Schuster, 1999), p. 818.

14. Ron Nessen, *The Ford White House: The Diary of a Speechwriter*, pp. 97–98; Gerald Ford, *A Time to Heal: The Autobiography of Gerald R. Ford* (New York: Harper & Row, 1979), pp. 253–54; for Kissinger's flawed decisions in the final two years of South Vietnam's existence, see the extensive documentation in Gregory Tien Hung Nguyen and Jerrold L. Schecter, *The Palace File* (New York: Harper & Row, 1986).

15. Tyler, *A World of Trouble*, on Kissinger and the Chase Manhattan Bank stake, pp. 241–42.

16. Interview with Dr. Bailey on January 15, 2010, Washington, D.C. Bailey had been a banker as well as a professor of economics. Such skills were previously absent on the NSC staff.

17. Afghanistan as "not enough" is reported by Mark Danner, "Words in a Time of War," *Los Angeles Times*, June 1, 2007; "salted peanuts," Woodward, *State of Denial*, p. 409.

18. The famous Oriana Fallaci interview is quoted in Margaret Talbot, "The Agitator," *New Yorker*, June 5, 2006.

19. In his "saga of the American people's continuous reinvention," Walter MacDougall offers a delightful collection of descriptions of American flimflam men at work, as in *Throes of Democracy: The American Civil War Era 1829–1877* (New York: HarperCollins, 2008).

20. "An expert on terrorism would be recognized as such by the usual criteria—publications, memberships, awards—that would apply to experts in any other field. It is odd to see so many 'experts on terrorism' on TV. I do hope they are kept out of the courtroom." E-mail to author from Philip Bobbitt, Herbert Wechsler Professor of Jurisprudence at Columbia University and author of *Terror and Consent: The Wars for the Twenty-first Century*, July 11, 2009.

21. Former CIA director James Woolsey was among those who insisted that Timothy McVeigh and Terry Nichols were tied to Saddam Hussein. Terrorism "experts" such as Laurie Mylroie, then at AEI, and Steven Emerson agreed, with the latter concluding that the bombing "showed 'a Middle Eastern trait' " because it "was done with the intent to inflict as many casualties as possible" (CBS News, April 1, 1995).

22. One of numerous instances can be seen in Council on Foreign Relations, "Multilateral Intervention in the Middle East," *Backgrounder*, July 24, 2006.

23. AEI's Danielle Pletka on "casualty averse" is from Ricks, *Fiasco*, p. 20, and on "politics of the region," p. 129.

24. "On the Media," NPR transcript of "Who Is Alexis Debat?" Bob Garfield interview with Laura Rozen, then of *Mother Jones*, September 21, 2007.

25. "A Senior Fellow at the Institute of Nonexistence," *New York Times*, November 12, 2008. Also see the impressive "think tank" website, www.hardinginstitute.org.

26. Transcript, "This Government Does Not Torture," ABC News, October 5, 2007.

27. "A Dangerous Step on Interrogations," editorial, *Washington Times*, January 27, 2009.

28. Stalin's torturers adopted the term "conveyor" because, leaving at the end of their shift, they passed the victim on to the next officer to maintain nonstop sleepless interrogation.

29. *Educing Information: Interrogation: Science and Art*, Intelligence Science Board Phase 1 Report (Washington, D.C.: National Defense Intelligence College Press, 2006), p. xiii.

30. Scott Shane, "2 U.S. Architects of Harsh Tactics," *New York Times*, August 12, 2009.

31. *Educing Information*, chapter 5, Steven M. Kleinman, "KUBARAK Counterintelligence Interrogation Review," p. 99.

32. A well considered book in this field bears precisely that title. See Jerry Richardson, *The Magic of Rapport* (Capitola, Calif.: Meta, 2000). The FBI also acknowledges that "the scientific community has never established that coercive interrogation methods are an effective means of obtaining reliable intelligence information." Like Shin Bet, the FBI implicitly flatters its subjects during interrogations. Saddam was asked to give his views on the history of modern Iraq. A bomb maker captured by Shin Bet will initially be interviewed by an Israeli explosives expert to discuss common skills, materials, and professional techniques.

33. Confidential source for material that remains classified.

34. Kleinman, "KUBARAK," p. 98.

35. Educing Information, Prologue, p. xiii.

36. Jane Mayer, "The Secret History," *New Yorker*, June 22, 2009, p. 56. Additional evidence of being "routinely inept" concerned the first detainees in Guantánamo from Afghanistan: U.S. Marines were astounded to discover some were octogenarians, others pubescent, and the marines into whose hands they were dumped had not been told that few spoke Arabic, as the awaiting Arabic translators expected. Karen Greenberg, author of *The Least Worst Place: Guantanamo's First 100 Days* (2009), elaborated at Politics and Prose, Washington, D.C., March 27, 2009.

37. Sidney Blumenthal, "Torture Policy," *Salon*, April 26, 2007.

38. *Educing Information*, p. 114.

39. Sadly, LBJ's overenthused acclaim of Diem as the "Churchill of Asia" is regarded as sufficiently significant to be included on the website of the U.S. Senate Historical Office; on "George Washington of Iraq," see *New Republic*, August 11, 2003, quoting William Luti.

40. Chiang Kai-shek himself barely spoke English, but was otherwise "just like us" as well—his clout was channeled through his wife and interpretor, a Wellesley grad, the *Atlantic* and *New York Times* essayist, and the first private citizen to address the Senate and the House of Representatives.

41. Steuck, *Rethinking the Korean War*, p. 193.

42. Tyler, *World of Trouble*, p. 429.

43. *Financial Times*, April 26, 2007, and Maureen Dowd column, *New York Times*, April 18, 2007. The former defense minister was Ali Allawi, a nephew of Chalabi.

44. I spoke with Peter Galbraith on October 13, 2008, after his talk at Politics and Prose, Washington, D.C., where he discussed his book *Unintended Consequences: How War in Iraq Strengthened American's Enemies*.

45. On "no choice," see the *New York Times*, editorial, December 26, 2009. "President Karzai's Inauspicious Start," re "Obama has no choice but to work with Mr. Krazai"; Kissinger, *Years of Renewal*, p. 803.

46. Dexter Filkins, "Afghan Leader Finds Himself Hero No More," *New York Times*, February 8, 2009, p. A1; the diplomat cited is Spanish envoy Frances Vendrell, in a report by Alison Smale, *New York Times*, September 15, 2008, p. A7. U.S. allies also endorsed Karzai, but not to Washington's heroizing extent.

47. Rich Oppel "Afghan Warlord Denies Links to '01 Killings," *New York Times*, July 18, 2009.

48. Woodward, *State of Denial*, op cit, p. 447.

49. Use of "terrorist mastermind" is pervasive, as by NBC News' excellent chief Pentagon correspondent, Jim Miklaszewski, concerning Zarqawi, March 2, 2004, or in general descriptions of bin Laden, as in the story "Obama Administration to Ratchet Up Hunt for bin Laden," CNN, November 12, 2008.

50. Doris Kearns Goodwin, *Lyndon Johnson and the American Dream* (New York: St. Martin's, 1991), p. 252.

51. Arkady Yedelev, quoted in the *Economist*, July 18, 2009, p. 50.

52. David Frum and Richard Perle, *An End to Evil: How to Win the War on Terror* (New York: Random House, 2003), p. 7.

53. Robert Skidelsky quoting former U.S. ambassador to the UN John Bolton: "if the choice is [Iran] continuing [towards a nuclear bomb] or the use of force, I think you're at a Hitler marching into the Rhineland point"; *Project Syndicate*, April 2008.

54. Bradley Graham, "Decline and Fall," *Washington Post Magazine*, June 14, 2009, p. 14.

55. "Bush Announces Hussein Capture," www.washingtonpost.com, December 14, 2003.

56. An example of an extraordinarily important book that gets sidetracked on this theme of "militarism" is Andrew J. Bacevich, *The New American Militarism* (New York: Oxford University Press, 2005).

57. Elisabeth Bumiller, "Clear Voice of Bush's Pentagon Has Become Harder to Hear," *New York Times*, October 5, 2009, p. A1.

58. Interview with Senator John McCain, by Dana Bash, *Situation Room*, CNN, April 8, 2008.

59. Senator Joe Lieberman made the comparison to General Ridgway during confirmation hearings for Lieutenant General Petraeus in January 2007. "Lead us to victory" was both voiced by William Kristol in an ABC News interview and written up in a typically restrained *Weekly Standard* editorial, "Idiocy in D.C., Progress in Baghdad," March 26, 2007.

60. General Schwarzkopf's book title is extracted from his self-effacing remark, "It doesn't take a hero to order men into battle. It takes a hero to be one of those men who goes into battle."

61. *Time*, January 7, 1966. "Man of the Year: Gen. Westmoreland, The Guardians at the Gate." Cover article.

62. Karnow, *Vietnam*, p. 361.

63. "Changing of the Guard," *Time*, April 19, 1968.

64. Halberstam, *The Best and the Brightest*, p. 468; this is a fascinating book to encounter nearly forty years after publication. But new readers need to be cautioned that Halberstam gives no account of the horrific scale of Viet Cong terror in the South, or of Ho Chin Minh's massacres in the North during mid-1950s collectivization—events that motivated Washington.

65. During 1975–76, I worked with General Taylor—several times at his Massachusetts Avenue apartment in Washington—on his essay for the inaugural issue of *International Security*, Summer 1976: "The United States—A Military Power Second to None?" He creatively reinterpreted the "balance between the US and the USSR." See pp. 49–55.

66. On Taylor's comparison of Korea and Vietnam, see Hersh, *Dark Side*, p. 264.

67. Taylor's myopic commitment to a high-tech "fence" is in Rufus Philips, *Why Vietnam Matters: An Eyewitness Account of Lessons Not Learned* (Annapolis, Md.: Naval Institute Press, 2008), p. 104.

68. On "armies of freedom," see Halberstam, *The Best and the Brightest*, p. 480.

69. The question about those "men who were said to be the ablest to serve" is at the core of Halberstam's book, and would be revisited in his obituaries. See George Packer, "Postscript: David Halberstam," *New Yorker*, May 7, 2007.

5. A WORLD TO BE LABELED, NOT UNDERSTOOD

1. I spoke with Robert Dallek, after his book presentation at Politics and Prose, Washington D.C., May 19, 2007. However, his core argument is wrong. No evidence suggests that the Nixon/Kissinger détente policies that allowed Moscow more trade with the West "eroded totalitarianism," as he also argued on *Face the Nation*, interviewed by Bob Schieffer, CBS, May 20, 2007.

2. James C. Thomson, Jr., "How Could Vietnam Happen?—An Autopsy," *Atlantic*, April 1968.

3. Stephen Earl Bennett, Richard S. Flickinger, John R. Baker, Staci L. Rhine, and Linda L. M. Bennett, "Citizens' Knowledge of Foreign Affairs," *Harvard International Journal of Press/Politics*, March 1996, vol. 1, p. 10. "Germans are the most knowledgeable about international politics, citizens in Britain, Canada, and France displayed moderate knowledge, and Americans had the least knowledge."

4. I am encapsulating the arguments of Marcus Hansen, the mid-twentieth-century historian of immigration, and the first ex-

traordinary mind to focus on questions of assimilation, as well as the author of *The Immigrant in American History* (posthumous, 1940). He posited a "law" of cultural tension: "what the son [of the immigrant] wishes to forget, the grandson wishes to remember," except that the latter projects a dated stereotype.

5. "Third world standard" is the wisdom of McCain campaign senior adviser Nancy Pfotenhauer, C-SPAN, *Washington Journal*, August 12, 2008. Concerning "vibrant social democracy," the belief that Europe has lost its economic dynamism is a classic case of pundits "seeing what they want to see." Such assertions are not reflected in per capita real GDP since 1980, rising at about the same rate in the United States and the European Union, in technology innovation or in EU and U.S. employment rates in adults aged 25–54.

6. That half of congressmen do *not* have passports is a very conservative estimate. No precise figures exist, but a starting estimate is that only a quarter to a third of U.S. citizens *do* hold passports and Congress by no means enjoys twice the ratio. The estimate was conducted with several U.S. Senate and House staffers, January 8, 2010, Washington, D.C. Half of U.S. civilian personnel in Baghdad have never previously left the United States comes from Chandrasekaran, *Imperial Life in the Emerald City*, p. 17.

7. Jeff Stein, "Can You Tell a Sunni from a Shiite?" op. ed, *New York Times*, October 17, 2006.

8. PRI's *The World*, March 10, 2009.

9. Halberstam, *The Best and the Brightest*, p. 162.

10. Contrary to legend, as was revived in the 2007 biography *Memories of a Soldier-Scholar*, such an expert at the beginning of the Vietnam War would not have been professor/author/journalist Bernard Fall, who did not speak Vietnamese, who blamed America for France's defeat in 1954, and who was the first person known to have called for U.S. bombing of the North, in 1962. George W. Allen moved over to the CIA in 1964 to become a renowned analyst on Vietnam and, in 2001, he wrote the classic *None So Blind: A Personal Account of the Intelligence Failure in Vietnam*. "Mythical country" is from Philips, *Why Vietnam Matters*, p. 306.

11. Author's interviews with C. Dennison Lane, 2001 and 2008, who

was U.S. deputy military attaché in Thailand at the time. The exception occurred in 1968, when French officers who had been at Dien Bien Phu were consulted on the siege of Khe Sanh as the U.S. Marine garrison was surrounded. See W. Scott Thompson's important article "Lessons from the French in Vietnam," *Naval War College Review* 27 (March–April 1975), pp. 43–52.

12. Khong, *Analogies At War*, p. 246.

13. Rice was asked by a journalist if she ever had doubts about the consequences of invading Iraq. Her response was "Quote of the Week" in the *Washington Post*, March 31, 2008.

14. Secretary Rice, in an exchange during congressional testimony with Senator John Kerry, March 5, 2007; President Bush on "make Plan A work" is *The Charlie Rose Show*, interview, April 24, 2007.

15. Halberstam, *The Best and the Brightest*, p. 528. The former aide to Ike, and an old friend of Bundy's, was Emmet John Hughes.

16. Frederick Kagan, "Plan B? Let's Give Plan 'A' Some Time First," op-ed, *New York Times*, May 6, 2008. Of course, there were other factors affecting the change of tempo in addition to "the surge": this included ethnic cleansing already accomplished, payouts to former opponents, and even shortages of 155mm shells to manufacture IEDs.

17. H. R. McMaster, *Dereliction of Duty: Johnson, McNamara, the Joint Chiefs of Staff, and the Lies that Led to Vietnam* (New York: Harper Perennial, 1998), p. 215.

18. Presidential debate transcript is in the *New York Times*, October 12, 2000. Almost half the ninety-minute debate in Winston-Salem, North Carolina, was devoted to foreign affairs.

19. James Baker and Lee Hamilton, co-chairs, *The Iraq Study Group Report* (New York: Vintage, 2006), p. 60, notes the U.S. language deficiencies. Comparisons with British and French capabilities are the author's personal observations.

20. Two examples of such misjudgment are: Foreign Service officer April Glaspie, with vast Middle Eastern experience, who as U.S. ambassador to Iraq in 1990 failed to anticipate Saddam's August invasion of Kuwait; and Robert Fisk, preeminent journalist on the Middle East, who went on holiday that month.

21. Nicholas Kristof, "Learning How to Think," *New York Times*, March

26, 2009. Among more than a hundred studies, such randomness is demonstrated lucidly by Berkeley psychology professor Philip Tetlock in *Expert Political Judgment: How Good Is It? How Can We Know?* We all fall in love with our hunches, hate to be proved wrong, and thereby tend to slight new information that doesn't fit with our preconceptions.

22. Bob Woodward, *Bush at War* (New York: Simon & Schuster, 2002), p. 137.

23. "Perles of Wisdom."

24. Mark Warren, "Brent Scowcroft: What I've Learned," *Esquire*, January 2009, p. 96.

25. Duelfer interview, PRI.

26. Thomson, "How Could Vietnam Happen?"

27. Kai Bird, *The Color of Truth: McGeorge Bundy and William Bundy: Brothers in Arms* (New York: Simon & Schuster, 1998), p. 297.

28. Halberstam on Bundy as "WASP" is from Bird, *The Color of Truth*, p. 134; Kraft on Milton is in Goldstein, *Lessons*, p. 15.

29. Author's conversation with Hugh Auchincloss, Jr., M.D., July 18, 2009, Washington, D.C.

30. Michael Beschloss, ed., *Taking Charge: The Johnson White House Tapes, 1963–1964* (New York: Simon & Schuster, 1997), p. 226.

31. Bird, *The Color of Truth*, p. 306.

32. Halberstam, *The Best and the Brightest*, p. 521, quoting LBJ.

33. Goldstein, *Lessons*, p. 115.

34. Beschloss, *Taking Charge*, p. 372.

35. Goldstein, *Lessons*, p. 199.

36. Bundy obituary in the *Washington Post*, September 18, 1996, p. A18; JFK on "saboteurs" comes from the Trade Mart Speech ("Kennedy's Last Speech"). President Kennedy was scheduled to deliver this speech the day he was assassinated, November 22, 1963.

37. Joseph Nye, "Scholars on the Sidelines," op-ed, *Washington Post*, April 13, 2009. The argument that "scholars are paying less attention to questions about how their work relates to the policy world" is credible only if one writes of social scientists, and forgets, say, engineers, physicists, biologists, etc. This again underscores the solipsism of the foreign policy field of study.

38. The London-based International Institute for Strategic Studies may appear to be an exception, but it is truly an international

institute rather than a national one, and is funded extensively by U.S. foundations and members.

39. I had spoken previously with Professor Coker on this topic, and he confirmed his quote via e-mail, January 18, 2010.

40. Rajiv Chandrasekaran, "Pentagon Worries Led to Command Change," *Washington Post*, August 17, 2009, p. A1. General McKiernan, this analysis observes, "did not fawn over visiting lawmakers like Petraeus did in Iraq."

41. On "best medicine," then president of the CFR Leslie Gelb is cited by Glenn Greenwald in "The Ongoing Exclusion of War Opponents from the Iraq Debate," *Salon*, March 25, 2008. Brookings being "AWOL" is the judgment of Steven Clemons, director of the Strategy Program at the New America Foundation, in *Washington Note*, November 25, 2005. AEI's "Black Coffee Briefings" were advertised in March 2003 on the AEI website and can still be found at www.aei.org/event/274. The author attended one and found it jejune.

42. The incisive scholar F. Stephen Larrabee, who holds one of RAND's five "Distinguished Chairs," suggests one reason for a shortfall in innovative thinking. He points to a redirection of Defense Department research funding, which for twenty-five years has become steadily preoccupied with backing short-term, tactical "flavor of the month" academic projects, like those concerning Iraq, "AfPak," China, and terror. Discussion with author, Washington, D.C., November 27, 2009.

43. More than eighteen thousand Americans as well as Frenchmen died in systematically brutal British captivity, twice as many as on the battlefield, and far more than recognized until today. See Edwin Burrows, *Forgotten Patriots: The Untold Story of American Prisoners During the Revolutionary War* (New York, Basic Books, 2008). My review essay in the *Washington Post Book World*, January 4, 2009, "Do Unto Others," spoke of "scenes akin to Dachau." The point is that the Americans refused to respond in kind.

44. "Perles of Wisdom."

45. Quoted in "U.S Importing Somali 'Pirate Jihadists,' " *Newsmax*, May 6, 2009.

46. Former senator Fred Thompson on "tough" and Senator Christopher Dodd on "take ownership," *Meet the Press*, NBC, June 21,

2009. Also see Paul Wolfowitz, " 'No Comment' Is Not an Option," op-ed, *Washington Post*, June 19, 2009.

47. Ken Silverstein, *Turkmeniscam* (New York: Random House, 2008), pp. 131, 147.

48. This episode was recounted to me and foreign policy scholar John Henry by Professor Walt's co-author, John Mearsheimer, on September 8, 2008, Washington, D.C.

49. The one day per week of relevant consulting has long been encouraged, as during my years as a research fellow at Harvard's Center for Science and International Affairs, and is a practice that endures among faculty and postdocs in public policy schools.

50. David Bromwich, "Advice to the President," *New York Review of Books*, July 16, 2009, p. 6. The CFR president at that time was Leslie Gelb.

51. Halberstam, *The Best and the Brightest*, p. 242.

52. "Lost ground" is from Schlesinger, *A Thousand Days*, p. 554.

53. Cited in Neal Barber and Willard Ronning, *Internal Security and Military Power: Counterinsurgency and Civic Action in Latin America* (Columbus: Ohio State University Press, 1966), p. 97. In my own conversations with General Taylor, in 1975–76, he reflected how counterinsurgency was "at the heart of things" during the Kennedy years.

54. Jacob Weisberg, "Party of Defeat," *Slate*, March 14, 2007.

55. "Take over Europe" is from a briefing with the editorial staff of the *Jerusalem Post*, as reported on jpost.com, January 29, 2007. "Get on with it" is cited by historian Manan Ahmed on the History News Network, November 17, 2004.

56. Fouad Ajami, "A Sage in Christendom," op-ed, *Wall Street Journal*, May 1, 2006.

57. Envisioning boom boxes is in *Washington Post*, October 7, 2002. Ajami urged a Pax Americana and "an overriding commitment to the defense of American primacy" in "A Cold Blooded Foreign Policy," op-ed, *Wall Street Journal*, December 31, 2009.

58. Senator Frank Church, as referenced in Loch Johnson, "It's Never a Quick Fix at the CIA," op-ed, *Washington Post*, August 30, 2009. Public understanding of the CIA's deficiencies has rarely been helped even by the Agency's best-known critics. Tim Weiner's *Legacy of Ashes: The History of the CIA* (2007) attempts to

explain the organization's deficiencies, but the author ended up playing into the hands of Langley's vigilant Center for the Study of Intelligence. His book was shredded on the basis of elementary fact-checking in *Studies in Intelligence*, CSI Publications, vol. 51, no. 3, 2007, which also reveals an instance of Weiner having invented dialogue.

59. Central Intelligence Agency, NIE 11-8-1960, August 1, 1960. Note chart 29157 7-60.

60. Among the flawed intelligence reports are SNIE 11-14-61, "The Soviet Strategic Military Posture, 1961–67; NIE 11-8-62, "Soviet Capabilities for Long-Range Attack," which did not forecast any specific new ICBMs; and NIE 11-8-63, "Soviet Capabilities for Surprise Attack," which only foresaw systems designed to strike cities and other "soft" targets. Note my discussion of the nuclear strategic debate—and the accompanying calculations—in *The Fifty-Year Wound*, pp. 368–73, plus notes 119 and 120. Also see the argument, and the calculations, on pp. 390–93, and notes 26, 27, and 32.

61. "Everybody thinks" comes from a report by Admiral David E. Jeremiah, that the CIA itself—under pressure from Congress—undertook after India's surprise nuclear detonation. See Tim Weiner, "Naïveté at the C.I.A.; Every Nation's Just Another U.S.," *New York Times*, June 7, 1998. As the article did not state, no one at Langley was fired or reprimanded.

62. Recruiting skills are evidenced by the nineteen agents (the "blue border" sources, or well-placed moles) who ultimately were executed due to treason (long undetected despite alarming evidence) within the CIA and FBI during the Soviet Union's final decade.

63. Tyler Drumheller, *On the Brink: An Insider's Account of How the White House Compromised U.S. Intelligence* (New York: PublicAffairs, 2006), p. 198; "magical thinking" is from my March 12, 2010, discussion with Drumheller. I explored these issues frequently with him during 2009–2010.

64. I discussed these issues with Bagley in Washington, D.C., in June 2009, and via e-mail, February 9, 2010. On CIA obstruction, see "KGB Spy Saga Won't Die," *New York Post*, June 29, 2007, and "Yale Press Log: News and Features from Yale University Press," July 3,

2007. A CIA spokesman said Bagley's talk was not canceled due to his message but because of questions regarding prepublication review of the book.

65. Former Soviet officials who concurred with Lee's analyses included Genrikh Trofimenko, of the Diplomatic Academy and the Institute of the USA and Canada. I worked closely with Lee during these years and spoke with him on the afternoon of September 11, 2001.

66. On information concerning the CIA and banks: this episode was shared by a senior CIA officer who had been involved directly in these decisions. Additionally, the decision to drop human assets within banks angered and frustrated the National Security Agency where this type of information was a mainstay of its work.

67. "Blackwater's Owner Has Spies for Hire," *Washington Post*, November 3, 2007.

68. Gerald Elbers and Paul Duncan, eds., *Scientific Revolution: Challenge and Promise* (Washington, D.C.: Public Affairs, 1959), p. 72. Translating these documents was thought "too expensive."

69. "Basically wasn't a limit" is quoted in Evan Thomas, *The Very Best Men: Four Who Dared, the Early Years of the CIA* (New York: Simon & Schuster, 1995), p. 181; Drumheller is in *On the Brink*, p. 71.

70. I spoke often with Mr. Richard about these CIA issues during 1998–2001. I also spoke with him extensively during his tenure at In-Q-Tel and participated in the analysis of business plans in the organization's Roslyn, Virginia, office, and spoke at length with him during and after his departure from In-Q-Tel, and in 2003 with investigative reporter Seymour Hersh about the In-Q-Tel mismanagement that led to Richard's departure. The glimpse offered by business reporter Christopher Byron is "Penny Stock Spies," *New York Post*, April 25, 2005, and related articles by Byron.

71. The extent of Soviet military spending made the difference between life and death of the overburdened communist order. Langley had no interest in listening to alternative—and correct—calculations, as from William T. Lee, thereby failing to grasp the extent of the Soviet predicament. But *after the U.S.S.R. collapsed*, the CIA sponsored conferences at Princeton and else-

where to insist its calculations had been correct. Panels of CIA managers and of academics, many of whom had been paid CIA consultants, such as RAND economist Charles Wolf, Jr., argued that they all had had a profounder grasp of the data than did even former Soviet officials, now siding with Lee.

The second example concerns the nearly universal belief, echoed by journalists such as Fareed Zakaria and Bill Keller, that the "Team B" assessments in 1976–77 of Soviet military capacity were wrong. Russian sources—including post-1991 regimental histories—now show them to have been fundamentally correct on all key issues: close approximations of missile accuracies, scope of Soviet civil defense, and violations of the ABM treaty. Team B did not even know the worst—Moscow's bioweapons program. Of interest to us: the CIA commissioned Sovietologist Raymond Garthoff to write a *post–Cold War assessment* of the Team B episode. "Garthoff did not disappoint," concludes one flawed study that addresses the subject (John Diamond, *The CIA and the Culture of Failure*, Stanford, CA: Stanford University Press, 2008, p. 50). A careful scholar on most matters, Garthoff unsurprisingly concurred with the CIA that "virtually all of Team B's criticisms . . . proved to be wrong." But here he was a prejudiced arbiter: he had been opposing such interpretations as Team B's even before I worked with him in publishing his views in *International Security* (Summer 1978). And earlier in the 1970s he had (unfairly) been railroaded off an arms control delegation for such judgments. For further reading, see my arguments, and the Russian sources, in *The Fifty-Year Wound*. Also see William T. Lee, "Soviet Strategic Nuclear Missiles: A Reassessment of Capabilities and Deployments," *Journal of Cold War Studies* 12, no. 3 (Spring 2010), pp. 111–81.

6. MYTHS OF HISTORY

1. George W. Bush, Address to Joint Session of Congress, September 20, 2001, referring to "different world"; Gary Hart, chairman, ASP, C-SPAN, May 4, 2009, referring to "a world fundamentally different" from that of the twentieth century; "not the same

people" is Thomas Kean, quoted in Albert R. Hunt, "Letter from Washington," *International Herald Tribune*, September 11, 2006.

2. Vice President Cheney, speech to VFW National Convention, August 26, 2002.

3. Kennedy referred to the "southern half" in "Special Message to Congress on Urgent National Needs," May 25, 1961. Thomson notes the fear of the "Golden Horde" in "How Could Vietnam Happen?"

4. "Mortal danger" is President Bush in the *San Francisco Chronicle*, October 5, 2005; "darker world" is from Charles E. Allen, now of the Chertoff Group and previously undersecretary of intelligence and analysis at the Department of Homeland Security, who has alternatively spoken of "in certain ways the world has grown darker," October 7, 2008, remarks to Maritime Security Council. G. John Ikenberry and Anne-Marie Slaughter, co directors, Woodrow Wilson School, Princeton University, in *Forging a World of Liberty Under Law: U.S. National Security in the 21st Century, Final Report of the Princeton Project on National Security*, September 2006, state that "the world seems a more menacing place than ever" (p. 11).

5. "How Rice Uses History Lessons," by Neil King, *Wall Street Journal*, January 19, 2007.

6. The use of analogies as "national style" was already observed by political scientist Stanley Hoffmann in 1968, as referenced by Khong, *Analogies at War*, p. 7; that most historical analogies are misleading has been documented by historian Ernest May, as cited in ibid., p. 7.

7. Discussion between Tony Blair and President Bush as cited by columnist Paul Krugman, *New York Times*, February 12, 2006.

8. Richard Norton Smith, C-SPAN, February 15, 2009, "Historical Presidential Leadership Survey." This impressive historian would emphasize "deservedly or not" when discussing the subject with the author, Washington, D.C., April 1, 2010; Burt Solomon, "Judging a War," *National Journal*, June 13, 2009, p. 37, cites "foreign policy experts" who believe that in 30 years a democratic Middle East would be attributable to Mr. Bush.

9. Karl Rove, "Bush Is a Book Lover," *Wall Street Journal*, December 26, 2008.

10. Maureen Dowd, "Aux Barricades!" *New York Times*, January 17, 2007, quoting Kissinger's authorized biographer Alistair Horne.

11. Scowcroft to author, op cit; Bundy's course title is often presented incorrectly. This correct version in the *1959/60 Harvard University Catalogue* also describes the course as "a study of American foreign policy since the second world war." (Thanks to Robin Carlaw of the Harvard University Archives.)

12. On JFK as "an historian," see Leebaert, *The Fifty-Year Wound*, p. 260.

13. The comparison to New York was made by L. Paul Bremer III, director of the Coalition Provisional Authority, August 2003. Ambassador Eikenberry questioned such wisdom—way too late, in the eighth year of war—as described in Carlotta Gall, "U.S. Envoy Vows to Help Avoid Civilian Deaths," *New York Times*, May 20, 2009.

14. "Simon and Schuster to Publish Cheney Memoir," *New York Times*, June 24, 2009, citing Lynn Cheney describing her husband as a "student of history."

15. April 15, 1994, interview with C-SPAN.

16. Jeffrey Birnbaum, "Mr. CEO Goes to Washington," *Fortune*, March 19, 2001.

17. Cheney to Dick Armey, quoted in Robert Draper, *Dead Certain: The Presidency of George W. Bush* (New York: Free Press, 2007) p. 178. Bernard Guetta, "Tout bien considéré," *L'Express*, February 20, 2003.

18. A. G. Sulzbelger "Cheney Says Obama Has Increased Risks," *New York Times*, March 15, 2009.

19. What became known as "the Bush Doctrine" was stated on June 1, 2002, by President Bush, in his West Point commencement address. It has been paraphrased and repeated often by Cheney.

20. Khong, *Analogies at War*, p. 262.

21. Daniel Mendelsohn, "Theaters of War: Why the Battle Over Ancient Athens Still Rages," *New Yorker*, January 12, 2004. See also Laura Miller, "My Favorite War," *New York Times Book Review*, March 21, 2004.

22. Admiral Zumwalt is generally considered the most distinguished CNO since World War II. He wrote a "memorandum of conversation" within minutes of his conversation with Kissinger. See Elmo R. Zumwalt, *On Watch: A Memoir* (New York: Times

Books, 1976), p. 319. Kissinger would denounce this account as a "fabrication" by a "dovish doltish admiral," at other times insisting that he had been misunderstood. See Isaacson, *Kissinger*, pp. 696–97.

23. Samuel Huntington, "The Clash of Civilizations?" *Foreign Affairs*, Summer 1993.

24. George W. Bush, speech to National Endowment for Democracy, October 6, 2005, as reported in *San Francisco Chronicle*, October 7, 2005.

25. Robert Kaplan, "A Gentler Hegemony," *Washington Post*, December 17, 2008.

26. Max Boot, "The Case for American Empire," *Weekly Standard*, October 15, 2001. Boot has also concluded that "Washington Needs a Colonial Office," in *Financial Times*, July 3, 2003. His eagerness for a "magical solution," Mark Ames argues in "Unreliable Sources," *Nation*, January 14, 2009, remains consistent.

27. Niall Ferguson, *Colossus: The Price of America's Empire* (New York: Penguin, 2004), p. 34. Ferguson also argues that, during World War II, British officials were struck by the "imperial character of American postwar planning." But that was their own worried perspective, and one soon to reverse itself. As foreign secretary from July 1945, Ernest Bevin was alarmed that the United States might retreat inward. Public Record Office documents to this end are cited in my *To Set the World Right*, forthcoming.

28. The earliest reference to "empire" in what would become the British Empire would be that by John Dee, scientist and astrologer to Elizabeth I. It referred to sovereignty over the British Isles.

29. "Abizaid Warns of Looming World War," *News from the Kennedy School*, November 20, 2006. Nor would one easily find a European officer who would churlishly mock a young woman with the temerity to politely challenge his analysis in the Q&A that followed his Kennedy School speech.

30. See Michael Barone, "The Misuses of Intelligence," op. ed, *Washington Times*, February 19, 2007.

31. Reference to the SS is Rice's fantasy, as stated in a speech to the 28th Annual Convention of the National Association of Black Journalists, August 7, 2008. Such silliness about "Werwolfkommandos" was echoed by, among many others, Michael Savage,

who described Nazi-like "hit teams" on his *Savage Nation* radio show, July 13, 2009.

32. Already in the fall of 2002, in anticipation of a U.S. invasion of Iraq, the U.S. Army J5 (Program Analysis and Evaluation) was scouring army archives to study the postwar occupation of Germany. Historian Bianka J. Adams, a naturalized American citizen from Germany, warned her Pentagon superiors that "Iraq is not Germany." Later she tried fruitlessly to head off the Werewolf references that drew on eccentric work by University of Victoria assistant professor Perry Biddiscombe. Author interview with Adams, August 18, 2009, Camp Liberty, Iraq.

33. "These dead-enders," as Brookings Institution researcher Michael O'Hanlon elaborated as chaos descended, "are few in number and have little ability to inspire a broader following among the Iraqi people." *Washington Times*, February 17, 2004.

34. The JFK-Obama "myth" concerning Kennedy opposing escalation is fostered in Goldstein, *Lessons in Disaster*, and is repeated by among other commentators, Frank Rich, in *New York Times*, January 24, 2010. On Kennedy's embarrassment, see Lawrence Freedman, *Kennedy's Wars: Berlin, Cuba, Laos, and Vietnam* (New York: Oxford University Press, 2000), p. 360.

35. Goldstein, *Lessons*, p. 99.

36. Ibid., p. 209.

37. John Lewis Gaddis, "Two Cold War Empires: Imposition vs. Multilateralism," *Major Problems in American Foreign Relations Volume II: Since 1914*, sixth edition, edited by Dennis Merrill and Thomas G. Paterson. Boston: Houghton Mifflin 2005, p. 239; an example of such recurring inaccuracy is seen in Steve Coll's essay, "The Cabinet of Dr. Strangelove," in the *New York Review of Books*, February 25, 2010. He repeats the myth that "Eisenhower knew that candidate John F. Kennedy's claims in 1960 about a 'missile gap' between the U.S. and the Soviet Union were untrue, but Eisenhower had to swallow his frustration in silence, lest he reveal the U-2's existence." See my response in the May 13, 2010, issue, pp. 69–70.

38. "Awake and Scream," op-ed, *New York Times*, September 16, 2006, as cited by Maureen Dowd.

39. See President George W. Bush's speech to the American Legion,

transcript, *New York Times*, August 31, 2006, which echoed the same words of General John Abizaid before the Senate Armed Services Committee, September 29, 2005. For the Vietnam war, the same statement was made by Colonel Harry Summers, as in his *On Strategy* (1982), and in congressional testimony by commanders.

40. Michael Gordon and Bernard Trainor, *Cobra II: The Inside Story of the Invasion and Occupation of Iraq* (New York: Pantheon, 2006), p. 317.

41. General McMaster is director of concept development and experimentation at the U.S. Army's Training and Doctrine Command. He is quoted from his article in *Survival*, as cited in *Herald Tribune*, February 9–10, 2008.

42. Michael R. Gordon, "Planning Seen in Iraqi Attack," *New York Times*, February 18, 2007, quoting Major General James E. Simmons, a deputy commander of the multinational force in Iraq, after his helicopter was shot down in 2007; "far more sophisticated" is Thom Shanker, "Report Cites Firefight as Lesson," *New York Times*, October 3, 2009, describing the firefight in Wanat; "surprising level" is also *New York Times*, p. A1, September 24, 2009; "not stupid" is Richard Oppel, "Iraq Veterans Find Afghan Enemy Even Bolder," *New York Times*, July 25, 2009.

43. "Obama Details New Policies in Response to Terror Threat," *New York Times*, January 7, 2010.

44. Sarah Kershaw, "The Terrorist Mind," *New York Times*, January 10, 2010, is just one example; she conflates the Pakistan schoolyard truck bomb with the strike against the CIA operatives.

45. Leebaert, *To Dare and to Conquer*, pp. 509–15.

46. Sir Robert Thompson had been permanent secretary of defense for Malaya and, in 1963, when this insight was offered to JFK, was head of the British Advisory Mission to South Vietnam.

47. Colin Kahl, "COIN of the Realm," review essay, *Foreign Affairs*, November/December 2007.

48. "McChrystal: Marines' gains are a model for counterinsurgency," *Stars and Stripes*, August 20, 2009.

49. Robert Dreyfuss, "The Generals Revolt," *Rolling Stone*, October 2009.

50. "Petraeus's Tougher Fight" David Ignatius, *Washington Post*, May 13,

2009; "invented counterterrorism" is the AEI's Frederick Kagan, *Financial Times*, October 11, 2009, cited in "Restive on the Frontier."

51. The emphasis is General McChrystal's, during his interview with *Frontline, Obama's War*, PBS, October 12, 2009.

52. On "Bundy," the quote has been powerfully repurposed for today by columnist Bob Herbert in "Reliving the Past," *New York Times*, September 4, 2009.

7. WE'LL SHOW THEM THE LIGHT

1. Schmertz, ed., *President Reagan and the World*, p. 141.

2. Remarks of Senator John F. Kennedy at University of Kentucky, Lexington, Kentucky, October 8, 1960, John F. Kennedy Presidential Library and Museum; Bob Woodward, *Plan of Attack* (New York: Simon & Schuster, 2004), p. 89; Scott McClellan, *What Happened Inside the Bush White House and Washington's Culture of Deception*, (New York: PublicAffairs, 2008), pp. 193–96.

3. "Transformational diplomacy" was a fad introduced at the U.S. State Department by Secretary Condoleezza Rice, who championed the spreading of democracy, as outlined in a speech at Georgetown University, January 18, 2006. The initiative had five core elements, but her theme of "ending tyranny in the world" was taken lightly by U.S. diplomats.

4. James Mann, author of *The China Fantasy: How Our Leaders Explain Away Chinese Repression* (2007), at Politics and Prose, Washington, D.C., February 24, 2007.

5. Condoleezza Rice, to the Chicago Council on Foreign Relations, Chicago, October 8, 2003.

6. Peter Grose, "U.S. Encouraged By Vietnam Vote," *New York Times*, September 4, 1967.

7. Quoted in James Fallows, "The Fifty-First State," *Atlantic*, November 2002.

8. *The Big Story*, Fox News, John Gibson interview with Woolsey, reported on WorldNet Daily, July 17, 2006. I have twice been invited to Woolsey's longtime Washington book club, the Leo Society, where his views on "Arabs" have been unsettling.

9. "The Case for Bombing Iran" is an article in *Commentary*, June 2007, by Norman Podhoretz. Podhoretz does not address other

similarly dramatic approaches to resolving nuclear weapons proliferation in the Middle East, such as, say, a nuclear-free zone encompassing all countries in the region.

10. David Ignatius, "Moment of Truth in Pakistan," *Washington Post*, May 3, 2009.

11. Secretary of State Hillary Clinton, "Remarks with Visiting Egyptian Democracy Activists Before Their Meeting," May 28, 2009, U.S. Department of State.

12. Benjamin Schemmer, *U.S. Special Operations Forces* (Tampa, Fla.: Special Operations Warrior Foundation, 2003), p. 11.

13. On General Stone, see "In Iraq, 'A Prison Full of Innocent Men,' " *Washington Post*, December 6, 2008; there is also the question of the actual qualifications of General Stone's mind readers: if one looked at their job requirements, as posted by the Multi-National Force–Iraq Joint Contracting Command, an applicant needed only "an Associate's Degree, though a Bachelor's degree is desired." Chertoff was interviewed on *Washington Journal*, September 18, 2009.

14. Eric Schmitt, "Pentagon Seeks to Overhaul Prisons" *New York Times*, July 19, 2009. The judge is John Bates, a 2001 appointee of President George W. Bush. See "A Bagram Reckoning," editorial, *New York Times*, January 17, 2010.

15. As quoted in Jonathan Mirsky, "The True Story of Izzy," *New York Review of Books*, September 24, 2009, p. 82.

16. This difference between Egyptians and Palestinians is underscored by Jehan Sadat in her interview with Deborah Solomon in "The War Widow," *New York Times Magazine*, March 10, 2009; "Self-govern" is President George W. Bush, as quoted by Woodward, *The War Within*, p. 424; "fear of dogs" is from General Ricardo Sanchez in *New York Times*, March 30, 2005.

17. The AEI's Frederick Kagan, C-SPAN, *Washington Journal*, July 20, 2008. Kagan anticipated a "fundamental change" in Iraqi society, due to the U.S. troop surge, and self-importantly intoned "I will only tell the American people the truth." "Magical powers" is Frank Rich, in "Two Wrongs Make Another Fiasco," *New York Times*, October 11, 2009.

18. Dobbins presentation in the CSIS Smart Power Speaker Series, "Nation-Building After Iraq," June 4, 2008.

19. Anne Applebaum, "The Smart Money in Afghanistan," *Washington Post*, September 23, 2008.

20. Dwight D. Eisenhower, *Waging Peace, 1956–1961: The White House Years* (New York: Doubleday, 1965), p. 498.

21. Elisabeth Bumiller and Mark Landler "Civilian Goals Largely Unmet in Afghanistan" "Heartbreaking" is in *New York Times*, October 12, 2009; "nightmare" is Anthony Cordesman in *New York Times*, October 12, 2009.

22. I interviewed Charles Abbott on October 23, 2009, Washington, D.C.; "superstar" is from a "senior aide" at State quoted in Philip Rucker, "Officials Hail USAID Administrator," *Washington Post*, January 15, 2010.

23. David Brooks, "Closing of a Nation," *New York Times*, September 24, 2006. Like so many "public intellectuals" eager for war in 2003, Brooks would reflect: "I was too enthusiastic. . . . Iraqi society was more complex than I anticipated. . . . [T]he attempt to radically reshape the country was doomed to fall victim to our own ignorance." Many of America's dead and maimed could have told him that beforehand. See Howard Kurtz, "David Brooks, Rankling Folks Right and Left," *Washington Post*, September 22, 2008.

24. "Obama Promises a Marshall Plan for the Twenty-First Century," *Guardian*, July 16, 2008. Pakistan's call was made by President Musharraf, *Times* (London), November 20, 2006.

25. William Pfaff, "Reality Is Its Own Caricature for US in Afghanistan and Pakistan," *International Herald Tribune*, August 21, 2009.

26. Joint Chiefs of Staff, news article, "From the Chairman—Strategic Communications: Getting Back to Basics," August 28, 2009. On the Internet, the comparison was made by Secretary Gates and is still correct. See "Hearts and Minds," *Washington Post*, July 24, 2008.

27. For the think-tankers' upbeat op-ed in March 2009 about having "no doubt," see Max Boot, Frederick Kagan, and Kimberley Kagan, "How to Surge the Taliban," *New York Times*, March 12, 2009. For the same think-tankers' sudden alarm in August about the supposed "weaker foes" in Afghanistan, see Robert Dreyfuss, "Afghanistan Apocalypse," *Nation*, August 26, 2009.

28. The PowerPoint slides are those by CSIS's Anthony Cordesman,

" 'Shape, Clear, Hold, and Build': The Uncertain Lessons of the Afghan & Iraq War: Part I," September 21, 2009.

29. Walter Pincus, "In Building Afghan Army It's Back to Basics," *Washington Post*, September 9, 2009.

30. Rod Norland "Iraq Swears by Bomb Detector," *New York Times*, November 4, 2009, p. A3. Anyone who observed Iraqi police checkpoints could see these shamanic devices at work into early 2010. U.S. officers immediately blamed the misplaced trust in them as an enabling factor behind the catastrophic "Bloody Wednesday" August 19, 2009, bombings in central Baghdad. Author's interviews in Baghdad.

31. I met with Kenneth Moorefield and his key aides in September 2009, after returning from Iraq, to discuss these force development challenges (September 18, 2009, Alexandria, Virginia). Moorefield's assessment of ARVN is supported by the scholarly work (and similar firsthand experience) of Lewis Sorley. See my evaluation of the ARVN—and comparison with America's NATO allies—in *The Fifty-Year Wound*, pp. 419–22.

32. Rory Stewart, "The Irresistible Illusion," *London Review of Books*, July 2009, pp. 3–6.

33. James Mann, *About Face: A History of America's Curious Relationship with China* (New York: Knopf, 1999), p. 79.

34. I discussed these force planning issues, known as PD-59, several times with Huntington as we flew together from Cambridge to Washington, D.C., for respective U.S. government consulting work during 1979–80.

35. Avi Shlaim, *Israel and Palestine: Reappraisals, Revisions, Refutations* (New York: Verso, 2009), p. 36. Oxford professor Shlaim is one of the world's foremost authorities on the Israel-Palestine conflict.

36. Author interview with Brown, November 22, 2009, Chevy Chase, Maryland. No one, of course, argues that "if only the Palestinian conflict were solved, all other Middle East conflicts would melt away." Authors Dennis Ross and David Makovsky rightly call this "the mother of all myths." But they have created that straw man, so the "myth" is all their own. See "Iran Talks Key to Peace Process," *Politico*, July 27, 2009, p. 37.

37. On killings in Gaza, one can reference not just conclusions of the *Report of the United Nations Fact-Finding Mission on the Gaza Conflict*

(Goldstein Report), September 25, 2009, but also to 1956 massacres as chronicled in *Footnotes in Gaza* (2010) and reviewed in Patrick Cockburn, "They Planted Hatred in Our Hearts," *New York Times Book Review*, December 27, 2009. Similarly the Jerusalem bus bomb may be one of many, like that of the No. 2 Egged bus in Jerusalem, August 19, 2003.

38. Durkee quotations are transcribed from notes made during our lunch December 8, 2009, Washington, D.C.

39. On taxes, see Josh Nathan-Kozis, "Can Tax-Free Donations Fund Settlements?" *Forward*, January 15, 2010, as well as David Ignatius, "A Tax Break Fuels Middle East Friction" *Washington Post*, March 6, 2009; on "gated communities" see Howard Schneider "Passions High Ahead of Talks," *Washington Post*, September 12, 2009, in which Mayor Ron Nachman states, "I don't call Ariel a settlement; it's a 'gated community.' "

40. The number of Lebanese civilian dead is of course disputed. One estimate is the twelve thousand cited twenty years later by *Le Monde diplómatique*, English edition, September 2002, "The past is always present," Pierre Pean. Robert Fisk in *Pity the Nation* (2002) cites Lebanese sources based on police, hospital, and Red Cross records that place the number of deaths in the first two weeks of invasion at fourteen thousand, most of them civilians. There were 368 Israeli dead from the invasion, all combatants. In any event, President Reagan's use of "holocuast" to describe these dead and maimed was intentional, as apparent from *The Reagan Diaries* (New York: HarperCollins, 2007) and is quoted in Deborah Strober and Gerald Strober, *Reagan: The Man and the Presidency* (Boston: Houghton Mifflin, 1998), p. 207. "Indiscriminate" is Tom Friedman's description of Israeli shelling of Beirut in August 1982, as discussed in his *From Beirut to Jerusalem* (New York: Anchor, 1990), p. 73.

41. Reuters "Hamas Calls Israeli Civilian Deaths a Mistake," *New York Times*, January 29, 2010; and Ian Austen "Canadian Inquiry Blames Israelis for Deaths in 2006," *New York Times*, February 2, 2008.

42. Israel supplied an embargoed VAX computer, material for the triggering mechanism, and an essential avionics package for delivery, plus technical guidance. CIA had eleven case officers in country during 1980–85, four with deep cover; "Project Circle" was penetrated, its enrichment facilities swiped regularly, and

the Mossad's TamCo "black station" monitored. I've extensively interviewed the key officer; "absolutely vital" are his words. "Devastating . . . espionage" is January 15, 2008, BBC News, also see Hersh, "Why Pollard Should Never Be Released," *New Yorker*, January 18, 1999, pp. 26–33. Israel granted Pollard citizenship in 1995 but denied complicity for thirteen years. Also see "Israel Might Have More Spies Here, Officials Say," Jeff Stein, *Congressional Quarterly*, April 25, 2008. On exports he deemed "deceptive," Rumsfeld was described as "incensed" by his China adviser Michael Pillsbury, interview, Washington, D.C., March 1, 2010. Also see "US Demands Answers from Israel Over China Arms Sales," *Agence France-Presse*, June 12, 2005.

CONCLUSION. FINDING OUR BETTER ANGELS

1. Gerald Seib cites the Pew Research and Council on Foreign Relations poll, and sees the attitudes as "isolationist sentiment," in *Wall Street Journal*, December 4, 2009.
2. The Islamic Republic of Iran stepped forward to help topple the Taliban and pledged $560 million for reconstruction, while Syria's Baathist regime shared intelligence with Washington, including results from Muhabarat secret police interrogations.
3. "This tough" is from Rice; "more complex" is from Brooks; "predictable in advance" is from another onetime advocate of the Iraq War, Francis Fukuyama, "The Neoconservative Moment," *National Interest*, Summer 2004. My own skepticism about invading Iraq was largely based, from experience, on minimal faith in CIA estimates, which in this case included CIA conclusions about WMD.
4. Tom Friedman, "It's All About Schools," *New York Times*, February 10, 2010.
5. Ikenberry and Slaughter, *Forging a World of Liberty Under Law*. Another conclusion from *Forging*, that "we must think of public health, economics, and other fields when we think of national security," is equally unoriginal (p. 55). That was essentially the founding charter of *International Security* in 1976.
6. "The Afghanistan Debate: Assessing the President's Policy Options," Brookings Institution, October 16, 2009, transcript.

7. "As Indonesia Debates Islam's Role, U.S. Stays Out," *Washington Post*, October 26, 2009, p. A1.

8. Krauthammer on "existential threat," to pick one reference, is in "The Neoconservative Convergence," *Wall Street Journal*, July 21, 2005. Evan Thomas at Politics and Prose discussing his new book *The War Lovers.*

9. Dexter Filkins, "His Long War," *New York Times Magazine*, October 18, 2009, p. 38.

10. David B. Rivkin, Jr., and Lee A. Casey, "The Memos Prove We Didn't Torture," *Wall Street Journal*, April 20, 2009. *The New Yorker's* Jane Mayer revisited the debate in "Courting Disaster," March 29, 2010. She in turn was deemed "dishonest" by a believer in the effectiveness of torture, an unconvincing former Bush speech writer. See "Jane Mayer's Disaster," NRO, April 14, 2010.

11. Similar guest positions in leading universities are occasionally offered to, say, a former Treasury official, but less frequently and without the publicity; and anyway he or she is more likely to bring substantive financial skills, as in finance or economics.

12. Steve Coll, *Ghost Wars: The Secret History of the CIA, Afghanistan, and bin Laden* (New York: Penguin, 2004), p. 22.

13. So observes Art Brown, twenty-five-year CIA veteran and former head of the Asia division of the Clandestine Service, in "Intelligence Boosters," op-ed, *New York Times*, December 14, 2008.

14. David Walker has long endorsed such audits, and he is quoted in the editorial, "Accounting for the Full Ante in Washington," *New York Times*, March 22, 2008.

15. See David Ignatius, "Slow Roll Time at Langley," *Washington Post*, April 22, 2009, and my response "Back to Basics at the CIA," on May 2, 2009. Ignatius based his column on interviews at Langley.

16. John Ross interview with author, Washington, D.C., December 13, 2009.

17. To glance at random at the *Wall Street Journal's* op-ed pages, one well-known historian cites 1930s militarism in Europe and Japan, plus America's "string of fighting presidents" since FDR, to make the case for boosting the 2010–2011 defense budget; a national security "senior fellow," in turn, suggests that Washington acquiesce in ongoing Israeli settlements in Palestine because endless conflict is inevitable no matter what we do, wrapping his brief

around the centuries of violent hatred between England and Scotland starting in 1296. Dates and sequence are wrong in both pieces. See Frederick W. Kagan, "Security Should Be the Deciding Issue," *Wall Street Journal*, October 31, 2008. On England and Scotland; see Max Boot, "Of Braveheart and Bush," *Wall Street Journal*, January 5, 2008. Boot misses the fact that the antagonism went back at least 158 years earlier, to the Battle of the Standard and beyond.

18. Senator Wherry's vision from 1940 is widely quoted in U.S. foreign policy writings. Tellingly, it's cited probably even more often in China. See, for instance, Lixin Wang, "With the Dragon as a Foil: America Imagining of China and the Construction of America's National Identity," *Social Sciences in China* 29, no. 4 (November 2008).

19. Counterinsurgency is being described as "new" by a cross section of politicians, defense thinkers, soldiers, and journalists, including Alissa Rubin, in "In Iraq, a Blunt Civilian Is a Fixture by the General's Side," a profile of anthropologist Emma Sky, *New York Times*, November 21, 2009.

20. James Kitfield, "New Lease on a 'Long War,'" *National Journal*, December 5, 2009, p. 30.

21. Ibid., quoting JCS chairman Mike Mullen.

22. David Ignatius, "Why Obama Needs to Send More Troops to Afghanistan," *Washington Post*, October 30, 2009; Kaplan, "Supremacy By Stealth"; The U.S. commander is Brigadier General Frederick Hodges, with General McChrystal adding the insight that "When you go to protect people, the people have to want you to protect them." See Karen DeYoung and Craig Whitlock, "Kandahar Offensive Not on Schedule," *Washington Post*, June 11, 2010.

23. Joseph McCarthy's speech in the U.S. Senate, June 14, 1951, ludicrously denouncing that "grim and solitary man," General of the Army George C. Marshall.

INDEX

ABOUT THE AUTHOR

Derek Leebaert, who has taught foreign policy at Georgetown University for fifteen years, is a partner in the Swiss management consulting firm MAP AG. His previous books include *The Fifty-Year Wound: How America's Cold War Victory Shapes Our World* (2002) and *To Dare and to Conquer: Special Operations and the Destiny of Nations from Achilles to Al Qaeda* (2006). He is also a co-author of the MIT Press trilogy on the information technology revolution, and a founding editor of *International Security* and *The International Economy*, as well as for a decade an editorial board member of *European Security*. He served in the U.S. Marine Corps Reserve and is a director of the U.S. Army Historical Foundation, Providence Hospital in Washington, D.C., and of other public service institutions.